"The King of the Cats"

"The King of the Cats" and other remarks on writers and writing

F. W. Dupee

Second Edition

The University of Chicago Press

Chicago and London

The University of Chicago Press, Chicago 60637
The University of Chicago Press, Ltd., London

©1945, 1951, 1953, 1954, 1956, 1957, 1958, 1959, 1960, 1962, 1963, 1964, 1965 by F. W. Dupee. ©1966, 1967, 1971 by the Estate of F. W. Dupee

Introduction ©1983 by Mary McCarthy

©1984 by The University of Chicago
All rights reserved. First edition published 1965
Second edition 1984
93 92 91 90 89 88 87 86 85 84   5 4 3 2 1

Library of Congress Cataloging in Publication Data

Dupee, F. W. (Frederick Wilcox), 1904–1979
   The king of the cats, and other remarks on writers and writing.

   1. Literature—History and criticism—Addresses, essays, lectures.
I. Title.
PN511.D8   1984   809   84–8475
ISBN 0–226–17286–4 (cloth)
ISBN 0–226–17287–2 (paper)

In memoriam
Richard Chase, 1914–1963

Acknowledgments

Acknowledgment is made to Farrar, Straus & Giroux for permission to reprint the Introduction (as "The Other Dickens") to *The Selected Letters of Charles Dickens;* to Random House, Inc., for permission to reprint "It Shows Shine: Notes on Gertrude Stein" from *The Selected Writings of Gertrude Stein,* edited by Carl Van Vechten, ©1962 by Random House, Inc.; and to Columbia University Press for permission to reprint "The Imagination of Duchesses" from the English Institute, *Society and Self in the Novel,* edited by Mark Schorer, ©1956 by Columbia University Press. Acknowledgment is made to the New American Library for permission to reprint the Afterword (as "Henry James and *The Wings of the Dove*") to *The Wings of the Dove* by Henry James, ©1956 by the New American Library; the Afterword (as "Max Beerbohm and the Rigors of Fantasy") to *Zuleika Dobson* by Max Beerbohm; the Afterword (as "Flaubert and *The Sentimental Education*") to *The Sentimental Education* by Gustave Flaubert, ©1972 by the New American Library; and the Introduction (as "Samuel Butler's Way") to *The Way of All Flesh* by Samuel Butler ©1967 by Fawcett Publications, Inc.

"Difficulty as Style" first appeared in *The American Scholar;* "A Preface to Lolita" in *Anchor Review, II;* "The Good European" (as "The More-Than-German Mann") and "Pieces of the Hour" in *Commentary;* "Lolita in America" in *Encounter;* "The Secret Life of Edward Windsor" in the *Nation;* "Memories of James Agee" (as "The Prodigious James Agee") and "Thomas Mann's Farewell" in the *New Leader;* "James Baldwin and 'The Man,' " "Kenneth Koch's Poetry" (as "You're Welcome"), "Nabokov: The Prose and Poetry of It All," "The Romance of Charles Chaplin," "Sir Richard and Ruffian Dick," "To Moscow Again," "Samuel Butler and *The Way of All Flesh*" (as "Samuel Butler's Way"), "Max Beerbohm and the Rigors of Fantasy," "Our Man in the Eighteenth Century?," "Truman Capote's *In Cold Blood*" (as "Truman Capote's Score"), "Wilson without Reputation," "Flaubert and *The Sentimental Education*," and the Foreword (as "On F. W. Dupee," by Mary McCarthy) in *The New York Review of Books;* "The Duke's Dilemma" (as "La Rochefoucald's Glory") in *The New York Times;* "England Now—Ariel or Caliban" (as "Theater Chronicles"), "Monstrous Dust," "The King of the Cats" (as "Dreams and Deeds of Yeats"), "The Muse as House Guest," "The Battle of Lowell," "In the Powers Country," and "Malamud: The Uses and Abuses of Commitment" (as "The Power of Positive Sex") in *Partisan Review;* and "Libido is a Latin Word" in *The Reporter.*

Contents

Literary Portraits

Literary Comment

Later Portraits and Comment

Foreword to the
First Edition

With few exceptions the essays and reviews here brought together were originally written for periodicals during the past fifteen years. They have all been much revised and, in some cases, re-titled. I have omitted from the list any extended comment on certain writers (for example Hemingway, Faulkner and Norman Mailer) about whom a profusion of recent criticism already exists in book form. I have given precedence to one type of literary journalism that seemed to me rather neglected when, some ten years ago, I first became aware of its possibilities for me. This is the type that I here call the "literary portrait." Based upon volumes of biography, letters and memoirs, the literary portrait is of course an old form of critical comment. Highly developed in the last century by such writers as Sainte-Beuve and Macaulay, it has not altogether lacked practitioners in the present century, one of them being Edmund Wilson. Naturally I do not pretend that literary portraiture is superior to, or a substitute for, good criticism of a more orthodox kind. I have attempted it only because, as I say, it seemed relatively uncommon in our time and because, for whatever psychological reasons, it has proved attractive to me personally.

No doubt this volume as a whole will strike some readers

as deplorably miscellaneous. Again, I can only plead that I have *liked* being miscellaneous, at whatever cost to outward consistency and inward commitment. I can best explain my liking for it by quoting from a memorial essay on André Gide that I wrote for the *Columbia Review* in 1951, the year of Gide's death. The essay as a whole has not seemed to me worth reprinting in this volume. The parts of it that defined Gide's idea of culture, as I understood it, do however correspond to what I think my own convictions on the subject are —allowing for all possible differences between Gide's mind and accomplishments and mine. The passage also suggests, perhaps, the extent to which his example, together with those of H. L. Mencken, the early T. S. Eliot, Edmund Wilson and other writers closer to home, helped me to piece together, years ago, a conception of culture and of criticism which I have tried in some measure to sustain through the decades:

André Gide did not often talk of culture in a theoretical way; and he never talked, as so many have done in our disrupted age, of the attractions of a *homogeneous* culture. He was conspicuous by the fact that the word "unity," save as a principle of art, had no power to captivate his imagination. If a kind of ideal of cultivation did emerge out of his life and writings and the long guerilla warfare of his ideas, it remained largely unformulated; above all, it was never projected nostalgically on the past or dogmatically on the future. It perhaps only amounted to what a gifted man, or body of such men, could accomplish for himself or themselves by way of the discovery of truth and the creation of beauty in any stage of culture short of barbarism. Gide was not, in my opinion, among the greatest artists of his time. The great poems and novels were written, in many cases, by the very men who dreamed of homogeneous societies: Rilke, Eliot, Yeats, Proust. It remained for Gide to make explicit, and to make *exciting*, the minimum faith, the practical faith in self, by which they all necessarily lived and wrote, and without which they would have been helpless.

Hence his own tireless habit of self-cultivation. In this respect he had always a frankly exalted and exploratory air, like that of a young man proudly getting up on subjects not included in the curriculum and reading Villon in the train. It is true that his moral ideas led a life of their own and did not exist merely to subserve his general culture. Yet they had a distinct bearing on it; even the extreme individualism and diabolism of his earlier years were a way of saying, as Henry James had said in his milder way, that culture was founded in experience, that experience begins with a knowledge of good and evil, and that knowledge is always primarily personal. Nor is it to impugn Gide's authority as an artist to suggest that his writing of tales and plays was itself entirely continuous with his other acts of self-cultivation: his incessant reading, his study of languages, his making of translations and anthologies, his editing and travelling and piano-playing and gardening, his pleasure in botany and entomology. He was a good artist in proportion as he was a good amateur— and in being so he helped to rehabilitate that word *amateur,* which has been made disreputable by the modern pride in pure creation and unremitting professionalism.

1965

Introduction
F. W. Dupee, 1904–1979

Mary McCarthy

"I have *liked* being miscellaneous," Dupee roundly declares in the foreword to *The King of the Cats* (1965), sounding a note of defiance, of boyish stubbornness, where to the ear of a different author an apology might have been called for. "Fred" was taking his stand as a literary journalist, a *flâneur*, a stroller, an idle saunterer, in an age of academic criticism, of "field" specialists on the one hand and fanatic "close readers" on the other. The shorter pieces of *The King of the Cats*, originally written for magazines, seem at first to bear out the confession: he turns from the letters of Dickens to a life of Sir Richard Burton, to "the secret life of Edward Windsor," to the letters of Yeats, to Kafka's letters to a Czech woman he was going to bed with, to Chaplin's autobiography. Quite a variety.

Yet Dupee was no butterfly, no moth singeing his wings at the flame of letters, no boulevardier. Or, rather, all that random sensuous delectation was both real and a masquerade. *The King of the Cats* was less miscellaneous than it appeared. It was not a series of peeps into literary shop windows where the mannequins were being undressed—stately Henry James, naughty Nabokov, Charlie the Tramp. In all its diversity that collection had a remarkable unity, which may or may not have been intentional—a unity of matter as well as of manner and style. Even the most fugitive of those essays (and

there is always something fugitive, some touch of "light housekeeping" in Dupee's approach) is pinned down by slender ties
to its fellows like Gulliver stoutly bound by the Lilliputians.
The point in common, the *trait d'union*, is that Dupee's "remarks," as he called them, tended to be about letters of authors, biographies of authors (La Rochefoucauld, Sir Richard
Burton), autobiographies of non-authors (Chaplin, the Duke
of Windsor), late works of authors (Thomas Mann, James
Agee), rather than about the primary work of authors. The big
exceptions were Gertrude Stein, Proust, Nabokov, and Robert
Lowell's *Life Studies*, which fitted, however, into the overall
Dupee pattern by being, itself, a prose-verse hybrid of autobiography and self-portraiture.

No doubt the unity I speak of was partly imposed by editors,
who "typed" Dupee as they do any regular contributor. He
was the right man to send a volume of Casanova to, a posthumous work of Jim Agee's (he *knew* him; they were friends
through Dwight Macdonald), anything marginally to do with
James, Proust, or Kafka, and, above all, any curio coming to
light in the collector's corners of literature, e.g., a new, unexpurgated translation of Petronius' *Satyricon*. The only misfit (from that point of view) I find in *The King of the Cats*
is a review of J. F. Powers's *Morte d'Urban*. Had I been an
editor at *Partisan Review* then, I would not have thought of
Powers as Dupee material. The Middle West, a golf-playing,
Chevrolet-driving, go-getter of a Catholic priest?—I would
have sent it to James T. Farrell or myself. But maybe Dupee
asked for the book, seeing Powers as a *writer* rather than as a
chronicler of Catholic rectories. Nevertheless the piece, even
more so than its companion, a review of Bernard Malamud's
Idiots First, seems a bit out of place in a collection so uncon-
cerned with grading current fiction. Malamud, too, would

hardly have been a "natural" for Dupee were it not for a curious resemblance noticed by him (and by no one else, surely) between *The Assistant* and *The Golden Bowl*. But there was something else: in the Chagall-like, Orthodox Malamud, Dupee had found an intriguing quality that he had already sensed in the Roman Catholic Powers—that of being *by choice* an outsider, a marginal figure, a minority, in the contemporary republic of letters, whose insiders at the moment of writing were Heller, Burroughs, Pynchon.

The essential art of Dupee is defined by himself in the foreword to *The King of the Cats* as literary portraiture. His models for that, he tells us, were Sainte-Beuve and Macaulay. More generally as influences he cites Gide, Mencken, the early T. S. Eliot, and Edmund Wilson. That is clear; it shines through his work with a wonderful perspicuity, and the visible line of descent going back to a vanishing point is a beauty of his criticism: every debt is gladly acknowledged, and if he with his favorites occupies a slightly larger space than his masters lined up behind, that is only the law of perspective, which requires the present to come forward.

Modesty is one of his critical traits, and he is mannerly, too: in the present collection of his work there is only *one* unfavorable review ("Leavis and Lawrence"); it advances the mild, sidelong suggestion that Leavis is a philistine. "What arrogant nonsense, one is tempted to say, while at the same time remarking on the amazing persistence and tortuous transformations of the philistine spirit in English letters."

The virtual absence of adverse comment is no sign of laxity. Luckily, too, his reviews are not free of mischief, even of delicate malice, as when he observes of Robert Lowell that Boston became "his Lake Country" and that the prose of *Life Studies* is "malign and dazzling." I am not sure whether it was mischief or malice that led him to say that there was something of the eternal bachelor in Yeats (and how true that was of Lady Gregory's star boarder!). Certainly a gleeful mischief dictated the following: "There are old photographs of Burton—dark, beetle-browed, his left cheek deeply scarred where a Somali warrior had put a spear through it, his gaze intensified by what is surely the Evil Eye, his mustaches six inches long and good for twirling. Such photographs suggest those sometimes reproduced on the jackets of books by our scarier contemporaries, Fiedler or Mailer." Blunter and less characteristic is: "*New Poets of England and America* [an anthology] assists us in penetrating the apparent anonymity, not to say nonentity, of the youthful band of men and women who make verse under these circumstances."

"He's French, you see," Edmund Wilson used to emphasize in his roaring voice, meaning, I suppose, that continental sophistication ran in the Dupee blood, making him suaver than his fellow *PR* editors—Rahv and Phillips and Dwight Macdonald. I don't know how much French blood Fred really had—perhaps a quarter or an eighth, certainly not as much as Wilson liked to imagine. In the distant past, Fred thought, the name had been "Dupuis." A true middle-westerner, from Joliet, Illinois, he had no more command of spoken French than Wilson and probably less of the written language. I doubt that it was his major field at Yale. Yet he was almost fatally attracted to French literature, starting with Stendhal. (I never heard him speak of the old authors, not even the likely ones— Montaigne, Louise Labé, Maurice Scève. . . . The exception was Rousseau, maybe not surprisingly in view of the *Confessions*. And there was also, I suddenly remember, Chateaubriand: *Mémoires d'outre-tombe*.) For *PR* in the early days, his undisputed "field" was French culture and politics.

Our interest in Gide was spurred mainly by him. At least it was at his urging that we published Gide's second thoughts on his trip to the Soviet Union, which I translated. And he was very much aware of Sartre—the Sartre of *Le Mur* and *La Nausée* in preference to the philosopher. When existentialism came in, after the war, our French specialist turned into William Barrett, who knew philosophy, the modern kind, and was able to read *L'Être et le néant*. But Dupee remained the magazine's authority on Malraux and the aesthetics of action; I remember a very long article, in several parts, I think, that he was writing on Malraux and could not seem to finish. Composition was hard for him then. There was no question with him of a "writing block," like the one Dwight Macdonald got when the wind of radicalism went out of his sails, but the act of writing was painful, and Malraux was his most agonizing subject. He did finally finish that study, shortly after we had despaired. But he did not choose to reprint it in *The King of the Cats* or schedule it for inclusion in the present collection.

The truth was, he wrote extremely well. I do not think that we on *PR* were fully conscious of that. Knowing the pain he suffered over those pieces, we were conscious of the process rather than of the result. Only now, reading the essays over, I see how brilliant they are in what appears to be an effortless way. He is amusing, observant, nonchalant. The tone is that of conversation. The continuing flashes of insight appear almost casually, like heat lightning. There are many offhand lines, let drop as it were negligently, in an undertone. Kafka's letters are reminders of "the lost art of being unhappy." James Baldwin's sentences "suggest the ideal prose of an ideal literary community, some aristocratic France of one's dreams." Writing of *Pale Fire*, he lightly observes that Nabokov has made a "team" of the poet and the novelist in himself. Recalling James Agee, he mentions the Luce connection and lets fall the dreadful phrase "captive genius," without stress, without follow-up. In his essay on "difficulty" (a theme that recently took George Steiner a whole book to deal with), he calmly wonders whether "a high degree of difficulty is not an aspect of the modern poetic style just as a peculiarly brilliant and aggressive clarity was a stylistic aspect of the school of Pope." And, of Flaubert, very simply: "He lived amid a clutter of dormant manuscripts."

He has a wonderful gift for quotation, bearing witness to a memory stuffed with luscious plums, which he pulls out one by one for our benefit. He gets his title for the 1965 collection from words Yeats is supposed to have spoken on hearing from his sister that Swinburne was dead: "I know, and now I am king of the cats." The quotations he pulls out often have juicy traces of anecdote clinging to them, e.g., the following, drawn from Burton's "Terminal Essay" to his translation of *The Arabian Nights:* "How is it possible for a sodomite Moslem prince to force a Christian missionary against his will and the strong resistance instinctively put up by his sphincter muscle? Burton could tell us: by the judicious use of a tent peg."

Dupee's criticism, in fact, is strongly anecdotal throughout. That is what gives it worldliness—both kinds, the terrestrial and the social. As he came to understand this of himself as a literary artist, we can watch his work grow. In his unsurpassed essay on *L'Éducation sentimental*—one of the last pieces he published—he asserts the sovereignty of the anecdote for a kind of new and modern epic, whose nature is "mock" or comic. The enthronement of the anecdotal means that the work affirming it will be flooded with irony. Flaubert's feat in *L'Éducation* was "to have made an epic novel out of an accumulation of anecdotes." It follows that "each episode extracts from the situation a maximum of irony and then, having made its point with a precision consonant with its brevity, is caught up in the furious current of the enveloping narrative." This accords with the mood of drift, so terribly modern, so twentieth-century, that pervades *L'Éducation*, which might have been subtitled "The Story of a Drifter," just as well as "The Story of a Young Man." No doubt it means something that our first glimpse of Frédéric Moreau is on a river boat that is bringing him home from Paris to Nogent-sur-Seine; he is susceptible to tidal currents, the ebb and flow of the age, the eddies of art and politics, and the net effect of the novel is of a general purposelessness. Dupee likens it to Joyce in its rigorous impersonality but distinguishes it from Joyce by the coldness Flaubert shows toward his characters, in comparison to which Joyce is "warm."

In this late and splendidly written essay, we seem to see Dupee at last finding himself. Always brilliant, succinct, intelligent, informative, "French," in Wilson's word, here he is decidedly more—emotionally moving, electric. I had often suspected, fancifully, that Fred identified himself with Frédéric Moreau, a bit because of the name and a bit because he, too, in his younger years, had known "the melancholy of steamboats," if not in the most literal sense. But this penetrating essay is an act of total self-recognition (if Frédéric is Flaubert, he is also, transparently, Fred); it is the apotheosis of a wry, self-observing nature, and, as always happens at such moments of confrontation, the reader feels caught in the mirror, too.

There is little left here of his faithful old models, Macaulay, Mencken, and the others. In some respect, even before this, he had left Wilson, his immediate mentor, behind: in the Gertrude Stein essay (cf. the *Axel's Castle* handling of her); in

the several essays on Nabokov and *Lolita;* in the Samuel Butler foreword ("In Butler, the man and the writer were entangled as the drowning man is entangled with his rescuer"),
which, after the Flaubert, is my favorite and shows a fineness
of intuition of which Wilson with his wounds and bows was
incapable; finally in his sympathetic short book on James (cf.
Wilson on "The Turn of the Screw"). The difference, as I see
it, is that Wilson took on himself the "heavy," huffing-and-
puffing role of educator to his readers while Dupee made
himself into a teacher in real life, first at Bard, then at Columbia, and in his writings did not seek to instruct but instead
learned from his subject with a jaunty grace. The result was
the sense of a mind and personality growing that buoys us up
as we reach the end of this volume, knowing regretfully there
will be no more. And it is perhaps not complete chance that
the visible growth of Dupee coincides with the birth of *The
New York Review* (1963) where he had not only a more
amused, appreciative, in short more sympathetic audience in
Barbara Epstein and Robert Silvers and also more space. The
earliest essay in the new collection that seems unmistakably
his is the Burton portrait—"Sir Richard and Ruffian Dick."
Moreover, it was in *The New York Review* that the final,
Flaubert essay appeared.

One aspect of Dupee I miss in what I have been saying is
the side that—after Yale, after a short-lived little magazine
called *The Miscellany* he and Dwight Macdonald edited with
another friend, after a year of semi-slumming in Mexico—
became an organizer for the Communist Party on the New
York waterfront and concurrently literary editor of the *New
Masses.* I do not see where a CP "streak" in him fits, unless
he got it from the *Zeitgeist,* like a Thirties Frédéric Moreau.
He was always against authority, but that fails to explain it—
the Party was authority incarnate. It was at some *good* urging,

I now feel, that he joined and bravely passed out leaflets. He wanted to be helpful to our poor, foolish, grotesque old society. Could that have had something to do with coming from Joliet, which after all is a prison town? Prison towns are sinister and hateful, and in Marxism he may have seen a set of burglar's tools to smuggle past the guards to the inmates. You cannot grow up in the shadow of prison walls without a few generous daydreams of escape for those inside.

Maybe so, but I wonder where the boyish idealism *went* when the Party let him down. Stalinism, now advertising itself as twentieth-century Americanism, had shown its colors in the Moscow trials and the Spanish betrayal and it was not too hard for Macdonald to convince him to leave the Party and the *New Masses*, taking the correspondence files with him. He appeared blithe about it; indeed, nobody breaking with Stalinism ever seemed to suffer regrets. And his sojourn there with Trachtenberg's "boys" had not been long: I first met him, just back from Mexico, at a party for the sharecroppers, given by Macdonald in 1935; by 1937, at the second congress of the League of American Writers, he was on our side. And I don't think he lost his idealism in the course of that adventure. It must have turned into an underground stream, making his teaching (he was very popular) fertile. Was it out of pure nonconformity that he never got his Ph.D.? I cannot find the idealism, as such, in his later writing. But it may be its long-term effects I notice in the growth indicators exuberantly branching and swelling in his later work. In 1968, anyway, at Columbia during the student strike, he risked some brand new dentistry to join a line of faculty drawn up to protect another group of "boyish idealists" from the forces of order and got a black eye for doing so.

1983

Literary
Portraits

The
Other
Dickens

In our time Dickens has been as thoroughly rediscovered as any writer of the past—assuming that he was ever really lost to view. His major novels are all once more in print, supplied with painstaking introductions by some of the best critics. In "Dickens: The Two Scrooges," Edmund Wilson has devoted to him one of his finest psychological studies; and Edgar Johnson's two-volume Life, *Charles Dickens: His Tragedy and Triumph,* is the definitive work in its field and a classic of modern biography. Only Dickens's letters have remained inaccessible, save in old, untrustworthy, out-of-print editions or in an enormous, expensive, out-of-print edition of more recent date. An exception is *The Heart of Charles Dickens,* the volume that Professor Johnson has made from Dickens's letters to Angela Burdett-Coutts. But these are his communications to a rather special lady with whom he had a rather special relationship. Meanwhile, in the bulk and variety of his labors as a correspondent Dickens made a great contribution to epistolary literature. His genius—as writer, friend, and public man—informs most of his letters, from the confident opening lines to the confident signature.

It was a remarkable signature for those days of emphatic identities asserted in fancy penmanship. The assertion of identity was emphatic but the penmanship was not fancy. It

said CHARLES DICKENS in large, easily legible characters; and when there was space left on the page, the pen
tended to race on, filling it with a long kite-tail of a flourish.
In those free, full, unembarrassed transfusions of personality
that were Dickens's letters, even the flourish seemed to say
something. One could read in it a reluctance to finish, a
promise of more to come, a sort of "to be continued" such as
he appended to the successive installments of his serially
published novels. One of the incidental attractions of the letters is that they are rather different in spirit—we shall presently see how—from the novels. Yet they obviously owe
some of their disciplined spontaneity to their origin in a
mind habituated to ready communication, affectionately
conscious of an affectionate audience, aware that its produc-
tions were being eagerly waited for. No doubt this awareness
sometimes weighed heavily on Dickens as a correspondent.
He was a prodigy of good will and fluency, not a monster of
them, and he could be perfunctory, slightly impatient, apolo-
getic for lapses and delays, like anybody else. One acquaintance living in Lausanne seems to have expected him to
report periodically on world affairs. This man inspired the
only dull sequence of letters Dickens wrote.

For the rest, the promise of more to come was generally
fulfilled with the expected liveliness. He wrote to a number
of friends through long, formidably busy years; while the unknown admirer of his work or petitioner for his charity was
reasonably certain to get a reply that was charming,
thoughtful and believable beyond the call of duty. For Dickens made duty a pleasure if anyone ever did, and as a correspondent it was his pleasure to breathe amiability upon what
he knew to be an unlovely world. His letters were acts of
friendship, even when they were about business. Any claims

they have on literature are primarily based on this consideration. He wrote them to further human intercourse, not to
further the art of letter-writing as such. Whatever thoughts
he may have had of posterity were probably attended by the
hope that posterity would be disappointed. He made bonfires
of the letters that came to him from others; and if he failed to
ask that all of his own be destroyed in turn, it was doubtless
from common sense. They were too numerous, too far-flung.
Sitting down to his correspondence nearly every day of his
life, when his literary work for that day was done, he wrote
as many as twelve letters at a stretch and sent them off just
about everywhere. Only a bonfire on a world scale could
have destroyed the letters of Charles Dickens.

His correspondents naturally tended to preserve them and
they survive today by the thousands. The known or suspected losses in their ranks are few. These include the letters
he wrote to Ellen Ternan, his mistress in his last years, which
exist so far only in rumor; and those parts of his letters to
John Forster that Forster disposed of after pasting the other,
and doubtless more significant parts, in the manuscript of his
Life of Charles Dickens. In the largest collection of Dickens's
letters to date, that of the Nonesuch edition of his work, they
fill three tall volumes of some nine hundred pages each, and
the projected Pilgrim edition of them will probably be larger
by several volumes.

Their very abundance is one of the essential characteristics of Dickens's letters. Without it they would not be that
"*auto-biography*, unrivaled in clearness and credibility,"
which Carlyle said they were. They would not be "in themselves a life work," as Lionel Trilling says they are. Dickens's
letters are a life work in themselves because they are distinct
in bulk and, as noted above, partly distinct in spirit from his

life work as a novelist, while being in their lesser way comparable to the novels in scope and quality. Their scope is Dickens's scope as the most popular good writer of his day and the master of his age in many of its extra-literary aspects. Their quality is his quality as a man and is as plain to see as it is intricate in its manifestations and causes.

A man of action if any literary man ever was, he writes his letters not as a spectator of events but as one who is in the thick of them. Indeed he is best at reporting events of his own making, and these were spectacular enough. Certain occasions excepted, he is no such social observer as Horace Walpole and Henry Adams are in their letters. Of affairs beyond his reach he is a diffident, even impatient, chronicler, unless he can project himself into them by some feat of comic fantasy. This he does, for example, in the case of Queen Victoria's marriage, which he proposes to prevent by storming the palace and carrying her off like Lochinvar; or in that of the Crystal Palace exposition, where a tale told of a little boy lost at the exposition and wandering out into London under the impression that he is still inside the grounds contains the writer's whole exasperated response to that famous showing of the trophies of human progress.

Dickens is a man of action for whom the troubled, often fruitless, distinctions between art and action, artist and man, artist and non-artist scarcely exist. His whole personal history works against them. His vocation for literature follows naturally, if by no means inevitably, from his youthful occupation as a reporter. He continues to identify that vocation with a regular trade or profession; and he labors to enhance its dignity in a society that is far from generous in granting dignity to the unestablished, whether persons or classes or professions. The society's cruel exclusiveness is hateful to him; yet he strives to establish himself and his fellow writers in it on their own terms.

In all this Dickens's passion for justice is inflamed by an undying sense of outrage which had its beginnings in the now famous ordeal of his boyhood. The distress of the twelve-year-old boy who saw his father suddenly imprisoned for debt and was himself made to drudge long hours in the unaccustomed squalor of a shoe-blacking plant lives on in the mature Dickens, although he confides these facts to John Forster alone. Indeed the events of his twelfth year seem to have constituted one of those family crises that cast their shadow back over the family's past and forward over its future. For young Dickens it was a crisis of the affections as well as a crisis in the Dickenses' social history. A nestling suddenly thrust from the nest, he never quite forgave his mother for her seeming indifference to his sufferings in the blacking plant. Grown up and married, he tends to visit his suspicions and resentments on his own wife, who, aided no doubt by her intrinsic faults, is finally made to re-enact the essentials of the mother's failure: she too is "apathetic" (his word) towards *their* children.

At the same time he has fears for the social well-being of the family. His paternal grandparents were domestic servants; and although his father, John Dickens, succeeded in extricating himself from that class—he was first a government employee, then a journalist of sorts—he was given to improvidence as to a kind of fate. There is reason to guess that he was morally unequal to his improved social position, remaining always in a state of partial dependency on others and his genial fecklessness turned into an ungenial, even criminal, parasitism in two of Charles Dickens's brothers. Hence Dickens's tremendous will to power, to success in the world, to respectability; and hence his affinity with another active type of his century (and ours), a type more ambitious than the craftsman or professional. Dickens is the artist as tycoon, dedicated to building up an impregnable personal empire, literary, domestic, and financial. His ambition throbs unmistakably in his letters. Like our Victorian grandfathers whose sense of power was manifested in their weighty tread on the floor, their heavily drawn breaths, their loudly ticking watches, Dickens is almost physically present in the assured rhythms and turns of speech of his epistolary prose. He knows, as he confides to his wife, "what a thing it is to have power." Yet his sense of power is infinitely refined by its supreme confidence in itself, in short by his consciousness of genius; and his greatness, unlike that of the legendary tycoon, is of the proudly accommodating kind. Much of the legendary life of that type is nevertheless in evidence in his letters. Three times he and his family make that significant move which Hardy will describe in one of his great poems.

> They change to a high new house,
> He, she, all of them—aye,
> Clocks and carpets and chairs
>   On the lawn all day . . .

Three times the Dickenses move, each time to a higher house. Indeed, no ordinary tycoon cared more for clocks and carpets and chairs—or mirrors and curtains and stairs—than Dickens does. In his householding capacity he combines the scruples of an ambitious hostess with the vigilance of a concierge. His passion for domestic order equals his sense of power but can seem more oppressive, for it often appears to operate at the expense of his wife. Poor "apathetic" incompetent Catherine Dickens, so tactless in company, so given to misdirecting letters, turning her ankle, falling through trap-doors on stages, dropping her bracelets in the soup—she is definitely not to be trusted as a householder. When he proposes to bring a guest home for the week end he must tell her to arrange the guest's room in such and such a manner and lay out a copy of the newly published *Scarlet Letter* for him to read (the guest is a judge).

Yet Dickens has real cause for anxiety in these respects. With his large and clamoring body of dependents, including the ten children that the listless but ineluctably fertile Catherine bears him, he is often a very put-upon man, a condition he supports with amazing humor, fortitude and cleverness. But he doesn't merely support this life; he turns it into elaborate gaiety with his inventive parties, games, theatricals, pet names. And if he generally adheres to the type of the tycoon, like Scott, the elder Dumas, Mark Twain and other writers of the nineteenth century, he avoids what was often their fate. His unsuccessful ventures are few and he never knows the ultimate Victorian disgrace of a bankruptcy.

This triumphant man of action naturally admires the active virtues and suspects the passive ones. "What a long time he is, growing up," Dickens remarks with dry indulgence about his father. "Manly," meaning what we mean by "mature," is a favorite word of praise with him; and his passion for maturity helps to determine the moral atmosphere of his letters. It is, however, an atmosphere in which the *style* of a deed, the tact or humor or pride that goes into its performance, contributes much to its value. In his feeling for the aesthetics of conduct he is not to be surpassed by Henry James. And in his moral sense the Dickens of the letters is more urbane, sinuous, experimental than the reader of his novels might expect him to be. Where the novelist is often instinctively identified with the stark taboos and inclusive judgments of the folk mind of his time, the letter-writer draws his standards more from his daily experience in the world, often ignoring the taboos, judging people according to their merits as individuals, or simply suspending judgment. The very firmness of his literary bond with the popular morality allows him a large liberty when it comes to particular cases. The Victorian smugness—there are other kinds—which in its sheer excess of feeling advertises an uneasy relation to the popular morality, is alien to Dickens. He probably could not write what Thackeray wrote to his mother, speaking of *Villette:* "I don't make my *good* women ready to fall in love with two men at once." Nor would he, in all likelihood, simply *refuse* to read the notorious Balzac, as George Eliot refused to do.

Sometimes Dickens appears to be surprised by his own susceptibility. During one of his philanthropic ventures he encounters a young woman whom circumstances have forced into genteel prostitution and who yet enjoys the love and respect of her brother and even humbly respects herself—"respects" is of course the key word and it is Dickens's. Her life, he asserts, is "a romance so astonishing and yet so intelligible as I never had the boldness to think of." It is: sexual vice is incompatible with respect and love in the world of his novels. Indeed Dickens's personal story as it appears in his letters must itself often seem a romance that he never thought of as a writer. It is a romance in which, for example, a nobleman (the Duke of Devonshire) can be really noble and a woman with a past (Lady Blessington) can be completely charming. It is a romance, too, in which the poor and the oppressed can arouse his unqualified ire, even when they are acting out of the very exigencies of their condition. This the unfortunate baker's man learns when he is caught urinating on Dickens's gate, is threatened with the Police Act by the great humanitarian himself, and can only demand to know, as Dickens reports, "what I should do 'if I was him.'" It is a romance, finally, in which the rhythms of existence itself are indifferent to moral impulses. Here Time alone is the great force for change and no one is hustled to his destiny by any patrol wagon of a plot. As distinguished from the characters in his novels, his acquaintances merely alter with the years, for better and worse, as people do in what we call "life" and in novels of the kind Dickens didn't write.

The differences are, however, far from absolute. Especially at moments of great emotional stress is the novelist firmly reunited with the letter-writer. The impulse of melodrama breaks out in him in the fierce accusations and final judgments he brings to the affair of his separation from his wife. On the other hand, his extravagantly idealizing tendency makes an unmitigated heroine of Mary Hogarth, his dead sister-in-law, as it does of the Little Nells and Esther Summersons of his novels.

Readers of Dickens's letters breathe not only an intriguing moral air but an exhilarating air of vast public acclaim. As between Dickens and his public, the acclaim is seen to be intensely heady, richly earned, cheerfully given, cheerfully accepted. Originating with the success of *The Pickwick Papers,* his fame is sustained by his continued performance as a novelist and by his other brilliant activities. The fame follows him all his days like a brass band and can be heard sounding from the distant square even when he is in seclusion. Indeed it has the peculiar interest of seeming to exceed its natural causes, as poetry does, or what is called "grace." A self-enhancing sort of fame, a celebrated celebrity, it is the kind of thing that people of all classes and tastes enjoy participating in. Dickens is the man you love to love, as Charlie Chaplin will be in his heyday, only Dickens is far more so. And Dickens never has a heyday followed by a fall from grace of the sort that often occurs in these situations. When opposition threatens, as it frequently does, especially in the easily stampeded American public which he confronts during his two stormy tours of the United States, he knows how to defy it and make it work for him. The band music never turns to jeers and never really stops.

His reporting of his exploits, in his letters, is a triumph of what I have called his accommodating pride. No other hero has ever made the life of heroism more attractive, more believable. Mere modesty is as foreign to him as mere vanity. He can delight in his fame without either exaggerating it or diminishing it, and his friends can become naturalized citizens of his privileged world without forfeiting their sense of the privilege. Sharing the pleasures of his celebrity with his correspondents, he is able to avoid the nemesis of egotism. The Dickens of the letters is superstitious in the profound way that other great men of action have been superstitious. Rarely does he announce any plan without adding "God willing," as if intent on appeasing a still greater planmaker than himself. So too with the news he gives his correspondents of his feats as a writer, actor, reader from his works, party giver, or whatever. He takes the curse off his ego by splitting his ego up. There is the Charles Dickens who writes the letters and there is "the inimitable Boz," that convenient alter-ego early bestowed on him by a former teacher. Dickens becomes, along with his friends, the fascinated observer of this phenomenal homunculus of a Boz. Boz can do anything. If he starts to break down under the strain, just feed him a dozen oysters and a pint of champagne and he will bounce back. Boz acts; Dickens watches, enjoys, and records the results in his letters. This process makes for accuracy as well as detachment on the letter-writer's part. The creator of the fantastic Mrs. Gamp and the fantastic Circumlocution Office is able to convey the assurance that he doesn't fancify facts in his letters. Nor do the facts require embroidering; they are fantastic in themselves.

With the years his fame only increases, reaching a high point when at last he takes to the road as a reader from his works, face to face with his tumultuous public. Meanwhile the letters testify to a counter-development in him, a growing consciousness of his inner self and its unappeasable desires. The "one happiness I have missed in life" begins to haunt him and make him fearfully restless. The one happiness is several things: sex, easy companionship, freedom from the self-imposed restraints of his impregnable personal empire, freedom to write in defiance of the Victorian taboos that he himself has done much to establish. All of these and more: he comes to know the intrinsic sense of loss that is common to the supreme genius who is exhausting the possibilities of his culture, of his very condition as a human being. Dickens does not respond to this tragic process as Tolstoy will do, by a mental flight, magnificent and quixotic, into the infinite. A man of action to the end, Dickens meets the situation as he can—by putting his wife away, secretly taking a mistress, going on the road, amassing still more fame and money. On the question of literary freedom he is assailed by an angry incoherence that is quite untypical of him. He blames the English morality, blames those who find fault with it, and does nothing except to avail himself more and more of the greater personal freedom of Paris. *His* flight is limited by geography; and the scrutiny of his inner self, carried on in letters to Forster and others, has comparable limits. He undertakes it not as one who makes a practice of introspection but as one who is driven to it by a great need and rises gallantly to the occasion. Thus the risks run by the *confirmed* introspective are, at least, not Dickens's risks. He is in no danger of talking himself morosely and glibly out of existence. In his unprecedented—for him—confession to Maria Winter, despite all the sad things he confesses to, there is the exhilaration of discovery, the freshness of a relatively untried passion and idiom.

His pleasure in friendship never lessens, however, and he adds to the sum of his acquaintances the rather racy and adventurous—one gathers—Wilkie Collins, his occasional companion in Paris and Italy. Friendship is Dickens's natural medium as a man. It remains generally unthreatened by the fierce demands he often makes upon his domestic intimates. He is obviously not a virtuoso of love but he is a virtuoso of friendship, practicing his art on all comers and thus transfiguring—as far as anyone can—the dreary realities of strife and boredom. But it is no improbable idyl of friendship that the letters record. His amiability can turn into bitterness and even physical revulsion. Beneath his manly good will, his hearty toleration of people, there is an aching fastidiousness. From egotism in its many guises he recoils exactly as he does in his novels, such vices manifesting themselves for him in deformities of body and speech. "The shape of his head (I see it now) was misery to me, and weighed me down in my youth," he says of Lord Grey, the statesman whom the young Dickens, as a reporter in the Parliament, had seen and heard too much of. So there is in the letters news of quarrels; and Dickens occasionally criticizes the people who are closest to him, complaining of Forster's loudness of speech and mildly caricaturing Collins's pretentious chatter about the arts. But there is a taboo on criticism for its own sake, and malice is definitely banned. Good will prevails, and not only for reasons of conscience. The friends addressed in Dickens's letters have a way of being more than friends in the abstract. He likes to put them to work, to associate them with him in various enterprises that redound to their common good and pleasure. John Forster is not only his intimate friend but his literary counselor and, on occasion, his collaborator in the financing and editing of periodicals. Forster is a special case of a general rule. Dickens involves others in his elaborate theatricals, interests them in his philanthropies, makes them contributors to his periodicals, engages them in strenuous well-planned excursions. A visit to the Honorable Richard Watson of Rockingham Castle is apt to center on the production of a play, with all present taking parts. Friendship may sometimes be tried by such exertions but it is kept from languishing. This Victorian Falstaff embroils almost everyone in his intricate frolics and as a result almost everyone shows unsuspected talent, helping the company to earn large sums for charity and to make the Queen laugh—she will not be excluded from the revels.

In most cases, it is true, his close friends are the kind of people who can profit from such exercises. Dickens's immediate circle consists of journalists like Douglas Jerrold, Mark Lemon and W. H. Wills, men of the theater like W. C. Macready, popular artists and illustrators like Daniel Maclise and Clarkson Stanfield, fellow novelists of wide appeal like Collins and Bulwer-Lytton. With all their differences and their often prominent egos, they have by trade or temperament a common accessibility to the gregarious London life

and the resounding public occasion. This does not keep some
of them from enjoying a high degree of intimacy with Dickens. Forster and Collins obviously share his confidences and
know his opinions on most subjects. It is not in any of them,
however, to be to Dickens what, say, Schiller was to Goethe,
or George Sand to Flaubert, or Hawthorne to Melville. Evidently it is not in Dickens to require friends and correspondents of this stature, and the absence of them is doubtless
felt as a loss to his letters considered as literary documents.
He is often discriminating in what he says about works of
literature, including his own works. But he is best in his
powerful feeling for the general responsibilities and privileges of the literary *profession*. He is untempted by those
further reaches of thought which, for many writers, make the
exchange of letters with their peers an adventure and a necessity.

The power of thought displayed in his letters is of quite
another kind. It springs from his concentration upon the
world of actual experience, above all the world of social experience, as he knows it in the mid-nineteenth century. The
imposition of a new industrial order on a feudal order of long
standing throws that world into confusion, misery and fear—
a fear of revolution comparable in its intensity to the fear of
atomic extinction pervading our own mid-century; and Dickens's mind is constantly harassed and exercised by the dis-
tressing spectacle. But he takes thought of the abuses only
with the intention of taking action against them. The *habit* of
reform, which afflicts others of his time and will afflict even
Bernard Shaw, is absent from Dickens's temperament. In his
letters he denounces the abuses rather less often than we
might expect of so famous a champion of the unfortunate. He
is too busy with his practical attempts at reform to devote

much passion to their manifestations and causes. It is during his first tour of the United States, where he is not only greatly disappointed but—as a foreigner—relatively helpless to do anything, that he is most fiercely and consistently the social observer. In America, therefore, the essential concern of all his criticism becomes unmistakably clear. It is directed chiefly against the failures of intelligence, courage and feeling in individuals. Whether he is assailing the new practice of solitary confinement in American prisons, or the tendency to conformity among American writers, or the national love of boasting and snooping, Dickens usually comes down to the problems of personality and the well-being of the single separate person, including the artist. "*You* live here, Macready, as I have sometimes heard you imagining!" he writes from Baltimore in 1842. "Macready, if I had been born here and had written my books in this country, producing them with no stamp of approval from other lands, it is my solemn belief that I should have lived and died poor, unnoticed, and a 'black sheep' to boot."

True, Dickens's name has become a byword for the reforming artist. Yet there is in all his letters, I think, no mention of an abuse, from the Ragged Schools to the pirating practices of editors, that the most ardent conservative of our own day would not find intolerable, an invasion not merely of the "rights" but of the bases of personality. In this way Dickens remains the friend of the race as well as of his numerous correspondents; and it is to the race that his letters, careless though he was of their future, finally belong.

1960

Sir Richard
and
Ruffian Dick

In high school a friend and I sometimes managed to get hold of the various volumes of *The Arabian Nights* in the privately printed translation by Richard Burton. There we found greater wonders than any in "Aladdin and His Lamp" and other expurgated or inauthentic examples of oriental story that had reached us as children. In Burton's "Terminal Essay" to the *Nights*, when we had the luck to get it also, were still better things, true things in plain prose with a minimum of Latin. How is it possible for a sodomite Moslem prince to force a Christian missionary against his will and the strong resistance instinctively put up by his sphincter muscle? Burton could tell us: by the judicious use of a tent peg. Not that we had really wondered about such things. Burton's attraction was that he set the questions as well as answered them, enlarging our curiosity even while he satisfied it—the perfect pedagogue. There was much also in the "Terminal Essay" to inflame the anti-Victorian passions we were beginning to feel. The Victorian age, Burton said, was "saturated with cant and hypocrisy." We knew that already but were always glad to hear it said again. But I doubt that we knew anything about the other exploits for which he had once been famous: his pilgrimage, in Moslem disguise, to Mecca; his expedition to the still more forbidden city of Harrar; his discovery of Lake Tanganyika, an adventure that inspired Livingstone and Stanley and helped to clear up the ancient mystery surrounding the sources of the Nile. It seems unlikely that we knew how very recently he had died (in 1890).

A revival of Burton in all his aspects appears a possibility at present. His translations of the *Kama Sutra* and *The Perfumed Garden*, those cheerful excursions into sexual physiology, have circulated both in hard covers and in paperback. Three new accounts of his career have come out in the recent years. Two of them (*That Blackguard Burton*, by Alfred Bercovici, and *Death Rides a Camel*, by Allen Edwardes) are potboilers; but the third, *Burton, A Biography of Sir Richard Francis Burton*, by Byron Farwell, is a thorough and conscientious book, chiefly factual, rarely reflective. Presumably the writers and publishers responsible for these books think of Burton as a timely subject. Is he by some chance a spiritual ancestor of the many who at present, and generally with reason, seek to accomplish a moral revolution, a "breakthrough" into realms of greater personal autonomy and sexual freedom? Possibly. There are old photographs of Burton —dark, beetle-browed, his left cheek deeply scarred where a Somali warrior had put a spear through it, his gaze intensified by what is surely the Evil Eye, his mustaches six inches long and good for twirling. Such photographs suggest those sometimes reproduced on the jackets of books by our scarier contemporaries, Fiedler or Mailer, their faces bearded, sweaty, hostile, furrowed with existential woe.

On the whole, though, it is a question whether Burton is an ancestor anyone would want to claim. On Mr. Farwell's evidence, he was a compulsive egocentric whose arrogance and xenophobia surpassed even those of the Baron de Charlus. Whether Burton was as large a bundle of vices as Proust's character was is not clear from this book, to which Mr. Farwell, an IBM executive stationed in Switzerland, brings an innocence that is in remarkable contrast to its subject (the book, unfortunately, is also innocent of footnotes). But rumors abound, flowing chiefly no doubt from such writings of Burton's as the "Terminal Essay," with its luxuriant account of the history and techniques of pederasty. And just as there can be little doubt that he "tried everything," so there is little doubt that his sexual interests were connected with, and largely subordinate to, his sadistic ones. Charlus merely liked to snub his inferiors and be beaten with chains. Burton's writings show him to have been fascinated with forms of torture, with the surgical processes of circumcision and castration, both of males and females; with the art of scalping as practiced by American Indians; with the size of the genitals of males and females and the degree of satisfaction or its opposite implied by their size (he was a great measurer of the sexual organs of obliging natives). What makes him so difficult a hero, however, is not his sexuality, hot or cold, but his insensate truculence, as of a human weapon in perpetual readiness to deliver. As such he provides a very good show. An extreme case of the aberrant Victorian, he can greatly fascinate, if nothing else. If there was ever an unlovable rogue before the heroes of *The Ginger Man* and *Look Back in Anger* it was Richard Burton.

It all began, possibly, when, aged about six, he was taken by the headmaster of his French school to watch the guillotining of a criminal. He seems to have remembered this and left some record of it, for Mr. Farwell is able to recount the incident in some detail. Anyway, Burton's career as a voyeur of the lurid and exotic was in motion. His parents were well born and well-to-do and chose to lead a wandering life on the Continent: Tours, Blois, Pisa, Siena, Rome, etc. In Naples, Burton, now aged fifteen, was collecting for burial the corpses of cholera victims in the streets and noting the curious phosphorescence the bodies gave off at night. Later, an officer in the Bombay Native Infantry, he was inspecting male brothels in Sind and submitting to the army authorities a report on techniques and finances (boys cost more than eunuchs). The report was unsolicited and unwelcome. A man that interested in vice was assumed to be vicious himself in those pre-Kinsey days. Future promotions for Burton were delayed, but lengthy leaves of absence were granted him several times.

His absences bring us to another side of Richard Burton. They were usually granted that he might pursue his study of oriental languages. This, naturally, was a subject of considerable utility to the invading British, and Burton had a genius and a passion for it. His delight in *any* learning acquired on his own was extreme—he had despised Oxford during a brief stay there and had got himself expelled. He was among the chief of the Victorian autodidacts just as he was among the most formidable eccentrics of the time, and the two roles were perhaps in his case related. "Eccentricity is, in fact, practical madness," V. S. Pritchett has said; it is resorted to "by those who are secretly up to something shameful or stupid or muddleheaded. And in England most of us are." Burton was muddleheaded but not stupid. His instinct of self-concealment, if he had one, took the form of a sheltering bravado which was in turn inseparable from his public personality. It earned him the nicknames of "Ruffian Dick" and "The White Negro" among his army messmates in India. At home he was to enjoy the friendship of Milnes, Swinburne,

Frederick Hankey, and other participants in, or connoisseurs of, *le vice anglais* (the phrase was used by Burton for sodomy and later by Mario Praz in *The Romantic Agony* for sadism). Thus his eccentricity was not in any simple sense a stratagem of self-concealment. It expressed, at least in part, an organic independence of English manners. This independence had been fostered by the years he spent abroad as child and boy, years prolonged in substance by the ceaseless changes of residence and the ever larger opportunities for graver and graver mischief (whores, swordplay, pyromania, attempted descents into the crater of Vesuvius).

Burton, it seems, reacted against his English origins in proportion as his feckless English parents proved incapable of controlling him and his younger brother (later beaten into lifelong idiocy by natives during an elephant hunt in India). England, Burton maintained, was hopelessly "lower class"; Oxford, apart from the gypsies camped in Bagley Wood, was dull. His expressed detestation of England seems to have exceeded in intensity any possible cause except one: an inverted nostalgia on his part, the will to defy what he had been deprived of. Perhaps this was the secret which he sought to disguise by his "practical madness." If so, the disguise was almost literal. His dark looks were alarmingly conspicuous in England and gave rise to suspicions that he had gypsy blood himself.

His love of learning was genuine, whatever its causes. True, the rage for collecting facts and impressions was, with him, indiscriminate. Tolstoy says of Vronsky when, self-exiled in Florence with Anna Karenina, Vronsky begins to be bored: "He was a sensible man and a Russian and could not merely go around looking at things, like an Englishman." The titles of Burton's 29-odd books give an idea of the variety of things he looked at: they range from *Etruscan Bologna: A Study* to *Falconry in the Valley of the Indus* to *A Glance at the* [Oberammergau] *"Passion Play."* Yet he was the opposite of the idle tourist Tolstoy had in mind. His traveling and looking were forms of participation in the community life of places other than England, places of his own choosing. He learned languages by taking native mistresses or, possibly, minions; he perfected them by assuming native disguises and setting up as a shopkeeper in the souks. In India once he acquired several monkeys, dressed a female of the troupe in silks and pearl earrings, and lived with them all as with a wife and family, meanwhile studying monkey language. Among the adherents of Sufism, an esoteric Islamic sect, he attained high rank.

Not that Burton gives much evidence of *enjoying* foreign places and peoples. On the contrary. Only among the desert Bedouins was he the utopian traveler. He admired the Bedouins for their "radiant innate idealism," their feudal grace, discipline, and pride of clan. Even so, he left it to Doughty to celebrate the Bedouins in a masterpiece. For the rest he was as fault-finding a traveler as Sterne's Smellfungus had been, viewing native "filth" and "corruption" with the cold eye of European superiority. On the American plains he was disappointed because the Indians, failing to attack, robbed him of the chance to kill some. In his later years, as an explorer and a consular officer in Africa (he eventually left the army for the foreign office), Burton served imperialism as shrewdly as his divided soul would permit. To the King of Dahomey he took presents from Queen Victoria, calming the king's annoyance at her failure to include a carriage drawn by white chargers.

Such were the contradictions that worked like madness in

the brain of this England-hating Englishman, who seems at moments to have been invented by Evelyn Waugh. No doubt the contradictions hampered him at just the moment when he might have won real glory at home and ended up—where his wife tried unsuccessfully to install him after his death— in a Westminster Abbey tomb. The moment came when he reached Tanganyika after incredible toils and dangers. There he halted, overcome with more than fatigue: with hatred for his bearers, the jungle and his fellow explorer, John Hanning Speke. Thus Speke could continue north on his own and become the sole discoverer of Lake Victoria, a really important prize. Speke's exploit caused the honors to be split between them; and Burton's quarrels with Speke, and Speke's later suicide, left the biggest trophies for Livingstone and Stanley. There were advantages to working, as Livingstone and Stanley did, for the glory of God or England or both. Burton could really only work for his divided soul. Thus East Africa failed him, as the army had, and his public role declined to that of a consular officer in relatively minor posts: Fernando Po, Santos in Brazil, Damascus, Trieste. Even in these places his energy and curiosity remained intact, until, confined chiefly to England by old age, he would interrupt his insular excursions to look at—for example—a mushroom farm.

Meanwhile, Mr. Farwell's reader, who has been panting after Burton through many crowded pages, undergoes a sharp reversal of feeling. He grows as bored with it all as Vronsky was in Florence. At first Burton's curiosity set Burton in violent motion across the world; and to the reader, as doubtless to Burton, the world looked like an infinitely capacious and inviting stage for those gratuitous prowls. But the same world has ended by resembling some place of dull confinement wherein Burton is forever and vainly, as he himself remarks, "kicking against the pricks." His talent for vaporizing romance was equaled by his talent for shrinking space.

But his adventures had come to include less strenuous kinds. There was his marriage and there were his translations, notably of *The Arabian Nights.*

Writing came all too easily to him. His numerous books tended to expand into garrulous monologues interrupted by garrulous footnotes. Or so I gather from what Mr. Farwell says about them and from the little I have been able to read of them myself. Sometimes the prose lights up and a scene materializes out of the vapors diffused by the writer's insistent personality. Curiously, though, the voice seems frequently to be not his own. Frequently it is the voice of some great Victorian gusher, Carlyle or Ruskin, caught at the moment of its thinnest flow. And the voice scolds, as Henry James said Ruskin often did, "like an angry governess." Burton is always passing sentence; his court is in perpetual session; no allusion is too insignificant to escape judgment even when the judgment is favorable: "says Bacon with his normal sound sense." Thus, rebel though he is, Burton reproduces and magnifies the worst fault of Victorian writing, its sententiousness. But sometimes the voice is that of a Persian poet, or, more happily, of Homer: the fleets of covered wagons he saw on a trip to the Mormon country were, "these long winding trains, in early morning like lines of white cranes trooping slowly over the prairies" (quoted by Mr. Farwell). My own "judgments" on his books are tentative and may be misleading. There could be better books in the Burton canon than those I have seen. His *Arabian Nights* was momentous for other reasons than its prose, whose somewhat labored archaisms align it with the Lang, Leaf and Myers *Iliad* rather than with the selective and inventive archaism of

Arabia Deserta, Doughty's masterpiece. Burton certainly cribbed from John Payne's translation (1882-84), as Mr. Joseph Campbell charges in his *Portable Arabian Nights* and as Mr. Farwell admits. Still, Burton's version was inclusive, unexpurgated. Through his courage and that of his associates in the Kamashastra Society, an informal organization of eroticists, it reached a large public. The "Terminal Essay," reread in middle age, remains a fascinating monument to curiosity.

Burton's marriage to Isabel Arundell proved more durable than his monkey household. It was nevertheless a bizarre romance. She was the conventionally brought up daughter of a Catholic family whose forebears had been in England since the Conquest. While still a young girl, she says, she had been told by a gypsy that she would marry a very dark man named Burton. Still quite young, she met Richard Burton during one of his brief stays in Europe and was instantly smitten. After many years and few meetings and despite her mother's objections she married him. Isabel's persistence, which had probably brought about the marriage in the first place, made it last. There is little evidence that she was interesting except for the extremes to which she carried both her romantic silliness and her pious prudery. Her "Rules For My Guidance As a Wife" survive. One rule reads: "Attend much to his creature comforts; allow smoking or anything else; for if you do not, *somebody else will.*" If nothing else linked this strange pair it was the capacity of each to embrace wildly antithetical impulses. Isabel probably drew strength from the tradition of the innocent girl who marries a rake to reform him. Perhaps Burton wanted at last to *be* reformed, a little.

Once married he tried to maintain a partly separate existence as a consul in West Africa. This failing, he accepted

Isabel's constant companionship, with few signs of discomfort. His erotomania pained her but she allowed it, as she did his smoking—so long as he was alive. It seems to have been through her efforts that his achievements were finally recognized by the Queen and he became Sir Richard. A rancorous lone wolf in so many instances, he was capable of great good nature with a few individuals. Stanley, one of these, wrote of him, "What a grand man! One of the great ones in England he might have been, if he had not been cursed with cynicism." He loved his parents, whose restlessness he had inherited and made a fantastic career of. Immediately following his death, Isabel signalized the triumph of Patient Grizzel over Ruffian Dick by burning all his papers. The task took her several days and the news of it made a scandal in London. She saw him buried in the graveyard of a Catholic church in Mortlake, a dingy London suburb. Over his grave she ordered erected a mass of marble carved to look like an Arab tent.

May every breakthrough artist of our time have as fitting a tomb. Yet Burton seems to me to have been our spiritual ancestor in only one respect and that a negative one. With him, as with some of us some of the time, the conquest of personal autonomy and sexual freedom was accompanied by a ferocious and boring egotism. Too much autonomy made him a kind of automaton of aggression and animal courage. The spectacle presented by his life, although certainly unique in the ingenuity of its wildness, and as "fabulous," almost, as *The Arabian Nights* itself, tends in the long run to make for weariness insofar as it doesn't make for laughs. It is now easy to see that he was not, alas, a free spirit, any more than Charlus is, and that he was not really in advance of his time but behind it. Burton was a displaced Regency Beau, an admirable enough type when *not* displaced, as he was, in Victorian England. As it was, his hatred of Victorian England was fatally counterbalanced by his desire to be a part of it on his own terms. As it was, the energy, confidence, curiosity, and courage of the age were his in sizable amounts, together with still more of its brutality and self-importance. He embodied all this with stunning finality and so remains a far from negligible figure, even though he may not merit the full revival treatment.

1964

The
Secret
Life of
Edward Windsor

With their famous subject, the Duke of Windsor's memoirs, *A King's Story*, are inevitably absorbing. They are dense with detail, painstaking in their reconstruction of the past, often charming and witty, and as consistently honest as they could be, considering their rather too obvious intent of pleasing rather too many people.

To my mind they are also a little sad, for their author is no free spirit despite his spectacular renunciation of public office. He professes to "draw comfort" from his marriage; at the same time he laments what that marriage entailed—"the sacrifice of my cherished British heritage along with all the years in its service." This balance of profit and loss he calls his "fate," describing himself as a "fatalist" by conviction. But surely it is a peculiar kind of fatalist who continues to argue with his fate as the Duke does here; and one recalls the cruelly perspicacious poem D. H. Lawrence wrote about him in the years when, as Prince of Wales, he was busily touring the empire and attending barbaric native ceremonies in his honor. What would the jungle men and the elephants think, Lawrence asked, "if they knew that his motto was *Ich dien?* And that he meant it."

Ich dien means "I serve," and the author of *A King's Story* still serves—serves his memories of past misfortunes, his hopes of future vindication. In no sense a fairy story, his book in a political sense is not a "story" at all but an unremitting defense of his life and work, indirectly an appeal for justice from the British people, perhaps a plea for reinstatement in some capacity among them. The Duke points to his long years of hard work as Prince of Wales; he makes clear how constraining is the monarch's position in a constitutional democracy. He argues that in abdicating he acceded, not necessarily to the wishes of the people but merely to the demands of the Baldwin circle.

Such is the Duke's defense, and to this reviewer it is not very convincing. Whether as morganatic wife or as queen, Mrs. Simpson would obviously have represented an absurd challenge to protocol and tradition, an affront to the dominions, the risk of annexing the monarchy to café society. And what would the situation be today if, besides having to acknowledge American supremacy in arms and money, Britons had also to live with the thought of an American woman in Buckingham Palace or in some adjacent hideaway? Better the Waldorf Towers! Better for the monarchy and the British people. Better for the Duke himself, if one may be so graceless as to tell a man his interests and interpret his story in a fashion contrary to his designs.

For although the Duke is ostensibly respectful toward the monarchy, he actually makes out a pretty bad case for it considered as something for a man to live with, especially a man of the Duke's English generation, for which a split notoriously developed between the claims of the public life and the claims of the private life. "Politics is the profession of the second-rate," Charles Whibley once wrote: Lytton Strachey resolved ancestral heroes into their idiosyncrasies as men and women; and only the other day E. M. Forster—an unregenerate survivor of that age—remarked that "greatness is a nineteenth-century perquisite." Clearly the Duke was once under the same spell as these typical English writers of his time. It is here that his "story" comes in and that it is seen to have the dignity of vivid truth, the fascination of being representative. For all the unique eminence of its hero, its theme is the now familiar one of spiritual dispossession. By writing his memoirs the Duke has realized his old aim of becoming one of us.

The Duke's father, George V, was a conscientious king, an exacting parent, and a profoundly simple man. He combined the monarchic with the domestic virtues to everyone's satisfaction; and he thus made very much his own position that is at once supremely magnificent in name and utterly powerless in fact. At worst there was, from the son's viewpoint, a failure of warmth on the father's part, a necessary sacrifice of family feeling to the observance of court routine and the ritual slaughter of animals in the hunt (Edward was to prefer golfing and riding to hunting). Upon this situation, not especially threatening in itself, alleviated for the Prince by his mother's unfailing tenderness, burst the war of 1914 with its terrible consequences for the stability of English society, for the youth of Edward's generation, for monarchism throughout Europe, for the prestige of authority everywhere. Edward yearned to share the dangers of war with his contemporaries but was obliged to observe them from a fairly safe distance. His sense of guilt on this score was unreasonable—no one seems to have expected him to fight—but it was nevertheless acute, and it made him tend to blame the whole monarchical system.

In the years that followed he could at least make up for his deficiencies, partly by sharing the frank pleasures and new freedoms of what was left of his generation, partly by pursuing conscientiously his prince's career. Now, in retrospect, he concedes scarcely more than Lawrence did to the amiable legend of him as the wild prince of the twenties. Instead, he recalls mainly his princely ordeals. The din of interminable parades and speeches still sounds on his page. One feels the horror entailed in the daily exposure of himself to vast crowds in which the mania to touch his person was intense and the risk of panic and death, including his own death, was always imminent. One experiences the vanity and folly of local officials, the oppressive smugness of Stanley Baldwin who, though invariably "correct," seems to have been intent on imposing himself, whether by treating his prince to long monologues or by obliging him to listen to the endless cracking of the ministerial fingers. Among the portraits of his former "subjects," as distinguished from those of his family, that of Baldwin is the most elaborate in the Duke's memoirs, where it has the symbolic purpose of showing that the king is himself a subject. Evidently Edward could not say, like his great-grandmother, "We are not amused."

Whether as prince or king, he is the captive of his position. The monarchy is a symbol of the past glories of absolutism; it can also act as a reminder of the fact that absolutism was vanquished by the people. So long as he accepts his present state, the royal personage is like a god; once he oversteps, "mixes in politics" even to the extent of saying "something must be done" to a group of unemployed miners, he is like Bajazeth in the cage provided for him by the conquering Tamburlane.

The Duke's response to this situation appears in the little things he remembers as well as in the general outlines of his career. Images of oppression and disintegration are congenial to his mind. He recalls the suffocating smell of mothballs in the robes of state, the distress of the musicians shut up in an airless hole at Windsor Castle, the jeweled cross that got dislodged from the royal crown and fell to the street during his father's funeral procession. Where the rest of us dream of glory, Edward dreamed of the commonplace. He dwells happily on those remembered moments when he or others— for he is constantly aware of others—asserted themselves against the royal routines, possessed themselves of something, however trivial. He remembers the time when his grandmother, Queen Alexandra, escaped her retinue and motored to Sandringham alone. He remembers how Henry Hansell, the tutor of the royal children, used to withdraw briefly every morning and stand alone on a low hill in the Sandringham grounds. For all its precious porcelains and Leonardo drawings, what he recalls most pleasantly about the Windsor Castle of his childhood is the launch which his parents acquired, like any bourgeois family of those years, and in which they went for excursions on the Thames. His father he pictures as sitting, at the point of death, wrapped in an old worn dressing-gown that someone had given him. His mother—who is here not at all the formidable Queen Mary of legend—is exclusively associated with the intimate and the domestic, now presiding in the nursery at the bedtime hour, now taking inventory of the family properties at Windsor.

In the thirties, as the empire tours fall off, the Prince takes to remodeling for himself a half-abandoned residence ("The Fort") on the Windsor grounds—like so many others in those years, he "fixes up an old house" in token of a desire to settle down. And presently there is Mrs. Simpson, whom he appreciates for "her American charm and energy" and because, like a Henry James heroine, she talks back to him. Ironically, he begins by admiring the gay cultivated life she shares with Simpson in their London flat, where the company, the conversation, and the cooking are of the best. And in possessing himself of her, does he not make the act doubly meaningful by taking her from another? Finally the abdication and the famous radio address. He is able at last to speak as an individual and in his own affectingly simple idiom, the idiom—almost—of the nursery; and he reprints the speech entire in his memoirs, noting that, save for two interpolations suggested by Churchill, it was entirely his work. "And now we all have a new King!"

The Duke's account of the abdication crisis is likely to become classic in the literature of memoirs. No master plotter among novelists, not even Henry James, could have invented a richer "situation" than the one that develops at this point. There is enmity without and treachery within; good motives are, however, abundant on all sides; everyone is tested to the full; and the action never flags, for no sooner has Edward decided to abdicate than a King's party materializes, led by Churchill and Beaverbrook in an adventuristic mood, and he is tempted to resist. Meanwhile Mrs. Simpson is, throughout the story, not actually divorced but only in the process of divorce; if she wished it herself or should be persuaded to it by others, she could at any moment halt the divorce proceedings and so relieve the crisis, at least momentarily. Finally, on the part of the protagonist, there is the compulsive innocence without which the plot would have been impossible in the first place. "I wish," Mrs. Simpson said to the King toward the end, "that I had had a clearer understanding of the constitutional questions." "I must take the blame for that," the King replied, "I thought it could be managed."

Only in the aftermath of the story does one feel a lack of the inevitability proper to good fiction. As one reads between the lines, takes note of the mild agonies of self-justification, feels the nostalgia for England and "The Fort," guesses how much England's grandeurs and miseries during the Blitz must have added to its stature in the Duke's eyes (as in everyone else's), one cannot but see that another ending was possible. This was a renunciation in reverse of the one actually effected by Edward: a forfeiture of private happiness, a sacrifice by which he might have secured his personal hold on the throne, made it "emotionally" his own, and then confirmed the transaction in the course of the common sufferings of himself and his subjects in wartime. But to point this out is worse than graceless, it is unrealistic; for the hero of *A King's Story* is no Henry James hero after all and his story is not a novel. It is an instance, perhaps, of what James used to call "life at its stupid work," and as such it is not without pathos and beauty.

1951

The
King
of the
Cats

For a man who lived a long time and was very active and ambitious, Yeats was unusually fortunate in his friends. Those in whom he was not so fortunate, who became his enemies, he mostly managed to outlive. "I did hate leaving the last word to George Moore," he wrote in a letter of 1927. And now after his own death he continues to be lucky in the same way. The editor of this monumental collection of Yeats's letters (*The Letters of W. B. Yeats,* edited by Allan Wade) was a member of the poet's London circle, an actor and a director of plays. He is also something that few such survivors of old times and intimates of great men ever are, a scholar. With patient labor he has assembled letters enough to fill some nine hundred pages. He has deciphered Yeats's wretched handwriting when that has been necessary, has figured out approximate dates where dates are missing, has written a commentary summarizing the events of Yeats's life from period to period, and—best of all—has identified the many obscure or semi-obscure persons addressed or alluded to in the letters. Who was Althea Gyles, of whom Yeats reports that "she brought a prosperous love-affair to an end by reading Browning to the poor man in the middle of the night"? Mr. Wade will tell you, and with just the right amount of detail.

To be sure, the volume is not as complete as its title and its huge bulk make you think it is. For one reason or another, Yeats's correspondence with several people of capital importance in his life—his wife, Maud Gonne, John Synge, Ezra Pound, Gordon Craig—had to be left out of the collection or be feebly represented in it. It is still a collection of great fascination and importance. Although some of the best things Yeats said in his letters have been used in the books about him published by Joseph Hone, Richard Ellmann and others having access to his papers, those things often sound still better in context. And of course it is context of the general as well as the specific kind that this volume supplies so plentifully. More than half a century of the poet's life is here in his own words, and with it much of the life of poetry itself from William Morris to W. H. Auden. If the ways of praising Yeats have grown dull with use and so have almost ceased to seem actively true, this book should help to renew them.

In themselves, however, his letters are not especially exhilarating. A few of them are that, in particular the later ones; and he is livelier with some of his correspondents than with others. Despite the good criticism they contain, the long series addressed to Katharine Tynan fails to reveal any adequate personal reason for its existence. Yeats seems to have thought she had the makings of a good Irish poet, but this was not enough; the letters become tedious with his effort to keep it up and not be patronizing. Even the letters to his father show the strain, and his father once complained that his son lacked "love" and made him feel like "a black beetle." (But the delightful J. B. Yeats *was* always a bit of a nag with his son.) With Olivia Shakespeare, on the other hand, Yeats is consistently engaging; she seems to have had no part in any of his projects but was simply a charming woman with whom he had once been briefly in love. For the most part, then, he had not the gift of writing letters as if he were a man living among men and women. If he has more of this feeling than, say, Wordsworth shows in his letters, he has less than, say, Byron or Keats show in theirs. Yeats's correspondents are mainly artists of some kind and are addressed by him as such. They are frankly his associates in what sometimes looks like a widespread conspiracy to be great, rather than simply to be. But he was ambitious for them as well as himself; and it is to the advantage of his letters, not to mention his poetry, that his ambition was that of the tortoise. He was a slow, patient, moral conspirator, seeking a triumph of merit. He may have said to his sister, when she told him Swinburne was dead, "I know, and now I am king of the cats," but he was no usurper. He aimed at what might be called legitimate succession, by way of a profound absorption in English poetry and a profound transformation of it. The size of his ambition, together with the conscientiousness of his methods, makes his letters extremely weighty and interesting in the mass. He was a meticulous correspondent, giving in abundance what he *could* give: ideas, plans, criticism, encouragement, anecdotes. He had a zest for the solving of problems, the meeting of situations,—a zest that his letters communicate to us. His ever-present tact did not prevent him from being quite firm, as in a long masterly letter to Sean O'Casey rejecting *The Silver Tassie* for the Abbey Theatre. His decision was probably wrong, but his reasons were compelling. The excellence with which he argues them is itself a testimonial to the importance of the occasion and the eminence of the rejected playwright. Conscious as he shows himself to be of the Irish temper—of George Moore's "incredible violence" and the "sour and argumentative" way of

Irishmen in England—he clearly cultivates amenity in his relations with people. "It's a poet's business to be amiable," he tells his publisher, A. H. Bullen. But this is not the same thing as being merely respectable: Yeats would not have relished the literary atmosphere of our bland 1950's.

Yeats was fortunate and he knew it and the knowledge colors all his letters. He seems alternately a true example of the happy warrior in literature and a case of clinical euphoria. He is constantly recounting his successes—with the poems or plays he is writing, the reviewers who review his books, the audiences who attend his plays or lectures, the famous people he meets at parties. And his satisfaction in the material arrangements of his life makes him purr like a cat. He rejoices in the comforts introduced into his lodgings by Lady Gregory: the port wine and the blankets. He rejoices in his periods of residence at Coole Park, her country house; the "great rooms" (in the plural) are splendidly silent and there are no fewer than seven woodlands, all magnificent. In all this there is something of the eternal spirit of the bachelor: he must make his nest all the cozier, and chirp the louder over it, because it is a nest for one. The spirit persists after Yeats's belated marriage, when he begins to celebrate his wife's feats of housekeeping and decorating, and the attractions of the houses that he himself is now in a position to acquire. But it must be noted that he does not long remain in the old tower that he calls "my castle," or the house in Dublin that he describes as a "mansion." He never really settles down; and of the money that comes to him in prizes and from lecturing in America, he gives much to other poets and to his various causes. In his letters he has an odd way of keeping the phenomena of his suffering in the background. From an allusion here and there, we may guess at the "ignominy of

boyhood" as he knew it, the hand-to-mouth existence he led
in youth with his loving improvident father, his detestation
of London in those days, the hardship of his life in ill-heated
and candle-lighted rooms, the pain caused by his bad eye-
sight and frequent failures of health, the unhappy consequences of his long vain wooing of Maud Gonne, the labor of
supporting himself by his writing and lecturing, the sheer
fatigue of being a great poet in the twentieth century. But
such experiences merely give a tragic accent to the strange
high comedy of his career. Even when, in the late twenties,
he breaks down and becomes very ill, he has a way of exult-
ing in the misfortune. "Yesterday the doctor gave me a shock.
I said, 'Why am I so exhausted?' He replied, 'The overwork
of years.'"

Complacency or courage? A little of the first, a great deal
more of the last. Yeats writes as one who has earned his good
fortune, made himself lucky. "They went forth to battle but
they always fell"—Matthew Arnold's motto for the Irish
spirit must have rung in his ears, as it did in Joyce's, not as a
knell but as a challenge. The waste of Irish genius in indo-
lence and backbiting, the waste of his father's genius in particular, seem to have determined him to husband his own.
He developed a system of thought, a method of style, an
entire economy of literary action. Primarily his thought
reached inward, to the power resident in the self. "Even
things seemingly beyond control answer strangely to what is
within," he told Florence Farr. This was applied spiritualism,
table-tapping become a way of life, magic raised to the proportions of an ethic. Among the scrappy dreamers and "peni-
tent frivolous" whom he describes as haunting Madame Bla-
vatsky and the Golden Dawn group, he alone was to achieve,
in his way, the transmutation of metals and the elixir of life.

But to his faith in the single soul was added an appreciation of the part of outward action. He had a conception of the poet's role in the world. What this was he suggests to John Quinn: "Keats's lines telling how Homer left great verses to a little clan seem[ed] to my imagination when I was a boy a description of the happiest fate that could come to a poet." This appears always to have remained his idea of the happy fate, and no doubt it was one he shared with Keats, Goethe, Whitman and others who have sought ideal audiences within the heterogeneous populations of modern nations. For Yeats the conviction that he had a little clan was some time in materializing. He might help to organize the Rhymers Club in the nineties but that was not it; and the absence in him of any strong sense of an audience helps to account for the tremulous vagueness of his early verse. In proportion as he acquired that sense, felt around him the "hearers and hearteners" of his work, he developed the *viva voce* quality, the manipulation of tone, the effect of address or posture, which animate his mature work. But just as he had to learn to write the "great verses," so he had to recruit the little clan to go with them. Actually there were many clans, ranging from his fellow occultists of the Golden Dawn to the audiences of the Abbey Theatre; and when he had despaired of tangible audiences he sought their Platonic counterpart in some ideal Byzantium of the past or simply among the self-delighting people of whatever time or place. He carried his dream into his cosmopolitan old age, determined to the last that he should know his audience, should feel it to be made up of men and women like himself. "It is time that I wrote my will: I choose upstanding men," he wrote in the great concluding passage of "The Tower." It is hard to think of another modern poet who would venture to cast his supreme thought in this testamentary form, or who, having ventured it, could carry it off with Yeats's poise.

His was a poise born of conviction and based on effort. If anyone is left in the world who supposes that Yeats practiced in his life only the "wasteful virtues" he sometimes praised in his poetry, these letters will undeceive him. They show how firmly he occupied that twilight realm between dreaming and doing which he celebrated in all his poetry—the realm where anything is possible. In the end he was really the king of the cats: the greatest *lyric* poet in the language.

1956

Monstrous
Dust

The recipient of these letters (*Letters to Milena* by Franz Kafka, edited by Willy Haas, translated by Tania and James Stern) was Milena Jesenká, the "M" of Kafka's later diaries. With her he corresponded at length in the early stages of a love affair that began in 1920 and lasted for some two years. He was very ill with consumption at the time; and after his death, in 1924, Milena preserved his letters, entrusting them to Willy Haas on the eve of the German invasion of Czechoslovakia. Her part in the correspondence has not survived and she herself died in a Nazi concentration camp. Mr. Haas, who tells her story in the introduction to this volume, knew her well as he had also known Kafka. He seems to have planned the book as a memorial to her.

She belonged, he writes, to a notable burgher family of Prague; and though Kafka was a native of the same city, he does not appear to have been acquainted with her there. Milena was of a younger generation and had been caught up "in the erotic and intellectual promiscuity of the Viennese literary café society in the wild years after 1918." Even in that setting she was a rarity: "passionate, intrepid," "a character such as Stendhal lifted out of the old Italian chronicles." When Kafka first knew her, Milena was twenty-four and lived in Vienna with a husband from whom she thought of separating. She taught school, wrote for the magazines, admired Stevenson as well as Dostoevsky, and had been quick to see the genius of Kafka's few published stories. She had undertaken to translate his *Metamorphosis* into Czech, and it was while corresponding about this project that they discovered one another.

To reconstruct the affair in its external developments would be tedious if not impossible in the present state of the letters, which the editor admits to be quite unsettled. Mostly undated, often unclear in their allusions to events and people, supplied with a minimum of editorial notes, and occasionally deleted "out of consideration for persons still alive," the letters must be read as a mere monologue. It hardly matters. So far as one can make out, "our relationship," as Kafka (or the translators) drearily term it, was probably uneventful. Kafka and Milena rarely met; and as Mr. Haas remarks, "their love was essentially a letter-love, like the love of Kierkegaard or Werther."

Not quite. Kafka was more enterprising than Kierkegaard, not to mention Werther. When he and Milena did meet, it was almost certainly to go to bed. Neither his diaries nor the present letters make any secret of his fierce intermittent sensuality. In this, he tells Milena, he had something in him of "the eternal Jew, wandering senselessly through a senselessly obscene world." It was the urge of the dispossessed for possession of the promised land, of the estranged for reunion with mankind. And although the affair with Milena looked hopeless from the start, neither of them abandoned it without a moral struggle as fierce as the sensuality. At first Kafka is tempted to continue it: he is eager for some permanent union. But before long he is writing, "we never can or will live together." His reasons are many: he is a Jew and she is not; he is too old, too sick; and anyway she is only "dazzled" by his writings. Conceivably, his very passion for her is generated by his mortal illness and despair. If he "belongs to her," it is by virtue of "this whole monstrous dust which 38 years have kicked up and which has settled in my lungs." She on her side combats and derides his scruples but cannot prevail against the monstrous dust, which is his accumulated experience of tragedy. She must remain his "angel of death."

They had, besides, a number of lesser misunderstandings. They brought into the affair too many of their friends. Kafka induces Milena to correspond with Max Brod: they fail to hit it off. Milena asks Kafka to hunt up in Prague an old acquaintance of hers named Jarmila: the issue is doubtful. Some acrimony is created by a mysterious mission that Milena has urged him to undertake and that she thinks he has bungled. Meanwhile there is Ernest, Milena's husband, toward whom Kafka is oddly propitiatory, not only because Ernest is a rival but because he is that—to Kafka—enviable thing, a Husband. Finally there is "the girl," Kafka's fiancée of several months (the "J.W." of the diaries), whom he is trying to break with: the girl also writes to Milena. Thinking of Milena, her husband and himself, Kafka describes the situation as "*torture à trois*," but he seems to have miscounted.

And indeed love, their love, is constantly depicted by Kafka as a disastrous experience. For Milena it will mean "to leap into an abyss"; for him she is "the knife which I turn within myself." Kafka's ambivalent feeling toward love and marriage is well known. It had, at this point, brought him failure in three major campaigns (the one engagement to "J.W.," the two separate engagements to "F.B."); and he was becoming intensely conscious of himself as a veteran with many wounds and no trophies. "Sisyphus was a bachelor," he noted

in his diaries during those years. In the case of Milena, however, one suspects that special irritants were at work and that
her being young, romantic, gentile, impelled him to a peculiar vehemence. He wants, perhaps, to divest her of her illu-
sions about life. So she is spared nothing of his situation—
past, present and to come. His oppressive father, his cruel
childhood, his "obscene" sexual history, his mortal thinness
of body, his insomnia, his coughing fits, his dreams—all are
made to contribute to her enlightenment. Increasingly, he
reminds her of his Jewishness. "This means, expressed with
exaggeration, that not one calm second is granted me, nothing is granted me, everything has to be earned." "My nature
is: Fear." At one moment Prague is full of Jewish refugees
from revolutionary Russia and there are anti-Semitic riots in
the streets. He spends an entire afternoon among the demon-
strators, "wallowing" in the spectacle. On this occasion his
cries are dreadful to overhear, like those of a man in the embrace of a nightmare. As Mr. Haas observes, for Kafka the
"love of a non-Jew was evidently a serious, tragic problem."

Yes, but all of life tended to become such a problem for
him. The inescapable unity of his experience was his despair,
his joke and his glory. His candor in expressing, in *feeling*,
his situation as a Jew was like a fire in which that situation
got refined of all local, temporal, special considerations and
so came to serve his great primary art. "Out of the quarrel
with ourselves, we make poetry," in Yeats's phrase. Elsewhere in the letters, at calmer moments, he writes about his
people in a spirit which has little to do with Milena, much to
do with his mind and art. "The insecure position of Jews,
insecure within themselves, insecure among people, would
make it above all comprehensible that they consider themselves to be allowed to own only what they hold in their

hands or between their teeth, that furthermore only palpable possessions give them the right to live, and that they will never regain what they once have lost but that instead it calmly swims away from them forever." A similar paradox gives energy to Kafka's fiction, in which man in general is shown as holding life "between his teeth" in return for the insecurity of his spiritual existence. And this conception, which distinguishes Kafka from Kierkegaard no less than from Eliot (for whom religion is so much a matter of "belief," and unbelief is so often associated with mere debility), Kafka owes to the tradition of Moses, Job and Ruth. His unique place among the great recent writers consists in his bringing that tradition to bear on the preoccupations of modernity.

There are in the *Letters to Milena* other evidences of the Kafka who had written *The Trial* and was soon to write *The Castle*. These, however, are mostly evidences of his general mind and style, rarely of his opinions or his reading. For all his distress, he usually sustains a good-humored composure: certainly it is often humorous, a kind of intricate teasing. Here as in his stories he keeps to the imponderable line between horror and farce, the physical and the spiritual, the intensely personal and the brilliantly impersonal. Even his macabre jokes at the expense of the Jews recall Swift's "A Modest Proposal," which he knew. For the rest, one constantly surprises his genius for invention at its characteristic work. Milena's husband, whom he used to see in the Prague cafés, had "the peculiarity of being called to the telephone several times during the evening. Presumably there must have been someone who, instead of sleeping, sat by the telephone dozing, his head on the back of his chair, and who sat up from time to time to call him." The letters abound in anecdote, parable, paradox (a little too much of this last). The entire experience with Milena is thus translated into Kafka's animated moral idiom—as he says, "rearranged for my orchestra." (The effects are probably much attenuated in English although the translation sounds convincing.)

But it would be to take an intolerably high line with these letters to assert that the humor and eloquence erase the impression of suffering. The impression of suffering is indelible; and to our present age, with its cult of the reconstructed ego and the busy life, Kafka's letters will come as intrusive reminders of the lost art of being unhappy. This art, which one may call the art of introspection, gives Kafka his peculiar authority in suffering. It permits him to see his own life in its entirety and to connect it, by way of observation and myth, with the life of everyone. It is with more than authority, with pride, that he says to Milena: "I believe I understand the Fall of Man as no one else."

1954

The
Romance
of Charles
Chaplin

One of the many fine things about Chaplin's *My Autobiography* is that it includes, along with an exhaustive index and a lot of photographs, a "List of the Films of Charles Chaplin." Thus we learn that his first movie—or if he insists, film —dates from 1914 and was entitled *Making a Living*. In all senses of the word "living," Chaplin has since made it. No other movie career, and few recent literary careers, have yielded so much continuous delight over so many years as his has. It has also included a period of what might be called "total crisis," one of those situations in which the hero of a mass society undergoes a bitter reversal of fortune, public and private, and becomes for a time a prominent scapegoat. In Chaplin's case, this deplorable turn has not proved ruinous. On the contrary, his present life as described in *My Autobiography* resembles the last act of a late-Shakespearean romance. Order has been restored, love is requited, paternity is triumphant, and there has been a general reunion with the universe—possibly excepting the United States. In this country, however, many of his films are again on view; and while you endure that "short wait in the lobby for seats," you are gratified to hear issuing from the auditorium gusts of unembarrassed, in fact uncontrollable, laughter. Even "the children," whom you have taken along, with some fear as to their possible reactions, soon get into the spirit and join the great collectivity of Chaplin-inspired mirth and adoration. A student did once tell the present writer that Chaplin's comic style lacked "moral reference" and was a little dated. It is the unfortunate student who seems a little dated now—if such things matter.

Charles Chaplin would therefore appear to be the perfect subject for an autobiography. Yet it has been reported that he was at first a reluctant subject and only yielded to his publishers' persuasion after much debate. No doubt the report is true. It was not in him to turn out an unconsidered performance inevitably labeled *The Charlie Chaplin Story*. And apart from the sheer labor of doing a thorough job, he may have felt some doubt about his competence to do it. True, he has shown a distinct largeness of ambition in those films where he was actor, director, script writer, and composer. But he has given no sign of thinking himself an accomplished man of letters with a command of literary form and style, and with the more or less settled convictions about life and art that are implied in those things. He commands them in his own elusive medium but the verbal medium is patently something else. Besides, the "person" behind Chaplin's work has always seemed a little inaccessible. And while these problems may or may not have figured in his deliberations before he decided to write his autobiography, they do figure for the reader of the completed work.

There are of course two Chaplins, Charles Chaplin and Charlie. The pair as such are well known in Chaplin lore; and their existence argues no large or lurid complexity on either's part, no war of rival identities between them. It is only a working partnership. The two get along so well together because they are so unlike. One of them is out of this world while the other is very much of it. Charlie the clown is an extreme case of artfully blended antitheses. He is a dandified tramp, a Pierrot of the industrial age, an ideally resourceful male with an ideal female's winning grace and solicitous sweetness. Charlie is a dream—but a dream that much solid stuff is made of. In the way he twitches a property mustache or slices with a knife a derby hat doused in a creamy sauce, believing the hat to be a real pudding, there is a multitude of all too human suggestions. Twitched mustaches are implausible by nature. All dinner party embarrassments approximate to the impact of cold steel on creamed felt, setting the teeth on edge.

Like a dream, too, Charlie is more eloquent for being silent. "The matrix out of which he was born was as mute as the rags he wore," Charles Chaplin remarks in the autobiography. By "matrix" he means, it will be seen, several things. In one of its senses, it is another word for the visual imagination, which Chaplin exploited and glorified in his pre-talkie films. At first he hated the sound track with its elaborate apparatus and specialized personnel. Charlie's essential being was threatened by electronic sound. It was an intruder upon the house of the visual imagination, a thief in the silence of Charlie's enchanted night. Charles Chaplin's job was to come to Charlie's assistance and rout the intruder, at least for a while. His role in the partnership was always to serve Charlie as guardian and general utility man. Charles took Charlie's measure when the future looked alarming. He foresaw that his alter ego's possibilities were relative to his alter ego's limitations, that his survival depended on his remaining what he had always been: an extreme case of refined artifice. No real concessions were to be made to new film technologies and styles of laughter. Thus Charlie was enabled to outlast many a less specialized, but also less conscious, artist who, through the competitive processes of comedy, was quickly to become a has-been or a hack or, like Walt Disney, an industry. When Charlie's time finally came he was put away, and his silence silenced, by a reluctant but realistic Charles.

Did a merger of the two take place after that, in the period of *Monsieur Verdoux* and *Limelight?* Or did Charlie Chaplin take over the whole firm? The question is silly. Half truths about dual identities can be manipulated to the point of becoming schematic. Yet in *My Autobiography* the author himself makes some random use of the Charles-Charlie duality, evidently with the purpose of enlivening the narrative and keeping its sprawling bulk in perspective.

The book does sprawl. It is a very strenuous exercise in total recall. Chaplin might have fixed upon a single representative moment or situation in his life, for example the making of *City Lights,* with all the important decisions, the professional problems, and the personalities that were involved in it. Instead he chose to attempt the usual full-blown survey and to present it in the usual chronological form. But is Chaplin's life, in its really significant aspects, conventional or usual? One's reading of the autobiography suggests the contrary. The career that was his essential glory seems much farther removed from the rest of his experience than would normally be the case if the autobiographer were a statesman or a writer or, for that matter, a different kind of actor. Given his beautifully specialized art, Chaplin's experiences as celebrity, lover, husband, and political prophet are of questionable relevance. At best they belong to the social history of movies. Yet he shows little talent or inclination for treating this subject. The people he portrays tend to remain indistinct; the conversations he reports, often in dialogue form, sound vaguely fabricated. It is as if everybody were on stilts, even jolly Douglas Fairbanks, Chaplin's most congenial friend. As a writer he can't work up enough feeling, either sympathetic or malicious, to make his associates—friends or non-friends—interesting. As a result, his own personality goes dim—becomes, as I say, inaccessible—for long stretches. He seems to be conducting a rather formal interview with himself. "What do I think of Mr. Churchill?" "I think Mr. Churchill is . . ." What is lacking is not candor; on the subject of people, as well as on his political and moral beliefs, he is generally forthright. An unrepentant exile from the United States, he is quite unafraid of giving offense to that ignorant and vindictive element of the American public that once found him *persona non grata. My Autobiography* is the work of a man who, in his own eyes, is not "controversial" but historic. His candor, however, is a quality of his moral intelligence alone. As an observer of persons and manners, Chaplin gets little help from it.

His adventures in Celebrityland are nevertheless told at length: those obligatory encounters with predictable personages from Shaw to Gandhi, Lady Astor to Elinor Glyn. Is anybody absent? Yes, Albert Schweitzer. But then, Albert Einstein is present. And Churchill, although he is everybody's star-celebrity, gets more space in the book than *Modern Times,* a unique masterpiece.

Is Chaplin aware of the irrelevance of it all? Probably. In the chapters concerning his travels and triumphs, Charlie the clown is, as I said, revived. He is invested with the skeptic's viewpoint and assigned the role of victim in the celebrity game. The procedure is too consistent to have been accidental; and the author's intentions, as I understand them, are of the best. He hopes to restore the balance by keeping his great comic counterpart in the picture. So the narrative is strewn with memories of small embarrassments suffered by himself and others in the Vanity Fair of world fame. Most of these incidents involve bits of brisk and punishing "business." In short they are "slapstick" and recall the comic routines in his movies. For example his contretemps with William Randolph Hearst. Once during luncheon at San Simeon the two of them disagree about a projected movie venture. Hearst becomes quite irritated. "When I say a thing is white you always say it is black," he tells Chaplin, who, feeling insulted, calls for a taxi and leaves the table. But he is quickly overtaken in another room by a remorseful Hearst who sits Chaplin down beside him in a small double seat of the Chippendale period and proceeds to make peace. Peace being made, the two then start to get up to return to the dining room. But they discover they are stuck in the valuable antique. With the insane splendors of San Simeon as background, this tale has a point.

A better story, with a more extended gag, has to do with Chaplin and Jean Cocteau. Indirectly, perhaps, it is also a comment on the strange logic of existence in Celebrityland, of which both men were of course ranking citizens and knew it. The two meet for the first time by chance on shipboard during a China Sea crossing. Cocteau expresses his joy that the long delayed meeting has finally taken place. They spend a night in rapturous conversation, although neither is well acquainted with the other's language and Cocteau's secretary makes an indifferent interpreter. They part towards dawn with enthusiastic assurances of future talks. But a couple of mornings later, when the two are about to collide on deck, Cocteau suddenly ducks into the ship's interior. And throughout the rest of the interminable day ahead, their relations will consist in a series of artful dodgings and hearty but decisive hails and farewells. It appears that a mysterious magnetic force is at work in Celebrityland to guarantee that any two of its ranking citizens will inevitably meet—somewhere, somehow. With Chaplin and Cocteau, the mysterious force seems to have got out of hand, like the feeding machine in *Modern Times*. Their off and on friendship also recalls that of the Tramp and the alcoholic millionaire in *City Lights*, made several years before Chaplin met Cocteau.

Charlie's interventions brighten a little the social picture in *My Autobiography*. And presently the picture changes. The social scene is more or less taken over by "Salka Viertel, the Clifford Odetses, the Hanns Eislers, the Feuchtwangers," and Thomas Mann and Bertolt Brecht. These friends reflected, possibly stimulated, Chaplin's increasingly explicit concern with what he calls "the fate of the world," a concern that was already apparent in the explicit satire of *Modern Times* (1936). For the world as for him the total crisis was at hand. Along with the Nazi horrors, the war, and Soviet Russia's entrance into it, there was the question of the Second Front. No doubt the arrival of the illustrious refugees in his vicinity brought home to him the human reality of the general terror. Chaplin's personal and professional life was similarly beset by difficulties. His labors on *Monsieur Verdoux*, a radically new venture, coincided with his forced participation in the grotesque "paternity suit." In eyes bleared by the prevailing hysteria, he stood convicted of moral turpitude and political unreliability, always a sinister compound. An impertinent reporter remarked to him during an interview: "Your public relations are not very good."

They were not, and his account of the crisis in his autobi-

ography is unlikely to improve them. Not that his public relations are the affair, or the real concern, of a sympathetic
reviewer. What must be said, however, is that he shows no
inclination to reconsider his own political attitudes of the
time, in the interests either of mere appeasement (God
forbid) or of historical truth and autobiographical self-
discovery. He emerges from the crisis in the role of pure victim—a role that is too exciting to be quite believable. With
such an embattled figure argument is fruitless, and where
Chaplin is concerned there are better things to do than argue
politics. As Robert Warshow, Chaplin's best critic, wrote:
"The impact of his art . . . was helped rather than hindered
by a certain simplicity in his conceptions of political and
social problems." "Conceptions?" A better word might be
"dreams."

My Autobiography is more convincing about family history and about the history of the movies as reflected in Chaplin's own work. One learns that he began asserting his authority as a film maker rather earlier than one had thought.
During his very first year (1914) in movies, while he was
still with the Keystone Company, Mack Sennett suddenly set
Mabel Normand to directing Chaplin's pictures. She was a
nice girl and pretty but "incompetent." He objected, pacified
Mabel, and became a part-time director himself. To be sure,
as he says, improvisation was rampant in the studios in those
days. He loved it. After touring for years in uninspired stage
plays he had, one guesses, stored up a wealth of unused inventiveness. It spilled out under the benign anarchy at Keystone. In time he seemed to us, his public, to inhabit a realm
where sheer inventiveness was the rule. Hence the peculiar
exhilaration his films imparted to his audiences, and the
bonus of personal affection his audiences gave him in return.

They understood what his "moral reference" consisted in. He made them feel agile, creative, free, happy. There was even something chancy about the origins of the Tramp's costume, inevitable as it seems now. Mack Sennett merely told him one day: "We need some gags here. Put on a comedy make-up. Anything will do." So Chaplin headed for the wardrobe and grabbed some "baggy pants, big shoes, a cane and a derby hat. I wanted everything a contradiction: the pants baggy, the coat tight, the hat small and the shoes large. I was undecided whether to look old or young, but remembering Sennett had expected me to be a much older man, I added a small moustache." He had "no idea of the character" at first, but once he was in costume the character was "fully born" and "gags and comedy ideas went racing through my mind." Still, improvisation had limits. There had to be a director like Mack Sennett to make decisions, as well as to reverse them, even while, like Mack Sennett himself, he "giggled until his body began to shake" at the doings of Fatty Arbuckle, Ford Sterling, Mabel Normand, and Charlie Chaplin.

As an autobiographer, then, Chaplin is more at home on the Keystone and Essanay lots than he will later be at San Simeon, Pickfair, and the Prince of Wales's Fort Belvedere (private residences which, incidentally, he tends to describe as if they were hotels, remarking critically on the "furnishings" and the "cuisine"). But he is most at ease in the first hundred or so pages, where the subject is his early experiences as a London waif and incipient actor. Those experiences were the ultimate "matrix" out of which Chaplin and Charlie emerged.

Most autobiographers are best on such distant and "formative" years. Chaplin's childhood seems exceptionally close to him and it was formative with a vengeance. His childhood was made to order to destroy a waif or foster a genius. In its concentrated burden of extreme situations it surpassed Dickens's famous childhood. Everything was extreme: the hardness of the hardship, the sweetness of the satisfactions. Home was the more ideally homelike because one was so often homeless. A mother's devotion was the more prized because it was frequently unavailable. Did "things happen," as children are always wishing things will? Things happened without let-up. The days were not only eventful; they were a perpetual flow, or flood, of elemental event. No wonder Chaplin was to be so different from his associates, in Hollywood and elsewhere. He tells us that the cockney-born H. G. Wells worried about his (Wells's) misplaced h's. In Chaplin's case some part of *himself* was misplaced by his early deprivations and has remained forever estranged from the world, even though capable of forming that working partnership with Charles Chaplin.

His Old World past, his almost *prehistoric* past, survives in Chaplin like a vital organ. Often though his family moved from flat to flat in South London, he remembers perfectly the street numbers and the "furnishings." He can recall, it appears, just about everything, and in the early chapters of *My Autobiography* he does so with a zest that is largely absent from the remainder of the book. The misery of that time speaks for itself. The autobiographer is thus at liberty to find satisfaction in the act of recall itself, in the precise art of retracing the child's million steps up and down greasy stairs, in and out of cheerless interiors, back and forth along dingy streets. (*Easy Street?* For something that resembles the *Easy Street* set, see the photograph in the book with the legend: "Where we lived, next to the slaughterhouse and the pickle factory, after Mother came out of the asylum.") So "real" is that entire past of his, so intimately and completely *his,* that the writer is freed from self-consciousness and can take a simple delight in the story, just as he will later show delight in recalling the time his mother said "shit."

Here, it may be assumed, memory works an uncommonly complete transformation even while it seems to be engaged in a powerful attempt at faithful representation. Chaplin's memory possesses it all too firmly for distortion to occur. Yet everything indicates that in actuality, at the time, the child was conscious of possessing little that he was sure was his own and could call "real." His childhood was the scene, not of poverty and neglect alone, but of a more inclusive kind of distress. People and places and things were constantly disappearing. Some of them turned up again and again. But would they turn up the next time? Life was a perpetual vanishing act. Or wasn't it?

"In my world of three and a half years, all things were possible; if Sydney, who was four years older than I, could perform legerdemain and swallow a coin and make it come out through the back of his head, I could do the same; so I swallowed a halfpenny and Mother was obliged to send for the doctor." Coins got scarcer later on. His parents, both of them originally popular performers in music halls, were separated and his father took to drink and his mother's health failed. The boy and his father became strangers or worse: intermittent relatives. They shared a flat when his mother was ill, then met at long intervals and by chance in streets and bars. His mother and Sydney (her son by a mysterious earlier union with an English gentleman in Africa) made up the family for Charles. In health, she was loving, attentive, amusing: a rare combination of maternal and theatrical instincts. There were recitations, impersonations, burlesques in the house. But her stage voice presently gave out and her theatrical engagements dwindled. At five, Charles replaced her on stage one night when she was suddenly incapacitated, and he finally made his exit showered with coins.

The family is now close to destitution. Mrs. Chaplin takes up religion and earns sixpences doing piecework as a seamstress. Her mind begins to distintegrate; there are spells of gentle madness, brought on, the doctors say, by malnutrition. She is in and out of asylums. The boys are in and out of workhouses where flogging is still routine and Charles on one occasion gets his. Somehow he and Sydney survive. The family's theatrical tradition is the legacy that saves them. At twelve, Charles gets his first important part (in *Jim: The Romance of a Cockney*) and although scarcely literate enough to read the script, he is a hit and on his way. With an act called The Eight Lancashire Lads, he tours the provinces: the ever-changing London habitations of his childhood are replaced by endless small town hotels. Being an actor is hard and lonely work, and not only in England. In America, where he eventually arrives with the Karno Company, he is again on tour and once more it is hotels, hotels. But something has been added, an American speciality of the period: the red light districts.

His love for his mother also survived. Of all the people mentioned in *My Autobiography*, she alone is portrayed fully and freely. His feeling for her puts aside the usual barriers of his constraint. She exists, and wonderfully, remembered in all the pity, the irony, the strange fun, of her condition. Amazingly, she herself survived, to spend her final years near Los Angeles after Chaplin had become famous and was able to tell her that he was worth five million dollars. In California, it appears, she still had spells of mild insanity, thus providing material for some of the weirder gags in the *Autobiography*. Once during a visit to an ostrich farm she was shown an ostrich egg by the keeper and, snatching it, she cried, "Give it back to the poor bloody ostrich!" and tossed the egg into the corral, "where it exploded with a loud report." Another time, out riding on a hot afternoon in her chauffeur-driven car, she leaned out to hand an ice cream cone to a workman in the street and accidentally threw it in his face. It seems that maternal instinct, like everything else, can go awry. Still another time she asked her son, "Wouldn't you rather be yourself than live in this theatrical world of unreality?" and he replied with a laugh, "You should talk."

Perhaps she wasn't so naïve. The problem of "being himself" has obviously vexed Chaplin even more than it does the rest of us. It forms a major theme, though an unformulated one, in *My Autobiography*. The circumstances that gave rise to the problem are written large in his account of his childhood. Considering the phantasmagoria of impermanence he lived in, it is a wonder the child could remember his name, let alone his latest address. Naturally, he clung to them, as to his mother's affection and other things, with a tenacity born of his very desperation. Naturally, too, the Tramp would eventually re-enact the essentials of that experience in terms of free invention and comic artifice. Homeless, speechless, nameless, indefinitely on the run, the Tramp finds his true love only to lose her, and possesses himself of the girl's grace and sweetness in lieu of possessing the girl. Nor is it unlikely, judging by his autobiography, that the Charles-Charlie partnership was his salvation as a person and an artist, just because it was, as already indicated, a *working* partnership. With actual women, on the other hand, his relations are somewhat obscured by his tact: many of the women are still alive. He does say, apropos of one early affair, that "No woman could measure up to that vague image I had in my mind." Possibly he means to suggest that he was perpetually trailed by the maternal presence, or absence, at least until his present marriage. In any case he brings a peculiar gaiety to his accounts of his more casual affairs. The girls include one nameless European who, after agreeing to a short-time affair, seems to have fallen for him and become a bother, until, re-signed at last to losing him, she accompanied him to his ship at Naples, waved a cheerful good-bye from the dock, and made off into the blue yonder walking the Charlie walk. Lucky girl. Lucky Charlie.

1964

It Shows
Shine: Notes
on Gertrude
Stein

There used to be something known to all readers as "Steinese." This was the peculiar literary idiom invented by Gertrude Stein around 1910 and made familiar to a large American public by her admirers and nonadmirers alike. Gnomic, repetitive, illogical, sparsely punctuated, Steinese became a scandal and a delight, lending itself equally to derisory parody and fierce denunciation. It had a formidable currency in writing and conversation throughout the teens, twenties, and thirties. "A rose is a rose is a rose" and "Pigeons on the grass alas" were encountered as frequently—almost— as the "Yes, we have no bananas," a nonsense phrase—later a song—of popular origin which may actually have been inspired by Steinese. "My little sentences have gotten under their skins," Gertrude Stein was at last able to say, with the pride of someone who craved recognition the more that she got mere notoriety. Her little sentences, originally quoted in scorn, had come in time to be repeated from something like affection; and thus the very theory that underlay her technique of reiteration was proved: what people loved they repeated, and what people repeated they loved.

Simple-minded though she sounded to the public, Gertrude Stein had her theories—few writers of note have had more stringent ones. If she was "the Mother Goose of Montparnasse," as someone said (such attempts to characterize her in a witty phrase were constantly repeated, too), she was a Mother Goose with a mind. She had studied psychology with William James at Radcliffe; conducted laboratory experiments there with Hugo Münsterberg; come close to getting an M.D. at Johns Hopkins; and then, settling in Paris with her brother Leo, had communed with Picasso in his Paris studio where a different kind of experiment was in progress: the plastic analysis of spatial relations which gave rise to Cubist painting.

Thus, behind the popular image, scornful or condescending, of Gertrude Stein there came to be a woman of immense purpose, equipped with astonishing powers of assimilation, concentration and hard work—as well as, to be sure, relaxation (she liked to lie in the sun and stare right into it). Her meeting with Picasso was in itself purely fortuitous; such a meeting might have befallen any tourist with a mildly questing spirit and enough money to buy paintings which, in any event, went almost begging. Gertrude Stein converted this meeting into the basis of a vocation and a life. It became for her the major case—her acquaintance with William James was a lesser case—of genius by association. Her scientific interests now fused with a passion, at last fully awakened, for art and literature. Out of this union of the laboratory and the studio came a body of theory and writing like none before or after it. True, there were elements in it of the Naturalism that was just then (*ca.* 1900) taking root in American literature. So far as these elements alone went, Gertrude Stein might have been a Dreiser *manqué*—except that, with her Cubist predilections, she became, as it were, post-Dreiser. Like Dreiser and other literary Naturalists she held quasi-scientific conceptions of race and individual character; life, moreover, expressed itself best in forms of "struggle" (the word was frequently hers as it was that of Dreiser's generation: "the class struggle," "the struggle for existence"). Her first mature work, *Three Lives,* was a triple portrait of the servant, a type of oppressed individual with a special appeal for novelists of the Naturalist tendency, from Flaubert and the Goncourt brothers to Dreiser himself; in addition, her trio, two German girls and a Negro girl, belonged to ethnic minorities, another staple Naturalist subject. Yet *Three Lives* proved to be a study in the language, syntax, and rhythms of consciousness rather than in the effects of oppression, social or cosmic. Here her aesthetic predilections checkmated and partially transformed the Dreiserian elements. *Three Lives* remains her most widely admired book.

The American writer who most attracted her was not Dreiser or any of his school but Henry James. And there may have been personal as well as aesthetic reasons for her refusal of Naturalist pessimism and protest and her liking for the less doctrinaire, the more free-spirited, realism of Henry James. Gertrude Stein felt no urgent identification with the oppressed; life was a struggle that she could very probably win. Her grandparents had been German-Jewish immigrants and they had prospered in the United States; her parents, prospering too, had been beguiled by art, languages, and educational theory. As children, Gertrude Stein and her sister and brothers, like the young Jameses at an earlier period, had been transported to Europe for a prolonged stay in some of its great cities. Thus the impression left by the elder Steins, at least on Gertrude Stein, was that of people who had to a considerable degree done as they liked and made themselves at home equally in America and Europe. No doubt their example, as she conceived of it, fortified her own determination to do the same, do even better. Hence the impulse, so patiently and passionately followed by her, to root herself in a profession, in the city of Paris, in a society of her choosing.

The consequences for her personality were, again, astonishing. In her maturity, she gave the impression, not merely of doing what she liked but of *being* almost anything she wanted to be. She seemed, as the many surviving likenesses of her suggest, at once female and male, Jew and non-Jew, American *pur sang* and European peasant, artist and public figure. She did not, however, create this intricate unity and sustain it without showing evidences of great strain. Her magnetic, almost magical, self-mastery was buttressed by frank self-indulgence and advertised to the world by a good deal of unashamed self-congratulation. A regular system of compensations characterized her ideas, her tastes, her associations—everything that made up her manner of life. Inclusions entailed exclusions in a virtually mechanical perfection of balance. For almost every idea she embraced, almost every person she befriended, there was some idea that remained pointedly alien to her, some person who was an outsider. Henry James had played something like this drama too, though with more compunction, it seems, and with himself often cast as the outsider. Gertrude Stein, never the outsider, seems not to have risen—or sunk—to the level of James's flexibility. Thus her combined residence, salon, and art gallery in the rue de Fleurus, where she presided with the aid of the devoted Miss Toklas, presented the aspects, now of an infinitely charming refuge, now of a bristling fortress. It was the citadel of that new spirit of connoisseurship which, applied to all things, from the writing of a sentence to the cooking of an artichoke, made life a joy and an ordeal for

so many young Americans of the period. The charming aspect of the rue de Fleurus predominated; the wariest visitor
was apt to be struck by things about Gertrude Stein that
were more literally magical than her self-mastery—things
that were not to be fully accounted for by will, intelligence,
or the principle of genius by association: her magnificent
head and features, her appealing voice, her elementally re-
freshing laugh.

II

But Gertrude Stein's family history cannot have been the
only source, or even the principal one, of her prodigious and
largely good-humored will to power. The same background
failed to supply her brother Leo with any such determination to make himself at home in the world. Brilliant, erratic,
eternally unfulfilled, Leo Stein became an early advocate
and perennial patient of psychoanalysis, finding a sort of
fatherland only in Freud. In Gertrude Stein's case, obviously,
it was her involvement in the profession of literature, and the
exacting mysteries attending it, that made the difference.
The profession was the more engrossing because of the variety of influences she brought to bear on it. If her conception
of literature included elements of Naturalism, it also anticipated the literary Modernism that was to culminate in the
chief works of such writers as Joyce, Eliot, Yeats, and Pound.
To her as to them (up to a point), literature in the twentieth
century presented itself as a problem in the reconstruction of
form and language. But where the solution of this problem
was a means to an end for these writers, it became, for her,
on the whole, a pursuit worthy in itself of her best efforts.

She had no quarrel, as they did, with culture, with history, with the self. Culture in her terminology becomes "composition," a neutral aggregate of institutions, technologies, and human relations which the artist, as artist, accepts as it is, eliciting its meanings primarily through eye and ear rather than through mind, memory, or imagination. And words, like the other materials of the literary medium, become useful to the artist, assume a character purely aesthetic, in proportion as they can be converted from bearers of established meaning and unconscious association into plastic entities.

Such, very briefly, was the theoretical basis of her work, a basis to which she added many refinements as she sought to find literary equivalents for the various experiments conducted by the Cubists. Her theories have been admirably expounded and criticized in a number of recent books. The usual conclusion is the common sense one. Literature is a temporal art rather than, like painting, a spatial one; and in being used as plastic entities, as things in themselves, words become not more but less alive, indeed peculiarly inert. Mr. Kenneth Burke has called Gertrude Stein's practice "art by subtraction," a phrase that expresses well the literal and merely negative aspect of her work at its least effective. Mr. B. L. Reid has made Burke's phrase the title of a hostile study of Gertrude Stein; and Mr. John Malcolm Brinnin, in *The Third Rose*, the best biography of her, sums up his investigations into her methods as follows:

> Language is plastic, but its plasticity must be informed and determined by the philosophy or, at least, by the information it conveys. In her earlier works, Gertrude Stein operated under this injunction naturally; but as she continued, her attraction to painting led her to wish for the same plastic freedom for literature, and eventually to write as though literature

were endowed with such freedom. "The painter," said Georges Braque, "knows things by sight; the writer, who knows them by name, profits by a prejudice in his favor." This was the profit Gertrude Stein threw away.

All this applies to darkest Stein. Mr. Brinnin and many others, including the present writer, find this territory difficult of access. Nor, of course, is one helped by having learned one's way around in, say, *Finnegans Wake* and *Four Quartets*. On the contrary, a knowledge of Joyce's or Eliot's methods sets one to looking in Gertrude Stein for meanings and values according to the principle of unconscious association. But this is the wrong principle to apply to, for example, *Tender Buttons*. Gertude Stein insisted that she was not practicing "automatic writing" or working in any literary convention, such as Surrealism, related to automatic writing. No release of unconscious impulses, her own or those of fictional characters, is intended. She must, in fact, have devoted much labor to eliminating such suggestions. Thus the body of her theory and writing at its most advanced occupies an anomalous position among the various modern schools. Where they all begin—by asserting the primacy of the literary "medium" (words)—Gertrude Stein for the most part begins and ends.

The usual theoretical objections to her work are persuasive; yet between them and her work itself there is always a certain accusing margin of doubt. Poets have found her work exciting, however inexplicably so, as if words in themselves might in certain circumstances appeal to some receptive apparatus in man that is comparable to what people call extrasensory perception. This is not, on the whole, the experience of the present writer in the farther reaches of Gertrude Stein. Yet, read aloud, certain passages in, say, *Tender Buttons*, do make their effect, especially if read in the company of people prepared to laugh or start or otherwise express the sudden access of the sense of wonder. The silent reader expects familiar rewards for his efforts. The *viva voce* reader is more apt to take what comes and make the most of it. To the ear, when it is lent freely to a given passage of Stein, the contrast stands out between, on the one hand, the perpetual flow of *non sequiturs* and, on the other, the air of conviction conveyed by the very definite words, the pregnant pauses, the pat summary phrases ("This is this," "It is surely cohesive," "It is not the same"); and the mingling of apparent conviction with transparent nonsense throughout such a passage takes on its own kind of momentary sense, giving rise (if the reader is lucky) to a wondering laugh. As one of her pat phrases suggests, "It shows shine." Does it also *show Stein?* If so, reading these tongue-twisting words aloud helps to bring the pun to light. So too with the occasional rhymes and jingles strewn through this prose: they also come alive better when spoken.

Tender Buttons is probably Gertrude Stein's most "private" performance. The verbal still-lifes in that book defy even Mr. Donald Sutherland, the critic who, in *Gertrude Stein: A Biography of Her Work,* has made more headway than anyone else in interpreting her prose. Here is a passage, surely very beautiful, from "Lend a Hand or Four Religions" (in *Useful Knowledge,* 1928), followed by Mr. Sutherland's comment:

> First religion. She is feeling that the grasses grow four times yearly and does she furnish a house as well. . . . Let her think of a stable man and a stable can be a place where they care for the Italians every day. And a mission of kneeling there where the water is flowing kneeling, a chinese christian,

and let her think of a stable man and wandering and a repetition of counting. Count to ten. He did. He did not. Count to ten. And did she gather the food as well. Did she gather the food as well. Did she separate the green grasses from one another. They grow four times yearly. Did she see some one as she was advancing and did she remove what she had and did she lose what she touched and did she touch it and the water there where she was kneeling where it was flowing. And are stables a place where they care for them as well.

One might say that the essence of this passage is the phrase "as well"—a sort of welcome to anything that is there to come into the composition, such a welcome being the genius of France and as often as not of America. The coherence of the passage, which consists in a sort of melodic progress of consideration, is between the rational French discursiveness and the rambling American sympathy as Whitman had it. But more important is the kind of existence expressed here. The existence of the woman in the passage is intimately involved with the existence, growth, and movement of things in the landscape. Her kneeling and the water flowing and the grass growing four times yearly and the caring for Italians are all part of the same slow natural living of the place and the world.

III

In serious literary circles, as distinguished from the large public, Gertrude Stein's real accomplishments were always known. There, her influence was at one time considerable, though it worked in very different ways and degrees on different individuals. It was known that her writing had influenced, in certain respects, Sherwood Anderson and, later, Hemingway. It was supposed that Steinese had found echoes in Don Marquis' *archy and mehitabel* as well as in the difficult poetry of Wallace Stevens, who once wrote "Twenty men crossing a bridge,/ Into a village,/ Are/ Twenty men crossing a bridge/ Into a village." Her insistence on the primacy of phenomena over ideas, of the magnificence of sheer unmediated reality, found, one assumes, a rapturous response in Stevens, a quiet one in Marianne Moore. In *Axel's Castle,* Edmund Wilson's discriminating study of modern literature published as early as 1931, she had a chapter to herself, as had, in each case, Yeats, Valéry, Eliot, Proust, and Joyce. *Axel's Castle* was a decisive event in the history of modern reputations. Wilson had some doubts as to Gertrude Stein's readableness in certain books but few doubts as to her general importance. Steinese and its inventor had become reputable.

By the time she died, Gertrude Stein had become something she wanted still more to be—she called it "historical." As early as 1923, *Vanity Fair* had printed "Miss Furr and Miss Skeene," her wonderful, and easily intelligible, exhibit of the vocabulary of genteel Bohemianism—"Mr. Furr was quite a pleasant man. Helen Furr had quite a pleasant voice a voice quite worth cultivating." Beginning with *The Autobiography of Alice B. Toklas* (1932) she had developed unsuspected capacities for writing still more intelligibly. The universal surprise at this fact, combined with the intrinsic fascination of the book, made it a best seller. And dire though the *Autobiography* is with special pleading, with that whole invidious system of inclusions and exclusions described above, it remains one of the best memoirs in American literature.

The improvement in her literary status disturbed for a while her firm sense of herself and her place in the world. "Money is funny," she said quizzically as the royalties poured in. But she soon mastered her new role and played it with good-humored dignity. Returning to America for the first time since 1903, she lectured to sizable audiences across the country. And following World War II she became a kind of oracle and motherly hostess to American military personnel in liberated Paris. Just before her death her sayings and doings over there were much in the news in America; and her later writings, cast in a much modified Steinese, were sought by the popular magazines.

Gertrude Stein died in Paris in 1946 at the age of 72. She seems to have died at peace with herself, her natural craving for recognition to some extent satisfied. At least she died firmly in character, having delivered from her hospital bed the last specimen, and one of the most searching specimens, of Steinese. "What is the answer?" she inquired, and getting no answer said, laughing, "In that case, what is the question?"

1962

Memories
of James
Agee

James Agee died in May 1955 at the age of 45. His death was a great loss and grief to those who had known him, including myself (though I knew him only intermittently). But to me, at least, his death was not exactly a shock. Agee lived with a life-consuming sort of intensity. In the circles he frequented, everyone was pretty intense. They smoked, drank, talked, sat up late, wandered around the Village looking for company, dreamed of greatness, fought off sterility, just as he did. But it was more or less understood at the time that Agee was special. There was a unique energy in him just as there was a unique beauty in his voice, eyes and hands.

His intensity was different from that of others we knew. He smoked and drank as if to appease an elemental hunger rather than to satisfy a nervous craving. His talk was a sort of rite. Rarely a monologue, it was most often, and quite literally, *tête-à-tête*. At parties, among the swirling ranks, he liked to put his head together with some other sympathetic head, nodding emphatically all the time they talked, while he sliced, carved and scooped words out of the air with his hands. The subject was, usually, not some matter of general opinion but a particular thing: a Russian movie, FDR's oratory, an episode in Hawthorne or Joyce. The method was passionately analytical, the purpose was praise. Let us now praise famous men. Argument was a false note in these confrontations. But it sometimes cropped up and he was capable of rage, hard and soft at the same time, stone and moss. "Men of letters are death, just death," he muttered in the course of a long dispute I once had with him about some such writer—was it Gide or Mann?

Mostly, though, he didn't dispute what you said; he refined on it. "Do you remember, Jim, how Edward G. Robinson gets shot down at the end of *Little Caesar?*" "Behind the billboards, yes," Agee would reply, with slow meditative ecstasy; and then he would go on to re-create the whole scene in amazing detail; the lighting of it, the sound made by the bullets in the empty night, the helpless death slump of the lonely little gangster. "*Little* Caesar he was—Charlie Chaplin turned criminal."

The topic was seldom abandoned until it had been treated thoroughly. Meanwhile, your place as Agee's interlocutor had probably been taken by other individuals in succession: there were always eager candidates. At last the party would have disintegrated—the aggrieved drunks have slouched out, the political-minded have marched off in groups, still debating—and there at 2 A.M. would be Agee with one interlocutor and two or three determined listeners, seated firmly in his chair, consuming the last of the host's last bottle, ducking his head, shaping his words with his hands, exhausting the topic, exhausting his insatiable listeners, exhausting himself.

"Agee is a genius," a woman writer of decided opinions once announced to a group of us. "Our *only* genius," she added, looking hard at us. But "genius" is one of those classifying words he resented. And if he *was* a genius, he was in some sense a captive genius. He was a captive of the Luce publications, for which he worked during long years. He was also the captive of an ideological age, in which he shone by contrast. Was he too comfortably uncomfortable in this position, occasionally snarling at his keepers but still accepting the ration of money or veneration they tossed into his cage, still on exhibit?

He had the sort of temperament which would have made him a great writer if he had been born just a little earlier. He belonged to the time of Fitzgerald, Hemingway, Faulkner, Cummings, Edmund Wilson. His own generation—it was to some extent mine as well—was as literary and ambitious as the older one. Agee, in particular, was very ambitious. But the younger ones seemed to lack the drive, the professional finesse, of the older ones. We tended to become something quite different: professional revolutionists, Freudians, Thomists, Southerners, journalists, critics, teachers. The authority that the older generation found in its literary talent, our generation found in systems of thought, political parties, business organizations, educational and other institutions, the examples of famous men. Yes, Agee's habit of praise, the piety that distinguished him from the reformist rancor of others, partly turned him inside out, too. It feasted to a considerable extent on what *had* been: his own past, the South's past, the recent past of art. As I make it out from his conversations and writings, his main struggle was to recapture a creativity which he associated with Joyce, Griffith, Chaplin and others. He labored to repossess a world that had been triumphantly realized by the modern masters.

If this is true, it helps to account for his piecemeal production as a writer, his occasional imitativeness and sentimentality, his difficulty in concentrating his mind on anything so definite as a story. Like Proust, he could only have *fully* realized himself in some super-work; but his *Remembrance of Things Past* remained unwritten.

What Agee did accomplish, between his movie reviews, his discursive but brilliant *Let Us Now Praise Famous Men,* his overwritten but moving short novel *The Morning Watch,* was magnificent, even though it seems fragmentary. I have space here to speak only of his posthumous novel, *A Death in the Family.*

As the publishers make clear in a note, the novel had to be assembled from a lot of manuscript left by the author when he died. The general subject is clear enough: the sudden death of a father and the consequences of it to his family, especially his small son. This central event, as well as the events immediately preceding it and immediately following from it, are accounted for in several chapters which appear finished. But there are six additional chapters, each more or less complete in itself, that deal with the same family, the same boy, but that do not seem either to presuppose or to anticipate the father's death. These chapters the editors have placed as best they could, printing them in italics. They have also included as a prelude a prose poem, "Knoxville: Summer 1915," which Agee published in *Partisan Review* twenty years ago.

A Death in the Family is, therefore, far from being a finished whole and it probably can't be understood or judged as such. It is, however, very wonderful in most of its parts. The jeweled prose that Agee sometimes resorted to elsewhere is occasionally, and disconcertingly, present here, too. There are also pages—including one that tries to render the noise of an auto starting—which sound too much like pages in *Ulysses.*

For the most part, however, the writing is in the colloquial

Mark Twain manner, which seems to come most naturally to Agee and which he makes fully his own, adding a certain richness of language and rhythm. An account of the family's visit to an ancient relative in the hills is in this style and is classic. So is the episode in which the son, Rufus, is bought a fancy cap by his aunt. He is essential boy and she is essential aunt and the cap is essential cap. As to the central subject, Agee renders the sheer shock of the death better than he renders any deeper realizations and consequences of it. Probably he would have got around to these: they seem to be assumed in *The Morning Watch*, which is about a similarly fatherless boy at a later stage of his development. *A Death in the Family* is incomplete, but it is full of superlative moments and confirms one's memories of the—literally—unforgettable man who wrote it.

1957

Literary
Comment

The
Duke's
Dilemma

The Life and Adventures of La Rochefoucauld is one of Morris Bishop's lively and learned biographies of historic Frenchmen. La Rochefoucauld, the seventeenth-century nobleman, soldier, lover, politician and author, is so brilliant a subject and Mr. Bishop presents him in such engaging detail that we remain convinced of the general worth of the book even when we dissent from some of its main conclusions.

La Rochefoucauld's story turns on one of those dilemmas which also preoccupied the dramatists of his time; in fact his story helps us to appreciate the elegant urgency of their plays. On the one hand he was possessed by a love of glory; on the other hand his glory could only be sustained by actions which inevitably diminished it. He was not in any foolish sense romantic or vain. His ambition had reference to that of his feudal family and class, both of which still enjoyed some power in France.

In the century of Richelieu and Louis XIV, however, that power was weakening; and no doubt the ambition of men like La Rochefoucauld was desperate in proportion as it was doomed. Their prestige had come to depend on privileges doled out by monarchs intent on consolidating their own power at the nobles' expense. La Rochefoucauld might protest that his glory was certified by his feudal past. In practice he had to engage in endless maneuvers in order that his wife should have the right of arriving at the Louvre door in her own carriage and of occupying a certain kind of stool in the queen's presence.

This was La Rochefoucauld's dilemma, which he tried to resolve in a life of action. In the course of it he resorted to almost every device of flattery, intrigue, seduction and open battle known to the time. Yet, in his capacity for self-awareness, for love and friendship, for wit, for gratuitous folly, and not least for boredom, he displayed an individual sensibility. If La Rochefoucauld harked back to the medieval hero Roland, he also foreshadowed the heroes of Stendhal. In him the great French ideal of *la gloire* was already fighting for its life.

His efforts largely failed. In the wars of the Fronde his castle was burned and he was almost blinded; his beloved natural son died in battle; his mistresses proved false; and in his poverty he had to marry his daughter to his former valet, now become rich. It was only when he turned to literature and friendship that he found any sort of lasting glory. By assisting Mme. de La Fayette to write her half-realistic stories of love and manners, he contributed to the inception of the modern novel, including of course the Stendhalian novel. And he wrote on his own the small bitter book of reflections by which he is chiefly known today. His shocked contemporaries received *The Maxims* as a classic and it has been one ever since. The work helped to fix French prose in its characteristic incisiveness; and it established La Rochefoucauld, in his concern with the psychology of self-interest, as the Machiavelli of the private life.

Dismayed by what he calls, without further qualification, their "cynicism," Bishop does not greatly admire *The Max-*

ims. And by incorporating a number of them into the text of his story, he tries to show that they were the mere fruit of La Rochefoucauld's personal disappointments. But the famous sentences resist Bishop's ingenuity; they remain stoutly and sometimes ludicrously unassimilated to the Duke's stream-of-consciousness as it is imagined by his biographer. If Bishop's experiment proves anything, it proves what Louis Kronenberger once suggested in his translation of *The Maxims:* that they are the essentially impersonal product of a definite method. This method Mr. Kronenberger defined as a "scientific cynicism . . . which tested vanity in a test-tube."

Meanwhile Bishop's account of the last years of La Rochefoucauld is full of grace and pity. The political rehabilitation of the old nobleman was never to be complete. He was excluded from the Academy and declared unfit—as he doubtless was—to be tutor to the Dauphin. Yet when someone presented the Dauphin with a gilded doll-house peopled by effigies of the leading contemporary writers, it was noticed that one of them represented La Rochefoucauld. Thus he was finally established at court in all his glory, if only as a doll.

1951

To Moscow
Again

"The profundity of Chekhov's works is inexhaustible to the actor," Stanislavsky said. But under present theater conditions, Chekhov's profundity, like Shakespeare's, can involve liabilities, for audience and actors alike. Perhaps it was so even in the patriarchal days of the archetypal Moscow Art Theater, Chekhov's shrine. There is evidence that things did not always go well there, although the playwright himself was at hand, or at least in Yalta, for consultation. He once complained that the officers' uniforms in *The Three Sisters* were too smart. The Russian military, he said, had ceased to be a glittering elite, had grown more cultured and shabbier. (The officers in *The Three Sisters* seem to have submitted wholly to the general bourgeoisifying trend, and the duel fought at the play's end, though fatal to one participant, is a travesty.)

But if the trouble was partly in the limitations to be found in any theater group, it was—and still is—largely in the profundity of Chekhov's art itself. While his plays were in rehearsal he was often asked by actors how such and such a scene or character should be done. And Chekhov, the kindliest of writers, would show a surprising impatience. "It's all there," he would reply. And no wonder. In his major plays, everything *is* there, in the script, from the state of people's

souls at a given moment to the state of the weather. His exclusive reputation for small-scale effects is quite unfounded.
The opposite is true of his effects. A principle of discreet
but forceful expansion is at work in his major plays. Each
interior implies an exterior. Often the exterior is a garden, and beyond the garden are fields, or streets and street
crowds, all Russia, birds in flight, the succession of day and
night, the seasonal cycle, Time, the universe. Nor is this almost epic range conveyed with any help from lengthy stage
directions, like O'Neill's, or prefaces, like Shaw's. It's all
there in the characters' talk, that munificent display of verbalism for which the term "dialogue" is a vulgar misnomer.

In her recent quarrel with the "theater arts" Establishment, in *The New York Review*, Elizabeth Hardwick insisted
upon the primacy of literary talent in the theatrical process.
"Drama is, after all, literature written for the stage," she said,
and her claim seems to me incontrovertible. But if it needs
any support it should find plenty in *The Three Sisters*, which
is having a conscientious revival at the Morosco Theater in
New York.

The usual Chekhovian profusion of detail swells into an
immense opulence in this play. Farce and tragedy coalesce in
an intricate, often bewildering, pattern of tonalities. The
number of characters, each with his peculiar destiny to make
manifest, his string of solo numbers to get off from time to
time as he wanders on and off stage, is large. It is large, at
least, by the standards of economy prevailing in the New
York theater, where a cast is rarely numerous enough to get
entangled, one with another, or with the furniture.

When the curtain goes up at the Morosco, the three sisters
are all on stage, but only Olga, the eldest, and Irina, the
youngest, are conversing. Masha, the other, is more or less

supine on her famous sofa, book in hand, silent except for an occasional mocking whistle. This is the parsimonious privacy we are accustomed on the New York stage. But it doesn't last. Masha's body uncoils and her tongue loosens: she has some cutting observation to make. And pretty soon three officers appear at the back of the set, chatting casually beside a long table in what is the dining room. It is Irina's birthday. A luncheon party is under way. And now, one by one, the others materialize: Colonel Vershinin, the new battery commander, with whom Masha will fall in love; Andrey, the morose brother of the three girls; Natasha, his brash upstart of a fiancée; the aged army doctor who has forgotten all his medical knowledge, who drinks, and who is the voice of despair, Chekhov's gloomiest spokesman; and Solyony, a buffoon to end all Russian literary buffoons, who turns out to be a killer. Thus the stage is soon full and it will only rarely return to the original state of comparative privacy. In this community of spiritual doom privacy is unwanted. For all their despair and their antagonisms, Chekhov's characters are still Russians. As we know from their classic literature, Russians have—or had—a quality denied to most other modern peoples: a certain gregariousness of the soul. Russians love Russians.

In this community, moreover, no one is fully capable of living in the present. No one, that is, who has any sensibility at all. The rest are clowns, buffoons, or bitches, all of them as self-deceived and self-destructive in their own way as the sensitive people are in theirs. But if the latter are incapable of living in the present, they do live, with a dreamy, often mad, intensity, in the past or in the future. The sisters are always pining for Moscow, the lost Eden, once the family home, where the girls hope to live, really live, again. Vershinin perpetually conjures up the coming millennium, and his enthusiasm for it is matched by his reluctance to fix the date of its arrival. "And when more time has passed—another two or three hundred years . . . Oh, what a wonderful life that will be!"

Meanwhile there is much talk of salvation through work. The work idea is a kind of compromise between the nostalgia and the futurism. Some members of the circle do have jobs. There are the schools to be staffed, and the army, the telegraph office, the administrative positions at the County Board. Between the jobs and the people who work at them, however, the disparity is in most cases total. So actual work doesn't pay off either, spiritually speaking. And therefore they talk and talk, creating themselves in conversation—if conversation is the word for the wonderfully disjointed flow of remark that goes on in the play: the irrelevancies, the non-sequiturs, the garbled quotations, the bad French and juvenile Latin, the animal cries, and—as a last resort—the forays into seeming nonsense. The verbalism of the play finds its ultimate form in nonsense. Solyony, the buffoon and future killer, torments his prospective victim with cries of "chook, chook, chook." Masha and Vershinin like to communicate by means of a sort of Slavic love call that goes "Tram-tam-tam." The old doctor voices his gentle despair in the syllables of the Offenbachian refrain: "Tarara-boom-de-ay." This phrase he hums softly to himself just before the final curtain falls. Famous last words. Tragedy into farce.

Thus the people seek salvation in talk, among other things. And thus *The Three Sisters*, considered as "literature written for the stage," finds its special language in their fantastic style. Paradoxically, however, its structure is determined, not by what they do but, for the most part, by what they don't do—by their habit of inaction or, at most, of action that is compulsive and unconsidered.

At their level, in fact, the usual distinctions between action and inaction, conscious will and sentient passivity, disappear as they do in dreams. And Chekhov, one of the chief progenitors of the modern tradition in drama, comes close to some of its most recent exponents, the Absurdists, as they may be called. Between the people who pine for Moscow and the people who wait for Godot, a family resemblance is detectable. In both groups there is a great urgency of salvation, and a professed belief that salvation is to be found, not really in work or talk, but in a dream of transcendence: the going to Moscow, the coming of Godot. In both, finally, there is a profound suspicion that this belief is illusory. Quite literally, they hope against hope. Thus it might be said that Beckett's people are merely Chekhov's people dispossessed of their furniture and stripped down to their reflexes. The former are dehumanized, the latter over-humanized, but the essential predicament is the same. For Chekhov's people, at any rate, the things that make up their humanity also constitute the symptoms of their failure. Their learning, their sensibility, their gentility, even their knowledge of the polite languages, are a burden to them. Their culture exists only that it may be forgotten, leaving them with the wistful pleasure of forever mourning its loss. "I've even forgotten the Italian for window, or ceiling," Irina remarks, apropos of nothing in particular and everything in general.

Yet one must avoid seeing Chekhov's work, and Beckett's for that matter, too exclusively in the light of such affinities and continuities. The works of both are far from being mere versions of moral history, mere stages in the evolution or devolution of humanism. To speak only of Chekhov: his sofas are as essential to his conception of life as they are to his stage sets, and so are the other amenities implied by the sofas. It was as a realist, however visionary, that he conceived his characters and wrote his plays, while Beckett, as I understand him, is a pure visionary of the "Absurd."

In its form and genre, too, *The Three Sisters* belongs to the end of the age of realism. It is a bourgeois melodrama *manqué*. The principals refuse to enact the roles assigned them by the original genre. Many of the original situations are present. The son of the family marries an ambitious village wench. He contracts gambling debts. The home is mortgaged. There are loveless marriages and adulterous goings-on. There is the duel. By degrees, the ambitious wench succeeds in largely dispossessing the family. The keys to the larder end by dangling from her belt rather than, as formerly, from that of Olga, the rightful chatelaine. In *The Three Sisters*, however, the family really dispossesses itself. The usual confrontations of melodrama fail to occur. What is lacking is not so much the will to resist aggression as the concentration of feeling needed to bring the will into play. Feeling is not absent, of course. It is all over the place. There are embraces, protestations, citations from the poets, flights of philosophy, and tears, tears, tears. But this tangle of emotions is unable to attach itself to any set of objects at all fitting. It thus fails to stimulate the will and to serve as a guide to conduct. The emotional confusion confuses the practical issues for the family members, even while investing those individuals with pathos and charm. In one of the few scenes that verge on a real confrontation, Olga is finally roused to anger against her brother's wife, Natasha. But it is not for her machinations, or even her affair with a leading citizen, that

Natasha is brought to book. It is because in a fit of temper she has spoken harshly to an old servant. "The very slightest rudeness, a tactless word upsets me," Olga cries. Her sensitivity to rudeness is admirable. One loves her for it. But in the light of the whole family situation, it falls quite short of the mark. It reminds us, and Natasha, of Olga's superior gentility but it doesn't get the house back.

1964

Thomas
Mann

I. The Good European

If all novelists are in some degree social historians, Thomas Mann was the great novelist-historian of the present crisis in Western culture. He made a magnificent spectacle out of what has since become a sad and desperate routine. Between the unlovely facts of disease and death on the one hand, and the glories of art and philosophy on the other, he discovered a metaphysical affinity. For Mann, and for his early readers, there was a sort of beauty in the contemplation of this affinity. It lent a grandeur to the slow disintegration of the Buddenbrooks, the rapid fall of Aschenbach in "Death in Venice," the up-and-down career of Hans Castorp in *The Magic Mountain*. Today, when the pressure of those unlovely facts and of the whole ever-worsening crisis seems to outweigh any current achievements in art and philosophy, Mann's metaphysics seem unconvincing.

Indeed, despite all his concern with decadence, there was in Thomas Mann an old-fashioned interest in soul cures, and an old-fashioned art went with it. The possibility of a cure was firmly implied in the story, even when the suggested cure failed to work for the hero in question. The cure consisted partly in an exposure to new experience, such as falling ill, falling in love, and traveling; partly in a submission to Socratic procedures: scarcely a novel or tale of Mann's is without some simulacrum of a Socratic dialogue in the course of which the hero's inherited ideas are subjected to intensive scrutiny by himself and others. The unexamined life is not worth living.

Mann's faith in the reality of ideas was profound. So was his genius for seeing ideas written large and grand, or small and droll, in the drama of human character, of manners, and of history. The peculiar attraction of his work—for a past generation that *did* find it attractive—lay in the relation of its drama to its ideas, its surface to its interior. The surface teems with anecdote: no modern novelist has given us more characters, happenings, and scenes that have the immediate charm of first-rate anecdote; while the interior is alive with dim but active intellectual presences: Spirit and Nature, Democracy and Aristocracy, North and South, and so on. The art of Mann consisted in fusing the surface with the interior, in thoroughly crystallizing the anecdotes into universal parables.

Nowadays it is often objected that all this is overdone in Mann's work. The crystallizing process is *too* thorough, the symbolism employed to accomplish it too obtrusive, the whole art of the man too surgically expert and complacently omniscient. To be sure, similar objections were heard even in the heyday of his reputation. There was always some doubt as to the ultimate creative intensity of his mind as compared with his greatest contemporaries in the novel. To go from Mann to Joyce or Proust or Kafka was, one said, like passing through the frame into the picture, or exchanging the doctor's office for the confessional. For what they are worth, these distinctions make sense now as they did in the past; and Mann has been under the further disadvantage that his complex German did not go into very acceptable English. Thus he has exerted far less influence than Joyce or Proust or Kafka on writing in this country. He has been the intelligent reader's novelist rather than the novelist's novelist.

The objections to Mann's work have become sharper in recent years. For beyond the merely technical criticisms lies a changed point of view upon literature and life—a change begotten, evidently, not by any lessening of the crisis in culture but by its vastly greater gravity. Mann's faith in ideas, his passion for explanations, have given way to an ethos of the Cool, of moral ingenuousness, in life as in literature. The *examined* life is not worth living.

It takes a really free-spirited critic to rehabilitate a dated classic. Mann is such a classic now and Mark Van Doren is such a critic; and Mr. Van Doren's small recent book on *Joseph and His Brothers* showed what could come of an encounter between such a pair. Where most critics have been engulfed by Mann's own omnivorous critical intelligence, Van Doren remains serenely visible. Between the German novelist with his elegant complexity and the American critic with his elegant simplicity there is a dramatic half-meeting of minds. It takes place, moreover, on Van Doren's chosen ground: the theory and practice of comedy. Thus one critic has made this dated writer his own, just as others may well in time make him theirs.

Here, meanwhile, are two further books on the subject, one about Mann, the other by him. Erich Heller's *The Ironic German* is a study of Mann's mind and work; and it has the immediate purpose, one gathers, of refurbishing Mann's image in the public mind. Mann's *Last Essays*, containing four literary portraits written during his later years, is a very personal and quite moving volume full of what appear to be tacit reflections on Mann's image as it came to exist in his own mind.

Anyone who is already familiar with his work will find comfort and instruction in *The Ironic German*. Mr. Heller's account of the novelist's intellectual composition and affinities is thorough; his defense of Mann in the dialogue that forms his chapter on *The Magic Mountain* is spirited; his analyses of the major works are excellent even though a little too lengthy and tortuous for what they contain. The point of view on Mann is not, however, very fresh or even very clear and well sustained. Unlike Mr. Van Doren, Mr. Heller does tend to fall victim to Mann's omnivorous mind, or at least to the similarities between their two minds.

For one thing, Mr. Heller's title seems unfortunate, almost a caricature. The "ironic" suggests a pose rather than a man and the "German" fastens on a world artist the fatalism of race. In part the book itself corrects the first of these impressions, showing that Mann's irony served a "moral intelligence" of the first order. Yet Mr. Heller is ultimately a little uncomfortable with the irony and with its philosophic basis. By way of gently suggesting Mann's supposed limitations, he cites Kierkegaard and his famous hierarchy of Being. Mann's early hero, Tonio Kröger, and by implication Mann himself, are said to have occupied "that border-region between the aesthetic and the ethical state" which lies considerably below the ultimate or religious state. But anybody can cite Kierkegaard and nowadays almost everybody does. The question is whether Kierkegaard is relevant to Mann, an uncompromising theist to an uncompromising humanist.

Then there is the difficulty of Mann's Germanism. Given Mr. Heller's background as a self-exiled writer of Middle European origins, and his position as an authority on German literature and thought, it is natural that he should see Mann largely in the light of their common traditions. And Mr. Heller undoubtedly contributes a great deal of subtly reasoned evidence to the study of Mann's antecedents. Yet Mann's conscious debt to, his veritable identification with, such figures as Goethe, Schopenhauer, Wagner and Nietzsche, are explored in *The Ironic German* to the point where one sometimes feels that one is participating in a mystery rather than reading about a novelist.

Concerning Mann's famous idea of the Bourgeois, Mr. Heller characteristically writes: "It seems an elusive but powerful organism capable of absorbing into its indefinitely expansive system a vast variety of incommensurable things: a measure of German piety and a measure of Will to Power, Goethe's doctrine of resignation and Nietzsche's dithyrambic excesses, Stifter's untempestuous ideal and Wagner's musical demon, Schopenhauer's will to saintliness and Bismarck's *Realpolitik*." Thus are Mann's many ghostly forebears summoned by Mr. Heller from their widely scattered graves. No wonder he concludes that Mann practiced a sort of "*Imitatio mystica*" of the dead, hoping thus to leave behind "a body of work which could truly claim to be the parodistic résumé of German Literary History."

But true as this may be, does it account for the living force and variety of Mann's work? Are not his German pieties a part of his private history as distinguished from whatever it was that made him a great novelist of modern experience? And is it not just as a great novelist of modern experience that his image needs to be refurbished?

The *Last Essays* evoke a less past-haunted Thomas Mann than we sometimes get from *The Ironic German,* despite its excellence in other respects. And although three of Mann's subjects in this book were German—they are Schiller, Goethe, and Nietzsche, the fourth and most reverently portrayed is Chekhov—the book recalls us to Mann's character as the German become the "Good European." Indeed, Nietzsche's famous formula seems to have been invented just for Mann, in this final phase as in most of his writing after *The Magic Mountain.* The *Last Essays* also reminds us of Mann's old genius as an essayist, his way of combining his extraordinary powers of intellectual analysis with his novelist's gift of creating characters and telling stories.

But what lends a peculiar interest to these characters and stories is the extent to which they add up to a gentle inquisition on his own character, life, and work. For one thing he seems to change sides, writing very warmly about Schiller and Chekhov, two figures who were in many ways his opposite numbers, and writing rather less sympathetically of Goethe and Nietzsche, a pair with whom he had formerly identified himself quite closely. "In Germany greatness tends to a kind of hypertrophy," he remarks in "Fantasy on Goethe," the last of his several studies of that poet. And he goes on to show how Goethe "had in his majestic old age a good deal of this absolutism and personal imperialism," and how "at his death there was to be heard not only the nymphs' lament for great Pan, but a distinct 'Whew' of relief." Nor does Mann spare us any of Nietzsche's vulgarity and brutality in his brilliant but perhaps too immediately political reconsideration of that figure, "Nietzsche in the Light of Recent History."

On the other hand, Schiller and Chekhov are praised for their relative humility and their steady devotion to principle. Where Nietzsche's fatal illness is related not only to his triumphs as a thinker but to his megalomaniac excesses, Chekhov's illness is said to have produced a "strange, skeptical and infinitely endearing modesty." He was, Mann says, "too modest even for passion." After all, Chekhov was a *real* doctor and knew too much about disease to glorify it as Nietzsche did and Mann after him. What Chekhov accomplished in the short story, a form that Mann says he himself scorned in his youth, is contrasted favorably with "works of monumental stature"—surely works like some of Mann's own. And Chekhov's narrative art is roundly declared to be (as it undoubtedly is) "unsurpassed in European literature." Yet, as Mann is at pains to show, Chekhov became a great artist more or less by accident: through the intervention of a forgotten Russian critic who saw promise in his early journalistic sketches. Here again there is an implied contrast, this time with Mann's own conception of the artist as an historically and metaphysically predestined entity.

It is in his account of Chekhov's ultimate beliefs, or lack of them, that the essay is most intimately revealing of the author's state of mind. A thinker ought to answer the question "What is to be done?" Chekhov believed; yet he could not say what was to be done to improve conditions in Czarist Russia or ameliorate the human condition in general. He did not, however, take refuge in irony or dialectical exercises but ruefully sought, as he said, "just to depict life as it is, without taking one step further." In other words, Chekhov avowed his uncertainties more clearly and humbly than Mann himself had ever done.

But it is not the implied self-criticism that matters in these essays so much as the impulse behind it. Despite his years, his fame, his achievement, Thomas Mann could still suffer, still reflect, still play Socrates to his own ideas. Like Chekhov, he lived to be greatly tried by personal ordeals, fearfully depressed by the state of the world; and both men sought relief in visions of a "perhaps imminent day when life will be bright and joyful as a peaceful Sunday morning." The words are Chekhov's but the dream is both Chekhov's and Mann's. Thus a writer as enormously complex as Mann had always been, and as complacent in his greatness as he had sometimes seemed, was capable at last of visions and other simplicities! This strange and wonderful fact underlies the *Last Essays* and gives them their peculiar preciousness. It also points to the more-than-German, the better-than-ironical, the magnificently universal artist that remains to be rediscovered in Mann's work as a whole.

1959

II. Thomas Mann's Farewell

Another substantial volume in black and gold has been added to the long shelf-full of such volumes that make up Thomas Mann's work for American readers. No doubt the present volume will be the last. Mann's works, like his days, have ended. They have ended well: *Confessions of Felix Krull, Confidence Man*, is an amusing comedy of ideas, a richly documented historical fantasy, and Mann's finest performance since *Doctor Faustus*.

The book had been gestating in the novelist's mind for many years. The early chapters were written as far back as 1911. Further chapters were added some ten years later, and the resulting fragment has long been familiar to us by reason of its inclusion among Mann's shorter writings in *Stories of Three Decades*. He spent his last years expanding the tale

into a sizable affair. Even now, we have only the first installment of a narrative which could have continued more or less
indefinitely, provided that the author had lived to continue
it. But it doesn't matter that *Felix Krull* is still formally incomplete, that the hero, impersonating the Marquis de Ve-
nosta, has yet to embark on his projected world travels.
Mann's is the kind of picaresque story that tends to complete itself as it proceeds.

True to its type, *Felix Krull* is the story of a rogue's progress. From small beginnings as the offspring of a ruined
Rhineland family, the hero goes on to cut a figure in the
great world of Paris and beyond. His career is a succession of
amiable ruses, thefts and seductions. Above all, it is a series
of impersonations, for Krull is disgusted with his own identity and constantly seeks to exchange it for others. He even
enacts a sick man—and does it so enthusiastically that his
draft board is fooled into rejecting him for the German
Army. Finding work in a fashionable Paris hotel, he is by
turns the perfect elevator boy, the perfect waiter, the perfect
thief, the perfect lover. A gushing poetess whom he has
robbed of some of her jewels finds him so remarkable a bed-
mate that, on learning of the theft, she gives him the rest of
her jewels. A Scottish lord, smitten in his way by Krull, seeks
to adopt him and make him his heir. But Krull disengages
himself from the insistent poetess and refuses the enamored
lord. He seems to be saving himself for something—for the
perfect adventure, it appears. And presently something of
this kind offers itself. A young Luxembourgian nobleman
whose parents wish him to make a world tour has his reasons
for preferring to remain in Paris. He bestows his name, rank,
and ample letter of credit on the willing Krull, who then sets
off for South America.

Mann's hero is the pretext for some admirable episodes, but he is not very interesting in himself. He seems just a little dated. His intellectual paraphernalia of masks and roles, the ironic glitter of his accomplished naughtiness, declare him to be a contemporary of Shaw's Don Juan, Gide's Lafcadio and other heroes of that Nietzsche-haunted age. It was a notable age, but to return to it by way of Mann's belated fantasy is to feel that it is distinctly distant and that the book itself is a period-piece. While reading it, one consents to play the Zarathustran as one might consent, at a costume party, to dance the tango in a ballroom conscientiously furnished with specimens of Art Nouveau. One knows all the time that it doesn't mean a thing.

The author himself seems to have felt this upon taking up *Felix Krull* again in his old age. Young or old, he was always intelligent, always resourceful; and it is a part of the book's endless game of impostures that the aged Mann is willfully impersonating the younger Mann. Thus Krull's later adventures are more broadly farcical than his earlier ones, and the atmosphere of psychological motivation and meaning has thinned. At the same time, the spirit of *pastiche* has grown franker. Krull is now reminiscent by turns of Rousseau, Casanova, Mr. Yorick, Rameau's Nephew and several other classic scamps of autobiography and fiction. Mann has even seen to it that he writes his confessions in a sober, sententious prose which recalls that of Goethe's *Wilhelm Meister*. Come to think of it, Krull and his adventures are not so much dated as simply historical. They form a sort of animated Mme. Tussaud's, although the exhibit is clearly contrived by a waxworker of genius.

In his authoritative little book on Mann, Henry Hatfield observes that the original Felix Krull belonged in Mann's gallery of portraits of the artist. Krull, says Mr. Hatfield, is "the artist as mountebank." For the later Mann, however, this hero seems to have been largely a pretext for abandoning himself to the pleasures of sheer invention. And barring the scenes of passion—here, as in *The Holy Sinner,* the frisky sensuality of the aged Mann is awful—his contrivances are brilliant. When Krull, posing as the Marquis, writes a long dutiful letter to the real Marquis's mother, and receives from her a lengthy reply, full of a serene and pedantic nobility, the writing is equal to Mann's in his heyday.

And for old devotees of his work there is a fascination in the way he returns in *Felix Krull* to his well-known themes and preoccupations. The familiar young man, from Lübeck or Hamburg or the land of Canaan, who takes leave of his family, breaks with his confining native circumstances and fares forth into the big alien world, is reincarnated in Felix Krull, though with less than the usual solemnity. And with the reappearance in full dress of Mann's old theme there is a resurgence of his old special skills and knowledges. One last time he rejoices in what he knows of the ways of hotels and restaurants, the rituals of travel, the feel of foreign places, the forms of class behavior and racial manners, the whole comedy of cosmopolitanism. By consenting merely to simulate creation, he accomplishes in *Felix Krull* something like the real article. "How inventive life is!" declares the hero. How inventive, to the last, was Thomas Mann.

1955

The
Imagination
of Duchesses

The novelist who writes familiarly of dukes and duchesses
has a special burden of proof to discharge. He must persuade
us that he really knows his privileged characters, that they
are worth knowing, and that they are at once like and unlike
ourselves. What he requires, in short, is a knowledge of them
in their common human nature as well as in the remarkable
forms that human nature may assume when it is combined
with uncommon privilege. Proust excelled at this complex insight; his portraits of the *beau monde* are vivid with it; he
was a master of the double exposure. In no other novelist are
there more amazing exhibitions of privileged human nature.

A la Recherche du temps perdu is something besides a
novel of social history. It is a portrait of the artist, a story of
how he achieves his vocation, an account of the processes by
which his imagination is delivered from its bondage to time
and passion. The other characters, however compelling in
themselves, are all securely drawn into the orbit of this central preoccupation. They may or may not be artists but they
have distinct creative endowments, and it is on their use or
misuse of these endowments that their several stories turn.
To be human for Proust is above all to have imagination.

I use the word in the sense that he appears to have had in

Originally a paper read before the English Institute.

mind when, writing to a friend, he described snobbishness as "a wonderful kind of imagination." In *A la Recherche du temps perdu* not only snobbishness but jealousy and other passions are seen as wonderful kinds of imagination. Imagination is as necessary to Proust's characters as generators are to automobiles. The generator converts mechanical into electrical energy, making the horn sound and the headlights shine. Imagination registers our desires and translates them into surprising forms of thought, speech and action. In this respect the men and women of *A la Recherche du temps perdu* are highly specialized. Whether they are duchesses, doctors, or procurers, the energy of desire is magnificently marked in them and so is the energy of mental invention.

In actual life, they would probably pass for geniuses. They *are* geniuses of a sort, even though most of them squander their endowment in a world of delusion. The power of invention is obvious and terrible in the major figures; it is also striking in cases where it is quite unexpected or is thoroughly malapropos—in short, where the effect of it tends to be comic. Such is the case of the very literal-minded Dr. Cottard with his outrageous puns; of Odette de Crécy with her small anxious lies and her brave show of Anglomania; of the elevator boy's sister who expresses her contempt for the poor by defecating on them in some unspecified manner; of the man who says he owns a painting by Rubens and then, when asked if it is signed, insists he cut off the signature to make the picture fit a frame that was already in his possession!

Montaigne observed that when the mind is insufficiently occupied "it brings forth many chimeras and fantastic monsters." Montaigne was referring to the intellectual dangers of being alone and idle; Proust finds such dangers in the busiest social life. The drawing room breeds its own chimeras. The abuse of imagination, the making it project selfish desire rather than seek out truth, is for Proust a very condition of social intercourse when pursued for its own sake. His worldly characters tend not only to think up monsters but, in doing so, to become monsters.

If, therefore, we compare Proust's idea of society with that of the great nineteenth century French novelists we see that a shift has occurred in the relations of the one and the many. Persons of marked imaginative powers were the exceptions in Balzac, Stendhal, and Flaubert. They were, or supposed themselves to be, the chosen few; and it was just the singularity of their minds and aims that made their adventures worth recording. Lucien de Rubempré, Julien Sorel, Emma Bovary—each may covet money or power or sexual adventure as other people covet those things; but in doing so each is essentially intent on realizing some idea he has of himself. We know, moreover, that it is usually from their reading, in romances or heroic memoirs, that they have learned the roles they propose to play. Each has in some fashion studied his part before embarking on his adventures; their indebtedness to literature makes clear how exceptional their aspirations are. And what are their adventures but a succession of collisions between their adopted roles and the hard surfaces of the social generality? Such is the impact for Julien Sorel that he can only maintain his idea of himself by finally courting imprisonment and death, while Emma Bovary sees her dreams succumb gradually to the prevailing materialism— sees them turn, as it were, into commodities: sheer sex, mere furniture, poplin by the yard.

The exceptional souls have taken over society in Proust's conception of it. Money-making, career-making, matchmaking and the other practical enterprises that provided the older novel with its characteristic intrigues are in the background of *A la Recherche du temps perdu*. The old struggle for tangible ends has given place to an all but universal struggle for prestige, and even this value seems precariously subjective, the stuff of ignorant supposition and willful desire. What almost everyone in Proust is intent upon is the projection of the self; this is now the enterprise of the many rather than of the distinguished few. There is, to be sure, the estimable Dr. Cottard who frequents the drawing room to further his career as a society physician ("plus de diagnostique Potain"); but it is Cottard's performance in the drawing room that matters. He too is "in society"—is there to shine as he believes a society doctor should shine. His literal mind flowers in its own fashion. He shines by his brusque, probing habits of speech and the painful surgery of his terrible puns. The various servants are in society too by reason of their occupations; Françoise, the chief of them, has her vivid ideas of herself; and we recall how brilliantly the haughty *"marquise"* of the W.C. in the Champs Elysées exemplifies the general condition.

The seekers of self are many and various in the novel, and so are their ways of representing themselves to the world. Each has a distinct quality of taste, a certain style of life, which he believes to be essential to the winning of prestige. Mme. Verdurin has her muscular music-lover's style, the foreign minister Norpois his musty diplomatic clichés and woolly Machiavellianism, Albertine her touching athlete's idiom, the young Marquise de Cambremer her determined patter of the person with advanced views on the arts. And though they all think of themselves as very special, even unique, they hasten to make common cause with others of similar style. They band together in protective and aggressive coteries based on the community of ideas. I refer, of course, to those characters who are definitely *dans le monde;* there are others—the painter Elstir, the narrator's grandmother—who cultivate their distinctive idioms and ideas of themselves in a wholly different spiritual climate.

Oriane, duchesse de Guermantes, is not only *in* the world, she *is* the world—in her own and certain other people's eyes. Her powers of imagination are limited but they are acute, and she is one of Proust's exemplary characterizations. In a medium where all is flux, she has the distinction of being relatively stable. Despite some vital changes in her nature and position, Mme. de Guermantes goes on and on.

On one occasion she is entertaining her dinner guests at the expense of an absent woman acquaintance when M. de Guermantes interrupts her. "Gad, Oriane," he explodes, "after all she's a duchess." Mme. de Guermantes feels the rebuke and falls silent. Several times in the course of the narrative the Duke thus calls her to order and she falls silent. Considering her usual effrontery, these are significant and somehow poignant moments. Her wit, so dear to her vanity and usually to her husband's, must give way to considerations of rank; and without her wit she is speechless, though never for long. Between her nature and her position there is a contradiction. She rejoices in a critical sensibility which exercises itself on all occasions and all comers. It is her pleasure to administer small shocks to the moral complacency of princesses, to take Tolstoy's side against visiting Russian grand dukes. Yet she is a member of a circle which constitutes her medium just as water is the medium of fish. Though chafing sometimes at its restrictions, she is unthinkable without it. She may imagine herself to be a free spirit but she is entirely a creature of contingencies. And when she surrenders to her husband it is not because she loves him—there is no affection between them—but because he is the living embodiment of the principle of necessity in her life. Faithless, brutal, stupid, he nevertheless represents the facts of money and rank without which she cannot operate.

To describe the Duke's incarnation of these things, Proust resorts to a comic exaggeration of his own grand manner, including the usual reference to the work of art. "Next to her, heavily seated, was M. de Guermantes, superb and Olympian. The sense of his vast riches seemed to be omnipresent in all his members and gave him a peculiar high density, as though he had been melted in a crucible into a human ingot to form this man who was worth so much. . . . I seemed to see that statue of Olympian Zeus which Phidias, they say, made all of gold."

Living with such a work of art is naturally uncomfortable for the Duchess but she cannot live without it. For she is like all the Guermantes family, and in a sense like all Proust's characters, in that she is possessed of a quality beyond her immediate social needs. There is a purposiveness about her which is in excess of the practical requirements of her position. Her great name, unlimited funds, considerable beauty, and unsullied reputation are enough in themselves to sustain her supreme position in the Faubourg Saint-Germain. Yet her special quality of imagination, her idea of herself, demands that she play a role enacted by no one else.

The Courvoisiers, a family of lay figures which Proust introduces for purposes of comparison with the Guermantes, are content with the actualities of their equally fine position. They are resigned to being what their status calls for, even if it means being rather dull. Oriane de Guermantes must be a wit to boot, must be in fact unique.

In this demand she resembles other members of the Guermantes family, all of whom are shown to share a peculiar type of *esprit*. One of them reads Nietzsche and aspires to be an intellectual. Another has had Bohemian adventures and is engaged in writing her memoirs. The greatest of them, the Baron de Charlus, is driven to elaborate perversities, cruelties, impostures. Primarily he has, along with his genuine endowments, an extravagant sense of his own privileged position. His gifts of mind entitle him, provided he translate them into a vocation, to legitimate privileges as a creative intelligence. With his knowledge of society, his eloquence, his original moral stamina, he might be, say, the Tacitus of his generation. But he fails to realize his artistic gifts; he confuses them with the virtues which supposedly inhere in his social position. In proportion as he fails to get the right kind of recognition, he demands more and more of the wrong kind. His defeatism in wartime, which Proust describes in penetrating detail in the last volume, represents the ultimate effort of his imagination in its political character. Starved for *his* kind of prestige, Charlus can finally envision the destruction of the nation that denies it to him. And meanwhile his homoerotic fantasies have turned frankly self-destructive. Instead of being a Tacitus, he has come to resemble one of Tacitus' malevolent emperors. He is a Nero of the imagination.

The Duchess' smaller range causes her to have a fate less drastic than her brother-in-law's. As time goes on, she merely sharpens and dwindles. Her wit, thoroughly charming at a time when it was stimulated by that of her friend Swann, grows coarser, crueler, more animalistic, more showy. We never see her from the inside; she has no private life save by implication. Still, we know her to be suffering more and more from her husband's brutality and from the fatigue of going round and round in her vicious circle. Her own pain leads her to give pain to others: to torment her servants, to forget her dying friends, to hasten their oblivion once they are dead, to dismiss from her mind the thought of death itself. She needs constantly to demonstrate her supposed freedom of spirit by exercising it in novel ways and so begins to consort with the Bohemian circles she had formerly despised. At last, when it is too late, she finds herself virtually outside that Faubourg Saint-Germain which was her natural province and only true arena. If the fish formerly scorned the water, the water now shuns the fish.

Yet Mme. de Guermantes retains always something of her original grace and gaiety and genius for fashion. She continues to exhibit some of the refinement that is the inalienable privilege of the Guermantes. And so do the other characters retain something of their original energy. *A la Recherche du temps perdu* is about men and art, and for Proust the world of art is continuous with that of other men. Social intercourse *for its own sake* is vanity, but people in society are distinguished by energy, eloquence, connoisseurship and a high evaluation of themselves. These qualities form a link between them and the mind of the artist. One of the paintings by Elstir, Proust's imaginary great Impressionist, shows the land and the sea partaking of the same substance and composing a reality superior to both. A similar interpenetration of values—social, moral, aesthetic—characterizes Proust's general sense of life. Everywhere in the novel, amid all the misery and corruption, there are occasions for beauty, intimations of immortality: Mme. de Guermantes's red shoes, the carnations that Odette's horses wear on their blinkers while her coachman wears a matching one in his lapel, the basket of fruit that Swann assembles lovingly from the various shops specializing in the several kinds of fruit—the peach here, the pear there, the grapes someplace else. Lionel Trilling has remarked that a reader of nineteenth century French novels, with their relentless social criticism, might be tempted to conclude that "society is a fraud." It would be a singularly unwary reader who would conclude as much from Proust's novel.

1955

The Coming
of Nabokov

I. A *Preface to* Lolita

In *Lolita* Vladimir Nabokov has made a notable tale out of notably forbidding matter and breathed fresh virulence into the great tradition, recently languishing, of the *roman noir*. The author of several novels, a first-rate memoir of his Russian childhood and exilic youth, a cranky study of Gogol, and some learned monographs on the subject of *Lepidoptera*, Mr. Nabokov is an experienced and no doubt widely read man of letters. But none of his previous ventures has quite prepared us for the impact of *Lolita*. The impact of *Lolita* on American publishers—the several who saw it in manuscript—was such that the book was finally brought out by a small press in Paris. American publishers are not greatly to blame. There is a real challenge in *Lolita*, and to say there is not would do the book itself an injustice. A largely sympathetic critic writing in *Partisan Review* (Mr. John Hollander) declares that *Lolita* "flames with a tremendous perversity of an unexpected kind." It does, and the flame would definitely singe a sleeve; and for just this reason *Lolita* is not for the mere fancier of erotica or consumer of pornography, if there are such people and if they matter. *Lolita* applies its heat to the entire sensibility, including the sense of humor. Instead of putting the desires in an agreeable simmer, it acts on them almost like a cautery, sterilizing them with horrid laughter. Between the horror and the hilarity of it, *Lolita* is a fascinating but very special sort of experience. It is a tale for the adult public; and should it sometime be published in the United States, it could be trusted, I think, to make its mark with that public as an original work of literature.

Meanwhile Mr. Nabokov's terrible infant circulates over here in its Paris format, gets itself reviewed in advanced periodicals and acquires a small celebrity. But this celebrity, if it is of the kind I think it is, could do the book a subtler injury than censorship can do, insisting as it mostly does that *Lolita* is no more than a very brilliant joke or literary burlesque. Mr. Hollander gives good reason for being of this opinion. He suggests that the book has, besides its tremendous perversity, a wealth of uproarious parody but "no clinical, sociological or mythic seriousness."

Lolita is very funny, very full of burlesque intentions, but the supreme laugh may be on the reviewers for failing to see how much of everyone's reality lurks in its fantastic shadow play. Surely the ways listed by Mr. Hollander—clinical, sociological, mythic—are not the only ways of making perversity pay off in literature; there are simpler ways of being serious. Mr. Nabokov has devoted much art to making *Lolita* yield reactions which I can only describe as "human." True, his hero is a thorough creep and no pitiable sick man or aspiring sick soul. He is contrived in such a way that he resists the charity of the clinic and refuses to be vaporized into allegory. Entangled in some of the most intricately sordid situations ever presented by a novelist, his hero tends to be in fact what some of Joyce's characters become in their guilty fantasies: a "sex fiend" pursued by angry bodies of righteous citizens. Incongruously, however, his situations are always assuming familiar forms, his horrid scrapes become our scrapes. The book's general effect is profoundly mischievous, like that of some diabolical distorting mirror in some particularly obscene amusement park. The images of life that *Lolita* gives back are ghastly but recognizable. If Mr. Nabokov's methods are the usual methods of comedy, they are here carried to new extremes.

Lolita purports to be the confession of a man who is in confinement awaiting trial for murder. But Humbert Humbert, as the hero-narrator calls himself, has something besides murder on his mind. He is attracted solely to "nymphets," girls of about twelve to fifteen years; and this anomaly of his nature, which has ended by ruining him, has also come close to destroying Lolita, his stepdaughter who at the age of twelve became his lover. Humbert begins by trying to account for his obsession. He refers us back to his childhood in Europe (he is a Swiss citizen but "a salad of racial genes") and to the small girl with whom he had an affair that was constantly disrupted by adult intruders and finally terminated forever by the girl's early death. Humbert is—or half thinks he is—a victim of interrupted coitus, and he continues to pursue the dead girl's image among the indifferent nymphets of the world. A regular marriage to a "life-sized woman" in Paris ends ridiculously, and Humbert makes his way to America. The time is the late 1940s.

Here, in a small New England town, he falls in with a Mrs. Haze, whom he detests, and her twelve-year-old daughter Lolita, whom he would like to possess. He doesn't think of taking full possession of her, though Lolita is rather flirtatious with him. He has slyer and less perilous gratifications which result from her clowning intimacies with him. He marries Charlotte Haze, the mother, in order to be in a position to continue these intimacies with the daughter. But

Charlotte is hostile to her daughter and resents her presence and keeps planning to send her off to camp or school, or to transport herself and her husband to Europe. She wants to be alone with her "deep-voiced D.P." Humbert, who had not of course counted on these developments, would like to murder Charlotte. But he finds it more in keeping with his character to let events take care of themselves, which they quickly do. He has been careless about leaving his diary around; and Charlotte, exercising her wifely right to poke among his papers, finds and reads the diary and learns the truth. Lolita is Humbert's real love and Charlotte herself is only an "old cat." "You're a monster," she cries to him, with considerable justice. "You're a detestable, abominable, criminal fraud. If you come near—I'll scream out the window." But instead she rushes from the house, is hit by a passing car, and killed.

Humbert is now in possession of the Haze house, the Haze car, and—almost—the Haze girl. His neighbors kindly condole with him, married so recently, a stranger in a strange land, and with a wild stepdaughter on his hands. The son of the man whose car hit Charlotte arrives with a carefully executed diagram of the accident and a document waiving his father's responsibility for the death. Humbert obligingly signs the waiver and accepts the man's offer to pay the funeral expenses. He now proceeds to the seduction of Lolita, but again without the intention of *fully* seducing her. Taking her to a suburban hotel, where they register as father and daughter, he administers what he believes to be potent sleeping pills to Lolita in the hope of rendering her insensible to his furtive explorations. But the pills are placebos: Humbert's conscientious doctor has feared that he meant to attempt suicide in his grief; and in the end it is Lolita who completes the seduction of herself. It turns out that she has already been corrupted in her small girl way by a small boy at a summer camp.

She is Humbert's willing mistress this first night but soon reverts to her childish state and rebels when the intimacy threatens to become permanent. She has lost a bossy unloving mother only to acquire a too doting and despotic father. Humbert, insane with passion, makes a virtual prisoner of Lolita, bribing her with clothes and money and sundaes, and reminding her that if she should give him away to the authorites he would promptly be arrested and she would be detained for observation as a juvenile delinquent. They embark on a nightmarish journey by car across the United States. It is a wild flight from legality and reality. It is also a horribly inverted variant of a father and daughter tour, with stops at the best hostelries and visits to the historic sites and famous beauty spots.

There is a period during which Humbert seeks to keep Lolita by normalizing, as it were, their relationship. He installs her in a progressive school and settles himself nearby but is soon told by the unsuspecting school authorities that Lolita is emotionally in a bad way, needs more "home duties," and would profit by his relaxing his stern attitudes of an old-fashioned European father. Maybe, in fact, she should be analyzed. He takes alarm, and soon the strange pair are off again on their travels. This time, however, it soon appears that they are being pursued by a rival of Humbert's in a red convertible. The identity of his rival is unknown to Humbert but we presently learn that he is another middle-aged man, even more disreputable than Humbert, whom Lolita has met at the school and fallen in love with. The "transference" of the small girl's affections from her "father" to another and similar man has occurred. All very normal and on schedule.

The other man catches up with them at last and spirits Lolita away in an elaborate simulacrum of an elopement. Humbert the pursued becomes Humbert the pursuer and follows the pair from town to town, led on by a series of gloriously cryptic clues dropped by his comedian of a rival. This rival has the advantage over Humbert that he is a playwright of sorts, instead of being the mere fumbling impersonator that poor Humbert is. And Humbert, unable to decipher the clues and find the treasure, must finally give up the hunt. Several years pass, and then, in an amazing scene, he does find Lolita. Now seventeen, she is married to a kindly ex-GI who is hard of hearing. They are very poor and Lolita is pregnant—a conscientious wife, though still secretly in love with the playwright, who abandoned her. Once again Humbert bribes her, this time to learn the name of his original rival. Learning it, he sets out to perform the one fully meditated and willed act of his life. He kills the terrible man in a farcically protracted scene of violence in which the victim, though full of bullet holes, keeps bouncing back to life. How hard it is to destroy a man, how hard to eliminate so well-matched a rival!

Such a summary of the action naturally excludes most of the values that give subtlety to *Lolita* in the reading of it. These values mainly inhere in what Mr. Nabokov makes of Humbert Humbert. In the falsest of false positions, Humbert has enough decency to feel his position as what it is. He impersonates the hero of a novel, even though he isn't a hero by nature; and by some curious law he is more interesting as his actions become more outrageous. The prologue, recounting his early life, rings with a Frenchy sort of jocularity and is the least convincing part of *Lolita,* just as it is the most innocent part. The jocular tone of the prologue probably arises

from its being in some measure a burlesque of those Freudian flashbacks resorted to by many novelists in order to
make clear how the hero "got that way." However Humbert
got that way, we are made to see that he has become something which, in its grimness, quite defies explanation. It defies statistics, too, although his psychiatrist has informed him
that "at least 12% of American adult males—a 'conservative'
estimate according to Dr. Blanche Schwarzmann (verbal
communication)—enjoy yearly, in one way or another, the
special experience 'H.H.' describes with such despair." He is
the impossible sort of person whom Freud can't help, or Kin-
sey either: cocky, humorous, perceptive, fastidious, and almost too well read, too articulate ("You can always count on
a murderer for a fancy prose style"). His qualities are pretty
much at the command of his obsession, but he naturally
seeks to avoid the implications of his servitude and, like any
Vautrin or Raskolnikov, he plays his roles, assumes his
masks. Yet these impostures are not so much chosen by him
as thrust upon him by the conditions of his life; and brutally,
one after another, they are snatched away, exposing an awk-
ward grin. His very name lends itself to indiscriminate gar-
bling and tends to resolve itself into Humburg. He marries the
full-sized woman in Paris under the consoling impression
that he is irresistible to her (he thinks all adult women are
mad about him, and some are). But off she goes with a poor
specimen of a White Russian taxi driver and Humbert is left
with another interrupted relationship on his record, another
shattered mask at his feet.

With his entry upon the American scene his impersonations become more profound and his story takes on true stature. Indeed *Lolita* at this point begins to impersonate an
"international novel" (of the journalistic Graham Greene or

Koestler type rather than the Henry James type). The deep unreality within Humbert is complemented by another kind of unreality in the place of his destiny. He becomes subject to the preposterous chances and changes of a wide-open society, a culture madly on the move. His fate hangs on the godlike motions of the motorcar and the wayward oracle of the telephone. There is an ambiguous promise in the friendliness of small towns, the lush convenience of omnipresent hotels and motels, the defiant come-on of little girls in blue jeans, the suggestive innocence of the instruction they receive at school and the literature they read. " 'Mr. Uterus (I quote from a girls' magazine) starts to build a thick soft wall on the chance a possible baby may have to be bedded down there.' "

"It's a free country!" Lolita cries when her mother tries to send her to bed. Humbert is an ironic portrait of the visiting European, and the Hazes help to complete the likeness. He is to them the prince of a lost realm—actually a luxury hotel kept by his father on the Riviera. He seems to have the superior sexual acumen and appeal so often assumed by Europeans and envied by Americans—but his sexuality is as peculiar as we know. Mrs. Haze's husband, a hazy figure at best, has long been dead, and she and her daughter have made their pointless way from the Middle West to this New England town where Humbert arrives to be their boarder, ostensibly with the idea of writing a book in a peaceful retreat. The Haze women and their appurtenances are familiar enough; they have been portrayed in many satirical novels and problem plays of modern manners. There is the arty, career-bent, unloving mother; the defiant unloved daughter with her eternal blue jeans, her deplorable manners and secrets, her loud cries of "You dope!" and "I think you stink!";

and there is the litter of lamps, sofas, coffee tables, magazines, Van Gogh prints, and pink toilet-seat tidies amid which they irritably and insubstantially live. But the observations and machinations of Humbert, the sinister outsider, project a fierce glare on this trite house and its trite occupants, re-creating them and investing them with a sour pathos. "The poor lady [Charlotte Haze] was in her middle thirties, she had a shiny forehead, plucked eyebrows, and quite simple but not unattractive features of a type that may be defined as a weak solution of Marlene Dietrich . . . Her smile was but a quizzical jerk of one eyebrow; and uncoiling herself from the sofa as she talked, she kept making spasmodic dashes at three ash trays and the near fender (where lay the brown core of an apple); whereupon she would sink back again, one leg folded under her."

Charlotte Haze will soon uncoil herself for a more urgent reason and then dash impulsively into eternity. She is an ominous figure, a resonant type. With her "principles" which bulk large but weigh little, her vacuous animation, her habit of asserting herself although she has next to nothing in her to assert, Charlotte is the immoral moralist, the loveless romantic, the laughless comic—whatever it is that spoils the party and dampens the honeymoon all across America. Once married to Humbert she naturally imagines herself to be deeply attractive to him. She looms alluringly in slacks or bathing suit, coils and uncoils herself with more nervous abandon than ever, buys the pair of them a brand-new bed, cooks up fetching little messes for dinner, and in a frenzy of misplaced homemaking decides to redecorate the entire house. But her taste in these matters, which she owes to her culture, is no more attractive to Humbert than her robust femininity, for which nature is to blame. Her diluted Dietrich charms are lost on him, preoccupied as he is by the skinny charms of Lolita; but so would Dietrich at full strength be lost on him. Thus Charlotte is made to act out a timeless travesty of Woman, and of Sex itself with the rigid specializations and fetishisms that attend it in its capitalized form, or whenever it is an end in itself. Noting Humbert's gravitation towards Lolita and away from Charlotte, we can only wonder at the small affective range of *anyone's* desires. Why the one female rather than the other? Can a few years more or less, an inch or two of flesh at thigh or bosom, make *that* much difference? Then, as we learn, there is Humbert's rich distaste for fully developed co-eds—those much publicized love objects—and his horror at realizing that Lolita herself will soon be just another woman. ("I see, maybe, the coffin of coarse female flesh in which my nymphets are buried alive.") One man's meat is another man's mummy. Humbert is heir to the merry old European tradition of libertinage but he has forgotten the point of it. Rather, he has reduced it to absurdity and is himself reduced to all kinds of anxious fantasies and substitutive pleasures. Where the Marquis de Sade, that other specialized libertine, fed poisoned bonbons to his victims in the hope of seeing them writhe, Humbert avails himself of sleeping pills which only leave *his* victim thoroughly awake.

The scene at the Enchanted Hunters, the suburban hotel where Humbert and Lolita finally seduce one another, is one long spasm of comic horror—though now with a different drift from the Charlotte scenes—and Nabokov spares us nothing of Humbert's soft misery and dubious triumph. The famous scene in Proust in which Charlus pays to have himself flogged by personable young men who are only turning an honest penny in the interim of caring for their families and fighting for *la Patrie*—that scene appears heroically comic, almost like some adventure of Falstaff or Don Quixote, compared to the mean ironies that beat upon Humbert Humbert through the long night, while a religious convention is in progress in the hotel, and the corridors creak and the toilets groan familiarly, and Lolita refuses to give up her restless spirit to sleep.

Their historic night at the Enchanted Hunters is an initiation into the impostures and discomfitures of the motel-hopping life that awaits them. " 'The name,' I said coldly [to the room clerk], 'is not Humberg, and not Humbug, but Herbert, I mean Humbert, and any room will do, just put in a cot for my little daughter. She is ten and very tired.' " Humbert's guilty fears constantly stalk him. An inspector at the state line peers suspiciously into the car and says, "Any honey?" Tires go flat with an accusing plap-plap beneath them. All hostelries seem hostile, whether they are merely called the Kumfy Kabins or are elaborate affairs with notices on the wall that read:

We wish you to feel at home while here. All equipment was carefully checked upon your arrival. Your license number is on record here. Use hot water sparingly. We reserve the right to eject without notice any objectionable person. Do not throw waste material of ANY kind in the toilet bowl. Thank you. Call again. The Management. P.S. We consider our guests the Finest People in the World.

In the course of this insane journey, Humbert undergoes a reversal of roles and in so doing registers more and more sharply the real horror and the real significance of his partnership with Lolita. He first impersonated her father in order to elude the authorities, but in time he comes to feel more and more like her actual father. Towards the end he begins to reflect on the whole affair in the spirit of a parent who has disappointed his child and been disappointed by her in turn. "I often noticed that, living as we did, she and I, in a world of total evil, we would become strangely embarrassed whenever I tried to discuss anything she and an older friend, she and a parent, she and a real healthy sweetheart . . . might have discussed . . . She would mail her invulnerability in trite brashness and boredom, whereas I, using for my desperately detached comments an artificial tone of voice that set my own last teeth on edge, provoked my audience to such outbursts of rudeness as made any further conversation impossible, oh, my poor, bruised child."

Humbert's remorse is more effective for not clothing itself in abstractly moral terms. He feels, not that he has betrayed a "trust" of the kind that traditionally inheres in parenthood, but that he has horribly let Lolita down as lover, friend, and fellow human being, as well as in his capacity as father. The consequence has been a complete sundering of human relations with her. Lolita herself, we learn at their last meeting, has not been destroyed; indeed, she has exhibited the strange capacity of the young to survive the worst abuses (other things being equal). Nor is any forgiveness of him on her part in question at this final meeting. Her career with him, so painfully vivid in his own memory, has for her fallen into place in a world of experience which she views as "just one gag after another." If she originally called him Dad in bitter irony, she now calls him Dad in sad earnest. But she doesn't mean anything by it, any real affection, and it's too late anyway. His betrayal, not of a trust but of her, has done its work. For of course he did betray her unspeakably. It did not constitute any justification of Humbert that she was his willing mistress at first and already knew the ropes. On the contrary this only deepened and complicated his guilt. Outright rape would conceivably have counted for less than this queasy collusion, especially considering the orphaned state of Lolita, to whom he was after all her only excuse for a parent.

In all this, the distorting mirrors have been continuously at work, giving back a monstrous picture of what is again, like the grim sexual comedy of the Charlotte episode, a desperately common experience. The perverse partnership of Humbert and Lolita reflects some of the painful comedy of family relations in general. There is, on Lolita's side, the recurrent childhood feeling of being misunderstood, abused, betrayed by one's parents until at last—if one is lucky enough to grow up to that stage—one can accept them as part of the gag that life is, or even love them if one is luckier than Lolita. From Humbert's point of view, which is the predominating one, the situation is even more complicated, in fact, quite hopeless. He is the parent who sadly suspects that communication has broken down between himself and his child. Instead of conversation there is only a weary compulsive banter. Mutual trust is replaced by a shameful system of bargains and bribes: the "normal" man's form of collusion with his child. Desiring an affectionate and willing compliance with his wishes, he is fortunate if he can purchase a temporary docility with gifts of money, clothes, or chocolate sundaes. In his own eyes he becomes a mere purveyor of such material favors, and day after day he pays the too large bills at the endless motels of life. All the time, his suffering over the failure of love in his child is enhanced by his suspicion that it is all his fault. While trying to count up the blessings he has bestowed on her he remembers, as he fears that *she* remembers, only his acts of cruelty or indifference. He attempts now and then to repair the damage, restore communications. But he is quickly rebuffed in some unexpected way which confirms his original fears. " 'A penny for your thoughts,' I said, and she stretched out her palm at once." Those inaccessible thoughts, that outstretched palm! Such are the cares of a family man.

Considering the weird shapes of sexuality that *Lolita* assumes, the novel might appear to invite Freudian interpretations of the usual kind. Fathers want to sleep with their daughters, daughters with their fathers. The reverse of any such intention is the burden of *Lolita*. By parading the theme of incest, with drums and banners, Mr. Nabokov makes it ridicule itself out of existence so far as *Lolita* is concerned; and the same holds for the other evidences of popular Freudianism with which the tale is strewn. *Lolita*, far from being mythic, is anti-mythic in this respect. Mr. Nabokov cultivates the groans and guffaws of the recalcitrant fact, the embarrassment that yields to neither myth nor clinic, the bitter commonplaces of life's indestructible surface.

To say this, however, is to take *Lolita* at its best. The novel has its less than superlative moments, when the ribald fantastication gives way to a thin facetiousness or a pastiche of Joyce. In confessional novels of the intensity of *Lolita*, moreover, there is frequently a disquieting note of unresolved tension. It is present even in the great narratives of this character by Constant and Proust. The hero of such self-scrutinizing novels is both the culprit and the judge, an unlikely situation, and he must strain and strain to persuade us that he is at once bad enough to sin and good enough to repent. Humbert's "world of total evil" seems out of character, or at least in conflict with his idiom. It is the author intervening on Humbert's behalf and playing the role straight in order to make a vital point. So, too, with Humbert's belated love cries for his Lolita, which seem to be dictated by some principle of compensation and ring a little false (to me). "I was a pentapod monster, but I loved you. I was despicable and brutal and turpid, and everything, *mais je t'aimais, je t'aimais!*" *Lolita* is partly a masterpiece of grotesque comedy, partly an unsubdued wilderness where the wolf howls—a real wolf howling for a real Red Riding Hood.

1957

These remarks appeared in *The Anchor Review 2*, together with some excerpts from *Lolita*, which had not then been published in any form in America and did not seem likely ever to attain full publication here.

II. Nabokov: The Prose and Poetry of It All

Readers of *Lolita* may recall that Humbert Humbert, who delivers himself of the contents of the book while in confinement awaiting trial for murder, is something of a poet. "You can always count on a murderer for a fancy prose style," he says, and you can count on this particular murderer for scattered flights of verse as well. His are "occasional poems" in the most invidious sense possible. Humbert's muse materializes only intermittently, and when she does it is in response to situations of a kind that do not, as a rule, give rise to *la poésie pure*—or whatever we may call the opposite of occasional poetry.

Hoping, for example, to calm his restless Lolita he improvises a bit of what he tells her is "nonsense verse."

> The Squirl and his Squirrel, the Rabs and their Rabbits
> Have certain obscure and peculiar habits.
> Male humming birds make the most exquisite rockets.
> The snake when he walks holds his hands in his pockets.

"Nonsense is correct," Lolita says mockingly, perhaps guessing that Humbert's weakness for nymphets like herself lends the poem a certain "obscure and peculiar" sense which she would prefer to ignore. As a poet, Humbert succeeds no better with Rita, a temporary replacement for Lolita, and one who knows her time is short. He tries to stop her accusing sobs by extemporizing some verses about a certain "blue hotel" they have just motored past. "Why blue when it is white, why blue for heaven's sake?" she protests and starts crying again. Humbert's lengthiest effort is a ballad, full of literary allusions, *double-entendres,* and straight French, which he writes to console himself for the loss of Lolita. One stanza reads:

> Happy, happy is gnarled McFate
> Touring the States with a child wife,
> Plowing his Molly in every State
> Among the protected wild life.

Humbert, like other of Nabokov's creatures, foreign or nutty or both, has a peculiar flair for knowing what is going on in the American literary world. He knows, for example, that "light verse" has been made respectable by Mr. W. H. Auden, whose own fine efforts in that form have rarely excelled Humbert's McFate ballad. He knows, too, that poetry of *any* weight lends itself nicely to depth analysis. His own analyst, Humbert says of his ballad: "It is really a maniac's masterpiece. The stark, stiff, lurid rhymes correspond very exactly to certain perspectiveless and terrible landscapes and figures . . . as drawn by psychopaths in tests devised by astute trainers." He is aware, too, of that specialty of American poetics, the belief that poetry inheres in phenomena themselves rather than in the poet and that to compose a poem one need only catalogue phenomena in sufficiently impressive numbers. So he pounces upon a mimeographed list of the names of Lolita's classmates, surnames and first names intriguingly reversed for the purpose of alphabetization (e.g., FANTAZIA, STELLA; FLASHMAN, IRVING; HAZE, DOLORES). "A poem, a poem, forsooth!" he exclaims, and goes on to imagine the occupants of the classroom: "Adorable Stella, who has let strangers touch her; Irving, for whom I am sorry, etc." Nor does Humbert's muse desert him on the ultimate occasion. When, gun in hand, he delivers sentence on his rival Clare Quilty prior to shooting him dead, he does so in the accents of a certain poem, well known to the literary world, about sin, penitence, and death:

> Because you took advantage of a sinner
> because you took advantage
> because you took
> because you took advantage of my disadvantage . . .

"That's damned good," says Quilty, providing Humbert with an approving, if captive, audience at last.

For Humbert, the uses of poetry are rather low. He might even be said to prostitute his muse. The uses of poetry for Mr. Nabokov are high, though not so high as to rule out the efforts of those who are compelled into song by mixed motives, including lust, revenge, and the hope of a check from *The New Yorker*. Like that other master of prose, James Joyce, Mr. Nabokov aspired in youth to be a poet. More than Joyce did, he has continued to write verse and to fill his novels with reflections on poetry. The reflections are often of major importance; the verse—the verse in English at least—is minor, as minor as verse could be and still remain interesting. His forthcoming translation of Pushkin's *Eugene Onegin* will conceivably stand as his main poetic achievement. For years he has been going on about Pushkin ("the gold reserve of our literature"), meanwhile preparing us for the *magnum opus* by translating other Russian poets. He brings to poetry and the informal criticism of poetry the same spirit of connoisseurship that enlivens his work as a whole—an impassioned connoisseurship that unites the naturalist in him with the literary artist in him and does duty, it would seem, for ideology. He has a mind too rich to be impoverished by ideas. His "commitment" (in the starkly fashionable sense) is to perceptions, discriminations, prejudices, and to the purveying, as he says, of "aesthetic bliss." Before 1940, when he came to live in the United States and started publishing in English, he contributed a number of poems to Russian *émigré* periodicals in Europe. Between 1943 and 1957 he wrote the fourteen poems which, described as "his complete poetic works in English," were collected in a miniature volume succinctly entitled *Poems* (1959). *Pale Fire,* his most recent novel in English (1962), consists of a long poem, or quasi-poem, ostensibly written by an American poet, and of lengthy notes ostensibly supplied by a European-born editor.

The last novel Mr. Nabokov wrote in Russian has lately come out in English—authentic Nabokovian English. *The Gift* is a delightful novel. It is also invaluable for what it tells us about its author's relation to the twin disciplines of poetry and prose, in the past as, I venture, at present. With *The Gift* as a main text, let me inquire into those relations, to the extent that I can do so in short space and with no knowledge of Russian.

The Gift has been widely and pleasantly reviewed during the months since it appeared. So far as I am aware, however, no one has pointed out that the book is a sort of hail and

farewell to the poetic muse considered as a full-time companion. A young poet formidably named Fyodor Godunov-
Cherdyntsev is the hero. (One of *The Gift*'s best reviewers,
Mr. Stanley Edgar Hyman, tells us this was Nabokov's own
pen name as a poet—he signed his novels V. Sirin.) An
émigré Russian who has forfeited much to the Bolsheviks—a
country estate, a St. Petersburg town house, probably a
father, possibly a future as a native writer, Fyodor lives an
exile's desultory life in Berlin. There he moves from furnished room to furnished room, gives stupid Germans reluctant Russian lessons, composes verses, imagines the fine reviews his recently published book of poems will get, recalls
his Russian childhood, mingles diffidently with his quarrelsome fellow exiles, loses his keys, gets his clothes stolen at the
Grünewald swimming lake. His life is almost as unreal as the
phenomenon we find him scrutinizing on the novel's first
page: a moving van with "the name of the moving company
in yard-high blue letters, each of which (including a square
dot) was shaded laterally with black paint—a dishonest attempt to climb into the next dimension." Fyodor seeks to
climb into the next dimension, the heaven of aesthetic bliss,
by the frail but not dishonest ladder of poetry alone. True, he
has a distinct "gift" for it, a charming craze for words, and a
capacity for hallucination that verges on secular mysticism.
The first chapter of *The Gift* is, among other things, a little
anthology of his poems. They are about incidents remembered from his childhood in Russia.

My ball has rolled under Nurse's commode.
On the floor a candle
Tugs at the ends of the shadows
This way and that, but the ball is gone . . .

Knocked from its hiding place by a poker, the ball *"Crosses the whole room and promptly goes under/The impregnable sofa."* The long line nicely reproduces the effect of the ball's trip across the room. And the ball stays lost.

As the novel unfolds, we see Fyodor's situation—which resembles the ball's—reflected back at him in various ways by the plight of other *émigrés* around him in Berlin. There is the tragedy (or tragic farce) of the young poet Yasha, a recent suicide, whose hopeless attachment to a German youth of the blond and blue-eyed type forms, incidentally, a grim parody of a familiar Thomas Mann theme. There is the pure farce of Mr. Busch, a Latvian with pretensions to poetic drama. Before an audience choking with stifled laughter, he reads his "new, philosophical tragedy." It is *Faust* out of *Brand* out of Busch, and includes the following conversation in a "Street of Sin":

FIRST PROSTITUTE
   All is water. That is what my client Phales* says.
SECOND PROSTITUTE
   All is air, young Anaximines told me.
THIRD PROSTITUTE
   All is number. My bald Pythagoras cannot be wrong.
FOURTH PROSTITUTE
   Heracles* caresses me whispering "All is fire."
LONE COMPANION (enters)
   All is fate.

"There is no great poetry without parody," Fyodor explains; and in *The Gift* the parodies tend to be better than the poems. So Fyodor begins to feel that he will eventually want "to speak in quite another way, not in miniature verse

---

* It is Busch's fault, not the proofreader's, that Thales becomes Phales, Anaximenes becomes Anaximines, and Heraclitus becomes Heracles. [F.W.D.]

with charms and chimes, but in very, very different manly words." Indeed, during an imaginary conversation with an older poet he respects, Fyodor hears the man say: "By the way, I've read your very remarkable volume of poems. Actually, of course, they are but models of your future novels." Fyodor then stops trying to recapture his childhood. Instead, he undertakes to reconstruct, first the final days of his beloved father, a celebrated naturalist who has vanished on a scientific expedition to Asia, the victim of an accident or of the Bolsheviks; second, the life of Chernyshevski, the celebrated social critic of the 1860's, father of Russian utlilitarianism, Lenin's mentor. For these projects, Fyodor abandons verse, wooing instead "the Muse of Russian prose-rhythms." His assault on Chernyshcvski's crude version of the liberal imagination strangely foreshadows the assault that Proust, at the start of *his* career as a serious writer, made for somewhat similar reasons on Sainte-Beuve. But *Contre Sainte-Beuve* (which, incidentally, is of recent discovery and could not therefore have been in Mr. Nabokov's mind during the years 1935-37 when *The Gift* was written) is the tirade of a tyro compared to Nabokov-Fyodor's explosive yet touching portrait of Chernyshevski, whose dreadful sufferings as a man effectively belied his doctrinaire optimism as a philosopher. Rejected by a publisher as "a syringe of sulphuric acid," the Chernyshevski portrait is really part of Fyodor's attempt to contemplate Russian history without nostalgia—that nostalgia of the exile which, in Nabokov's view, so often ends in the exile's paranoia. "Why," he asks, "had everything in Russia become so shoddy, so crabbed and gray, how could she have become so befooled and befuddled? Or had the old 'urge toward the light' concealed a fatal flaw, which in the course of progress toward the objective had grown more and more evident, until it was revealed that this 'light' was burning in the window of a prison overseer, and that was all?"

But Fyodor's attempt to climb into the next dimension depends on other things than writing. He must unite himself, with a pretty, intelligent, hard-working girl who loves him and his poems, her name being Zina Mertz. Zina embodies, along with a poetic sensibility, the advantages—figuratively speaking—of good prose. Is this putting it too neatly? I think not. The novel itself has a rather pat way of making its points, a somewhat mechanical way of contriving its games of reality and appearance. After all, *The Gift* is a comparatively early work. In most respects, though, the mature Nabokov is already in command. Fyodor and Zina meet in a setting that is prosaic with a vengeance. It is one of those superlatively dreary interiors, epitomized by the communal bathroom and the communal bar of soap with the single hair in it, which Nabokov loves to swoop down on, whether in Berlin or the U.S.A., from the high wire of fantasy. This feeling for the commonplace at its commonest shows that his affinity with Joyce equals his affinity (more obvious in *The Gift*) with Proust. Fyodor writes a poem addressed to Zina but printed as prose. "Look at that street—it runs to China straight, and yonder star above the Volga glows!" Thus, in a fashion, the man and the woman, the exile and his homeland, the poet and the prose writer are all momentarily united.

Need we conclude that Mr. Nabokov himself has "sacrificed" poetry to prose? I doubt it. The English poems, all but two of them first printed in *The New Yorker,* are, it is true, of a kind often called, with a certain condescension, "lapidary." Nevertheless, as Mr. Nathaniel Reicheck has suggested, "the poet goes beyond the limits of his art [the "light verse" art] without violating its canon. This enlargement of a traditional form is made possible by his campaign to re-design the English language. His prosody is a unique and subtle parody of the original." This, again, may be overstating things, but not by much. The English poems do have a peculiar miniature excellence: perfect lucidity, precise wit, the glow of a lighted candle cupped in an expert hand against the windy verse roundabout. "A Literary Dinner" turns on a misunderstanding such as might occur between an American hostess whose enunciation was unclear and a foreign guest whose ear was imperfectly tuned to slurred English. "I want you, she murmured, to eat Dr. James." And so, amid dull talk at the table, he does eat Dr. James.

> All was good and well-cooked, but the tastiest part
> was his nut-flavored, crisp cerebellum. The heart
> resembled a shiny brown date,
> and I stowed all his studs on the edge of my plate.

Such a *nice* foreign guest, obliging, hungry, and neat. For wit mingled with lyrical delight, "An Evening of Russian Poetry" comes closest to being "great"—besides being a helpful treatise on versification. Referring to the Russian poets' "passion for expansion," the lecturer goes on to exemplify it in several asides, by turns paranoiac and nostalgic in mood.

> My back is Argus-eyed. I live in danger.
> False shadows turn to track me as I pass . . .
>
> Beyond the seas where I have lost a sceptre
> I hear the neighing of my dappled nouns,
> soft participles coming down the steps,
> treading on leaves, trailing their rustling gowns,
> and liquid verbs in *ahla* and in *ili,*
> Aonian grottoes, nights in the Altai,
> black pools of sound with 'L's' for water lilies.

The empty glass I touched is tinkling still,
but now 'tis covered by a hand and dies . . .

While writing his English verses Nabokov was elaborating the English prose which, somewhat subdued in *Sebastian Knight,* sometimes out of hand in *Bend Sinister,* would culminate in the controlled sinuosities of *Lolita,* the almost paranoid eloquence of *Pale Fire.* Kinbote's eloquence, I mean, for the point of the novel, rhetorically speaking, seems to lie in the contrast between the inflamed yet often beautiful writing of Kinbote's editorial notes and the paler fires, the intermittent beauties, of John Shade's poem. Mary McCarthy has said much about the book in her superb analysis and panegyric in *The New Republic.* One need only add a few words on Shade's poem itself. Distressed by his daughter's suicide, the father tries to convey his grief, his thoughts on death in general, in a kind of Popian four-part epistle constructed of the appropriate couplets. But he cannot rise either to Pope's scarifying realism or to the dashing architectonics of Pope's verse. Shade starts to quote the great lines from the *Essay on Man:*

See the blind beggar dance, the cripple sing,
The sot a hero, lunatic a king.

But he breaks the lines midway, explaining that "they smack of their heartless age." Shade's poem has an inner subject that goes unperceived by either Shade or his editor, who imagines the poem is about him and *his* "lost sceptre," *his* living "in danger." The inner subject is the blindness of Shade's grief, his helplessness before the extremities of passion and death, the spiritual deformity which was his daughter's sole inheritance from him but which the singing cripple of Pope's lines and the crippled Pope himself do not share. So the poem maunders along, lovely in spots, penetrating in other spots, now elegiac, now cheery. It clothes itself in a simulacrum of Popian couplets without attaining to the hard antitheses, the decisive pauses, which are the prosodic mirror of Pope's tougher mind.

John Shade is a kindly, even affectionate, portrait of the American poet-in-residence. Like Robert Frost he maintains a stoic patience and a well-ordered life in the face of domestic disaster. As with lesser specimens of the type his muse is so thoroughly "in residence," so domesticated, that he is impelled, on one hand into academic verse, on the other into drink. Indeed, he could do with some of Kinbote's madness and passion, just as Kinbote could do with a lot of Shade's common sense. But the exchange of qualities does not take place. Instead, Shade gets the bullet intended for Kinbote—or, more accurately, for Kinbote's landlord. In *Pale Fire*, as so often in our author's work, it takes two men to make a proper Nabokovian man—two men who, however, rarely succeed in uniting. With a writer, if he is a genius, the duality may be made to work for him, just as the Siamese twins in the story, "Scenes from the Life of a Double Monster," are finally put to work by Uncle Novus. Nabokov has done the same with the poet and novelist in him, made of them a team. Thus he has been able to perfect an English prose medium whose flexibility is adapted to the astonishing range, the endless contradictions, of his nature, of Nature itself. Some of those future novels of which Fyodor's poems were the models have, we know, already come into being. After the translation of Pushkin's novel in verse, others may follow.

1963

III. Lolita *in America*

Seeing copies of *Lolita* in the bookstores here at the end of last summer (1958), in a regular American edition with no conditions attached to its sale but the $5 price on its cover, was a curious experience for anyone with a prior knowledge of this magnificently outrageous novel and its earlier history. And what has happened to the book since—its conquest of the top place on the best-seller lists—as well as what has *not* happened to it so far—the failure of the expected opposition to materialize—makes another chapter of surprises.

But the surprises are getting to be an old story. Only three years of age, going on four, Vladimir Nabokov's little masterpiece has had a paradoxical history since its first appearance in print, in 1955, by way of an edition put out by the Olympia Press of Paris. What is in question is obviously not only a novel but a phenomenon, and a many-sided one. Like some flamboyant actress of the old school, *Lolita* has made her way by her personality as well as her art. Besides figuring as a work of literature which excites a variety of serious responses, *Lolita* represents a prodigy of the publishing business, a formidable addition to popular mythology, a major event in the career—already pretty fantastic—of its author.

Its publishing history goes back to the spring of 1954, when, Nabokov writes, "I finished copying the thing out in longhand . . . and at once began casting around for a publisher."* He failed to find one among the four well-known American firms

---

* This, like other quotations from the author that follow, is from "On a Book Entitled *Lolita*," which Nabokov wrote to accompany some selections from the novel that appeared in *The Anchor Review* (June 1957), and which is also appended to the present "official" edition, published by G. P. Putnam's Sons (New York). There is also the pamphlet, *L'Affaire Lolita: Défense d'Écrivain*, The Olympia Press (Paris, 1957).

to which he submitted the manuscript by turns. Rejections tended to be decisive even though accompanied as a rule by rueful compliments on the book's undoubted merits. A novel that described so vividly the mutual seduction of a middle-aged man and a twelve-year-old girl, as well as the disturbing events that precede and follow it, was likely to scandalize the press, mobilize the pressure groups, and finally bring about the sort of action in the federal courts which doomed Edmund Wilson's *Memoirs of Hecate County* a decade ago. Grotesque improvements were suggested by certain publishers, such as that Lolita be changed into a boy (an item I would include under "mythology" if the author had not vouched for its authenticity). So, refusing compromises, Nabokov turned to the Paris publishers.

It is not surprising that the American firms turned the book down in 1954. They would probably have done so even if the author had been as celebrated as William Faulkner. But Nabokov's literary reputation did not then, one gathers, make him a particularly good risk, whatever the nature of the book he offered. Admirable but rather scattered, his work in English—as distinguished from his many earlier writings in Russian, all virtually unknown here—consisted for the most part of *Bend Sinister* and *The Real Life of Sebastian Knight*, two novels which seemed to belong to the then obsolescent category of avant-garde writing; a critical book on Gogol which defied the prevailing modes of criticism; and *Speak, Memory* (*Conclusive Evidence*, in the English edition), a volume of memoirs which had always the reputation of being very beautiful and penetrating but was not exactly a public triumph.

So much for the fear of censorship and the comparative obscurity of Nabokov considered as probable reasons for the rejection of *Lolita* by publishers here. There was also a general literary situation which, although it may not have influenced them, ought to be taken into account, because it provided some of the background for the novel's subsequent success and because it probably affected to some extent the nature of the novel itself.

Nabokov and his book were at odds with the general literary situation in at least two ways. In his personal and literary antecedents Nabokov was a hybrid, an unregenerate cosmopolitan, in a period which had gone native with a vengeance. By "gone native" I mean "become preoccupied with the national origins of literature, convinced of the sanctity of tribal traditions." The rediscovery of the ancestral Anglo-American pattern came first. Here was a neglected fireside which could be made to give out heat again; and the most prodigal of prodigal sons, all the old wanderers from Henry James to D. H. Lawrence, were hustled back there to be warmed. But any fireside would do for which a Great Tradition, a moral center, could be claimed, with whatever disregard for the complexities of the particular case or of literary inspiration in general. And just as the "idea of the nation," in one critic's phrase, was thus rehabilitated, so the word "moral" became compulsory in criticism. Into this situation Nabokov failed to fit at all, not because of his actually mixed origins but because they show in his work, are proudly explicit in it, help to make it what it is. Where to place Nabokov, of whom someone has said that he is "Dostoevsky crossed with Voltaire," especially since this brilliant example of hybridization eventuated in *Lolita*, a book too shocking for any great tradition to want to own? Enter here the second negative consideration. *Lolita* was notoriously about sex and murder, subjects which modern American fiction had seemed to make compulsory on its side. Better a new William Dean Howells with his smiling horizons than another writer of the violent *Sanctuary* type. Indeed William Faulkner did not become the enormously respectable figure he now is until he had been naturalized, as it were, under the rubric of the "Southern Myth" and photographed at his ease in his hometown square between the Jail and the Courthouse. Nor did his violences become fully acceptable until they had been moralized, so to speak, as "melodrama." Thus I would myself have predicted at that time that the next really new novel would not even be melodrama but would glorify those "common routines" which Lionel Trilling once tasked Mr. Eliot with having condemned; it would be a sort of sophisticated *Little Women*.

Not that *Lolita* is really without its complicated relations to the sentiments of those years, although the opposite would seem to be true. If, as a reviewer has recently said, "the mind behind it is so original that it might have arrived here by flying saucer," that mind has nevertheless had us under observation from afar. Here, in *Lolita*, are the common routines in plenty: the American small town; the house with the Van Gogh prints; the humdrum poetry of cars, schools, neighbors, swimming lakes, and country inns; the women big *and* little. Here also is melodrama, but of so bitter a kind that the label doesn't sweeten it. The melodrama turns this country of common routines into Lolitaland, a world of obscene innuendo, where the notices posted in motel bathrooms are cautionary come-ons and the very highway signs are helpful-sinister. This raffish conjunction of the ordinary and the ghastly wasn't what influential people had in mind for the novel in 1954. No wonder the present victory of *Lolita* and its author could not be foreseen by American publishers when the manuscript was first submitted to them.

By itself, melodrama is only disappointed tragedy, inviting

laughter. This, at least, is the way Nabokov seems to understand it, aided perhaps by the mating in him of Dostoevsky and Voltaire (or whatever pair of opposite numbers). The American *pur sang* comes up with *The Bad Seed*. But Nabokov did not arrive by flying saucer, even figuratively. He came from nearer by, and *Lolita*, as I have suggested, was highly relevant in 1954, in the ironic way that original works are apt to be relevant to received opinion at any given time. A resident of the United States since 1940, a citizen for several years, the author has long made this country the center of his life and observation, even submitting to the common routine of being an artist-in-residence (he has taught literature at Cornell University). Furthermore, the present book had been in his mind for many years.

"The first little throb of *Lolita* went through me in 1939," he says. He then lived in Paris, after having spent his youth in his native Russia, exiling himself in 1919 from the Revolution which had demolished the aristocracy he belonged to and undone his father, the famous Liberal statesman. For *Lolita*, "the initial shiver of inspiration was somehow prompted by a newspaper story about an ape in the Jardin des Plantes who, after months of coaxing by a scientist, produced the first drawing ever charcoaled by an animal: the sketch showed the bars of the poor creature's cage." This too Kafka-like inspiration led to a thirty-page story with an all-French setting, the prototype of Lolita being of that nationality while the original of Humbert Humbert, her *homme fatal*, was a Central European. In this form the story didn't satisfy the author. Some infusion of radically new experience seems to have been needed, and evidently his coming to America supplied it. "Around 1949, in Ithaca, upstate New York [seat of Cornell University], the throbbing, which had never quite ceased, began to plague me again." But now he wrote in English and what he began to bring forth "was new and had grown in secret the claws and wings of a novel." Much of it was written while he was on summer tours in the far West in his capacity as a part-time lepidopterist. While hunting rare butterflies in this cross-country fashion, he undoubtedly collected many specimens of common *vita Americana* for his novel.

Thus, from the point of view of Nabokov's development as a writer, *Lolita* probably sums up the process, compounded of fear and fascination, disgust and laughter, by which he has become an American writer. He laughs off such interpretations, and sounds most like a know-nothing native writer when he does so. But as D. H. Lawrence said, "Never trust the artist. Trust the tale." Trusting the tale in this case means seeing that Nabokov's naturalization has been on his own terms and is a triumph.

Meanwhile *Lolita* passed from his mind into literary and publishing history, and soon into "myth," when it found a sponsor in the Olympia Press of Paris. Assorted works in English, some belonging to the category of frank erotica, a few to that of literature as well, are the speciality of this house. Out of *Lolita* it made an attractive pair of volumes, which some tourists began to bring home, while people at home began to order them by mail, often under the impression that another *Ulysses* or *Lady Chatterley's Lover* was being sneaked past the United States Customs. But one of *Lolita*'s many surprises was in store for them. In response to a query from the Olympia Press, the Collector of Customs in New York City replied that "certain copies of this book have been before this Office and they have been released." Surprise turned into large-scale paradox when it became known that the book released by the traditionally strict American authorities was suddenly under a sort of ban in traditionally free-for-all Paris. Acting on an order signed by the French Minister of the Interior, as of December 10, 1956, the Paris police had descended upon the Olympia Press, prohibiting the further sale and circulation on French territory of twenty-five titles, including *Lolita,* published by that firm. An appeal to the Ministry by a legal representative of the Press brought a belated reply, saying plainly, over an illegible signature, that "la mesure d'interdiction visant les dites publications" must stand. An appeal was also made to the *Syndicat National des Éditeurs,* but this powerful organization of publishers stood by the Ministry just as the Ministry stood by the police. As sanction for their act, the authorities cited certain French statutes relating to the immunities and responsibilities of the press. But the Olympia Press was able to produce, and to reproduce in print, a letter headed "Home Office, Whitehall, Ministry of the Interior," dated September 3, 1953, and addressed to the *section des Services de la Police Judiciare* of the French Ministry, calling attention to the International Convention for the Suppression of Obscene Publications and charging the Olympia Press with sending by post "des livres d'un caractère hautement obscène."

The gendarmes were unwelcome enough in themselves; but the possibility that they had been set in motion by the British Home Office, after whatever lapse of time, made a literary scandal in France. The Olympia issued *L'Affaire Lolita,* a pamphlet containing the relevant documents as well as various appeals to traditional French liberty. The response of writers everywhere was sympathetic. And presently the Olympia Press was able to resume business, under a curious compromise evolved by the ministry. *Lolita* and the rest of her prohibited sisterhood could be sold, on the premises and by mail, but they could not be exhibited in the windows or otherwise advertised.

It was in the glare of these international ironies that *Lolita* came to the attention of the American press at large, most notably *Time* magazine, which made all the ironies plain in an article on the case (March 17, 1957). Considering so much publicity, an American publisher could now probably take the chance of bringing the book out in the regular way in this country. Indeed the respectably sponsored *Anchor Review* not only got away with printing large sections of *Lolita*, together with my own detailed commentary, but also got enthusiastic reviews in many different quarters. What had formerly seemed a wonderful literary curiosity now began to be spoken of as an absolute masterpiece. It had its detractors too, and they sounded just angry or hurt enough to provide a further stimulus to interest.

With its publication here (August 1958) by the dignified firm of G. P. Putnam's Sons, *Lolita* therefore quickly became the best-seller it still is at this writing. Inevitably, yet surprisingly again (considering the grim subject), the movie rights were acquired—for the usual "sum in six figures"—by the independent producers, James B. Harris and Stanley Kubrick, Inc. These gentlemen are reported to be busy on the phone all day coping with Hollywood mothers who would like to see their youngest daughters in the leading role. Serio-comic speculations as to what the movie-makers will do to make *Lolita* palatable, stories of all kinds and all degrees of veracity, public controversies more or less earnest, witticisms delivered in print and in conversation, make up what I call the "mythology" of *Lolita*. But the mythology tends to be self-defeating, for reasons having to do with the nature of the book itself. *Lolita* is like Falstaff to the extent, at least, of being the cause that others feel witty. But what can others produce in this way that Humbert Humbert, the humbugging hero and purported author of the book, hasn't anticipated, hasn't said better? One's double-entendres have a way of being turned against one by that far more resounding frame of reference. Humbert is as knowing, or more so, than the people who, inspired by a remark in the charming review of the book in the Sunday *New York Times*, have been filling the correspondence columns of that paper with news of the girl-child cult from Dante to Lewis Carroll. So, too, with Humbert's language. "Nymphet" and other new words, old words in shady new senses, are being fed into the vernacular by that eloquent source without their ever meaning half as much mischief as they mean in the original. Even the innocently intended remarks one hears or reads on the subject often seem to have been invented by Nabokov's hero, in a lesser moment. A firm that specializes in advising libraries on purchases writes (I have its filing card on *Lolita* before me): "Thousands of library patrons conditioned to near-incest by *Peyton Place* may take this in their stride. However, better read before buying." This is minor Humbert. Nor does a woman pleasantly reviewing the book in the Cedar Rapids (Iowa) *Gazette* improve on his mastery of the dying fall when she says: "The writing is pure delight, the syntax admirable."

Pure or not, the delight given by the book appears to have exceeded any distress it has caused, thus immobilizing the opposition. That there would be opposition and that it would try to take action seems to have been expected on all sides. A state of nerves braced by conscious courage may be felt in many of the early reviews, from New York to Texas. The courage seems to have had its effect, especially as represented in such a widely syndicated notice as that by W. G. Rogers, of the Associated Press, who wrote that *Lolita* is "concerned ostensibly with the flesh but [is] fascinating principally for the brilliant game of the mind." So far as action by censorship is concerned, therefore, *Lolita's* story is a story without a plot. Two public libraries, those of Newark and Cincinnati, have refused to acquire the book, the director of the latter institution saying that "the theme of perversion seems to me obscene." *Lolita* is still sold in Boston despite some indignant notices in the local papers and the demand for a ban made by a Massachusetts state senator. The published advice of Dr. James Alexander Hamilton of the San Francisco Medical Society is probably typical of the more usual approach of disapproving authorities. He proposes that the book be given "the silent treatment" in San Francisco, which "is already a haven for wandering psychotics and goofballs of every description." So far as I can make out, the various religious groups are also applying the formula of silence. A brief, uninformative notice of *Lolita* in *The Catholic World* concludes that it is "a romp which does not amuse."

The Catholic World's refusal to be amused saves the dignity of religious institutions. It also spares *Lolita* the indignity of a whitewashing. This last has been the book's fate in many quarters where sincere admiration and unexceptionable literary judgment have otherwise prevailed. No doubt it was from a fear of scaring their readers and alerting the potential crusaders that many reviewers exercised restraint in reporting the starker aspects of *Lolita* considered as an imaginative experience. The tendency has been, as with W. G. Rogers, to leap athletically from the flesh to the word game. A review of the American edition in *Time* came to the consoling conclusion, missed by *The Catholic World*, that "Nabokov seems to be asserting that all of Creation is God." A Comic Masterpiece—again and again reviewers have arrived at some-

thing like this ultimate tribute without traversing the exqui-
sitely painful ground between, the rank necessary purlieus of
disgust and horror in *Lolita*. The book, they tend to say, is not
pornographic, having no four-letter words in it. And again
Humbert Humbert can be heard to chuckle, this time at such
saving formalities. In the person of his author he has been
heard to say that pornography is only "the copulation of
clichés"; there are worse things. He has also expressed amaze-
ment at the tendency of some of the best critics to get out on
their favorite limbs—moral, metaphysical, or mythic—while
trying to prune *Lolita* to shape. Trusting the tale means stick-
ing to it. What he would say of Lionel Trilling's sober appraisal
(*Encounter*, October 1958) can't be guessed. For this distinguished critic, the grimnesses of *Lolita*, to which he does
full justice, are redeemed by its being about Love, a neglected
subject in our merely sex-ridden literature, and he doesn't
seem to allow the book a single laugh.

In his reserves concerning the book's stature, however, Mr.
Trilling is far more compelling than most of the outright enemies of *Lolita* have been. They have put on a poor show,
lacking the theoretical equipment for a good attack, not to
mention the rhetorical force, and falling back on the weakest
strategies. These consist for the most part either in rude plain-
speaking ("disgusting") or in attempts to sound superior and
bored ("achingly tedious," "dull, dull, dull"). Both devices are
so personal that they are likely to provoke only personal responses from the reader; and when the man who says "dull,
dull, dull" happens to be the not famously brilliant daily reviewer of the *New York Times*, Orville Prescott, the reaction
can be explosive.

The admirers of the book have certainly had the best of it,
for several reasons. *Lolita* is a wonderful novel, however you

take it. It acts with intricate force on anyone who lets himself be acted on. It has also had the luck to make its American appearance at just the right moment. The state of literary feeling—to speak only of that—has been undergoing something of a change here during the past year, from a kind of yearning conformism to a kind of yearning dissidence. *Lolita* has both profited by the change and helped to crystallize it. There have been many similar manifestations; but no other novel, no periodical or work of criticism, no group of like-minded writers acting in concert, has done so much. *Lolita* works its magic in circles where the efforts of the Beat Generation, for example, pass for only further symptoms—there are so many already. Moreover, these approving circles are not exclusively made up of any of the familiar types into which literary Americans are commonly said to fall. All the brows—high, middle, and low—are to be found in them, celebrating together. It was someone writing in racy obscurity in the Louisville *Courier-Journal* who described *Lolita* as "undoubtedly one of the great comic novels of all time." It was a well-known younger critic writing with the conscious austerity of his kind (and in *The New Republic*) who called the book "a major literary event, worth all the attention we can spare." It was the book editor of the middling *Atlantic Monthly* who called it "an assertion of the comic spirit to wrest delight and truth from the most outlandish materials." It was a quite unclassifiable voice in the Milwaukee *Journal* that spoke out for Nabokov's style: "sparkling and volatile, a marvel beyond the reach of most of our own best writers." Nor are the detractors to be found only where one would expect to find them. They are in the fairly advanced *Nation* and, of all places, the New York *Village Voice*, as well as in the newspapers of Dallas and Worcester. The old ranks will undoubtedly form again over other issues. Meanwhile, *Lolita* has contributed to a spectacle which many assorted individuals find irresistible. It has helped to make the fading smile of the Eisenhower Age give way to a terrible grin.

1959

Libido
is a Latin
Word

Thanks to the University of Michigan Press, the scandalous old *Satyricon* of Petronius now circulates freely in a candid translation at moderate cost. Mr. Arrowsmith is explicit where former translators recoiled prudently into the original Latin or into coy English double talk. He also tries to foster, by his choice of an idiom, the "illusion," as he calls it in his introduction, "of contemporaneity." The idiom is not his own idiom as a writer but, as he explains, is composed of a selection from current American speech and literary prose. Thus it is a frankly experimental, not to say artificial, idiom and in practice it has the limitations you might expect from such a creation. Expressions such as "cheap bastard," "for kicks," "just peanuts," and "running around like crazy" appear frequently, and they seem not to consort well either with each other or with the passages of more standard prose. Unlike Ezra Pound in his adaptations from the Latin of Propertius, Mr. Arrowsmith does not, as a rule, succeed in fostering the illusion of contemporaneity.

With that, however, I reach the end of my complaints. The Latin of *The Satyricon* is even more complicated than Propertius's Latin. Now racy, now formal, charged with sudden ironies, tending always to parody, and strewn with poems in various meters and styles, it has been a problem to translators at all periods. Mr. Arrowsmith renders the poems exceedingly well; each is a true *tour de force*. And if his prose tends to sound artificial in the very act of trying to sound natural, it has great advantages over the fake Elizabethanese of J. M. Mitchell, author of a popular rendering of *The Satyricon* in the old Broadway Translations series. Based, moreover, on the latest editions of a much abused and emended text, the Arrowsmith rendering is trustworthy, clear, easy to follow, and, as I said, explicit. Here, then, is the inflammatory *Satyricon* in a form that all may read. The democratization of culture and the liberation of sex could go no further.

For the book belongs, of course, to literary culture as well as to that interesting department of writing called "erotica" and thus has a double claim on our attention at present. T. S. Eliot's complaint, in the erotica-loving 1920's, that *The Satyricon* seemed to be the one work of classical literature universally known to modern readers, no longer applies. The combined efforts of the Great Books advocates and our intrepid poet-scholar-translators have restored much of classical literature to the schoolroom and the bookshelf. A consciousness of ancient myth and drama now broods over current literature and criticism and sometimes appears to haunt them. If Arrowsmith's *Satyricon* follows in *Lolita*'s wake, it also forms an item in a series of "Classics in Translation" issued by the same university press and led off by the morally impeccable Hesiod. A modern rendering of *The Satyricon* was in order and has been needed. Long a prize puzzle to scholars and a mighty challenge to moralists, the book has also been an inspiration to writers from Voltaire and Flaubert to Gide, Joyce, Fitzgerald, and Eliot himself. A passage from *The Satyricon*, about the caged sybil who wants only to die, forms the epigraph of *The Waste Land;* and both works are filled with the shapes of impotence and death. Yet the differences between the two are, to say the least, striking. The one is as implacably tragic and Christian as the other is implacably comic and pagan.

Nothing, however, can really be said about the work's meanings until some account has been given of the mysteries and problems that have accumulated around the text. Like its hero, the luckless but indomitable Encolpius, *The Satyricon* has had a fugitive career in time and space, coming down to us in a sadly mutilated form, and with no fully accredited author or date of composition to lend it historical respectability. When, where, and by whom was this improbable farrago of sex and sensibility conceived? What went on in the infinitely receding distances of a story that seems to begin, as it certainly ends, in the air? What, for that matter, went on during those lapses of continuity—grimly called lacunae by scholars—that are always making the scene go dark in the surviving sections? Was the book ever really completed or did the author's creative purpose, like the amorous purpose of Encolpius himself, flag at the climactic moment? Whatever its original form was, why are there no known allusions to *The Satyricon* among ancient writings?

Questions of date and authorship are settled with one stroke if one accepts, as many classicists including Mr. Arrowsmith now do, the tradition that Petronius Arbiter, Nero's sometime courtier and ultimate victim, wrote *The Satyricon* during the latter half of the first century A.D. A distinguished modern scholar, Mr. Gilbert Highet, goes on to claim that *The Satyricon* was composed by Petronius with the idea of treating Nero to a vicarious slumming trip through the lower depths and outer fringes of Roman society. Others tend to doubt—on principle, since facts are lacking—that a book of this highly original character could have been written by any mere courtier of this world, ancient or modern. On the contrary, the author might well have been some provincial of genius, on the order if not the scale of Shakespeare and Joyce. Besides, the evidence of history (Tacitus and Suetonius) suggests that Nero was not shy about slumming on his own.

The novelty of *The Satyricon* is generally acknowledged by classicists even while they struggle to supply the book with a prominent author and to fit it into one or another of the established genres of Roman literature. The author's originality, and his consciousness of it, appear in the uncommon energy of his language, the boldness of his comic inventions, and the uncompromising thought implicit in his story. Using the first person, itself a rare practice in classical narrative, he makes it pay off in his feats of characterization and specialized speech. The traditional device of mistaken or disguised identities here takes on new dimensions.

Encolpius, the narrator, has a number of roles but is thrown among people who mostly play their own roles more successfully than he plays his. A knight among rich and powerful freedmen, a poor tutor among established teachers of rhetoric, a part-time con man among more skilled practitioners of the game, a sincere lover among unscrupulous libertines, he is above all a mere man living among the shadows and memories of the more heroic males of epic and romance. Like Odysseus, he has offended deity and been obliged to suffer for it through long wanderings. But the deity Encolpius offended is not any Olympian, only the half-serious lust god Priapus; and Encolpius' sufferings consist in his being set upon—most unheroically—by lustful females and eunuchs, doused with aphrodisiacs, shaved of his hair, fitted out in women's wigs, tumbled in fishponds.

In short, Encolpius seems to embody one of those backhanded tributes to common humanity which—as in the case of Mr. Bloom of *Ulysses*—are ridden with ironic contradictions. On the one hand Encolpius is only what Mr. Arrowsmith says his name implies, "the Crotch," a poor, bare, forked animal. On the other hand he is gallant, charming, idealistic, and indomitable: our own man, however absurd.

Encolpius' adventures generally involve sexual experiences of the most flagrant kind. *Libido*, a word that occurs in the Latin text, is more than a life force animating all the characters. It suggests a live wire with which they have all come into galvanizing contact. They enter on sexual relations as readily as we shake hands with an acquaintance. Just as no one is reproved except out of jealousy, so there are no innocents and no common "norms" to govern the choice of a sexual partner. In the gay unformulated pragmatism of this world anything goes if it works; one takes one's "love object" where one finds it, in persons of either sex or any age. And it is no dream, no projection of the unconscious such as gives a basis in psychological realism to the Night Town scenes in *Ulysses* and other examples of modern literary fantasy. What happens in *The Satyricon* happens in the clearest of Mediterranean lights to people who may be, as it were, electrified, but who are wide awake and in their right minds.

Mr. Arrowsmith theorizes about all this promiscuity in a way that may make the book more acceptable to modern readers but that seems to me to distort its meaning, besides receiving no support that I can discover from the text. As in

Lolita, he says, we here view the world's disorder through the eyes of a still more disordered individual, through "the prejudiced eyes of a first-person pederast" (Encolpius); "in this way the mocker is mocked in return, his pretensions exposed in his own rhetorical passion, and his cool raffish eye clouded by what he cannot see: his own absurdity." But isn't Encolpius absurd, as I have suggested, because he is "human" and not because of his love affairs alone? How, moreover, does his pederasty differ from that of the other characters? And how does his "rhetorical passion" differ from the rhetorical passion indulged in by most of them in one way or another?

All eyes are "prejudiced" here. The divorce between sensibility and actuality is a constant theme of the book. In particular, a comic exaltation of sexual actuality unites with the ironic exaltation of common humanity in Encolpius and others. All this makes *The Satyricon* at once relevant and irrelevant to an age like ours—an age divided at the top between philosophical sensualists and philosophical ascetics, Lawrences and Eliots, all of them intent on rationalizing, pro or con, something that in itself resists such efforts, namely sex. As Mr. Gore Vidal has remarked, "Sex *is.*"

To the sensualist, the book makes its appeal solely through the frankness of its sexual scenes. But these are rarely idyllic, and even then they are subject to rude interruptions. Orgies become roughhouses, dealing out pain and humiliation, though of a slapstick kind. Expurgate these images rather thoroughly and you have the hurly-burly of an early Chaplin film. In the author's unrelenting comic view, sex is as supremely funny as it is ineradicably "human."

"Wholesome" is Mr. Arrowsmith's oddly chosen word for

The Satyricon's impact on the ethical constitution of readers. He claims that it is not only "moral," in the cant of our time, but positively good for you. And in an odd way, he may be right.

1960

In the
Powers
Country

J. F. Powers has long enjoyed an inconspicuous fame as the author of two volumes of short stories, *The Prince of Darkness* and *The Presence of Grace*. These volumes, together with his recently published novel, *Morte d'Urban*, make up Powers's entire work. The outcome of twenty years of writing, the work is obviously not extensive but it is very good. And *Morte d'Urban*, a comic novel of great charm and point, casts its glow back over the short stories, of which it seems the inevitable extension.

Mr. Powers's work is all the more interesting because its prime subject is one that has been little exploited by American writers and that would seem, in fact, to hold little promise for them. His subject is the contradictions that beset Catholicism, in practice if not in theory, because of its claim to an earthly as well as a divine mission and authority. Powers is, however, a very down to earth, very American, Catholic. In his work, the contradictions are expressed, not in any of those flagrant dramas of sin and redemption which form the staples of Christian romance, but in the simple spectacle of priests going about the ordinary business of their professions. From this spectacle, however, he evokes a mingling of severity and raillery that is not simple. It seems to have confused several reviewers of *Morte d'Urban*, even one as intelligent as Stanley Edgar Hyman, who wrote: "It is very funny when Father Urban . . . is wet on by a hamster but it is not the Dark Night of the Soul." Definitely not, and J. F. Powers is not Graham Greene, with whom Mr. Hyman rather unfortunately compared him. In the soul, as we glimpse it in Powers's stories, it is not always three o'clock in the morning; it practically never is. By stating his objections to *Morte d'Urban*, however, Mr. Hyman indirectly defined the grounds of Powers's special excellence. In his own way he is a thorough realist, even a regionalist. His explorations into novelistic reality are confined to a locale that is small enough and distinct enough to be knowable in terms of what he wants to know about it. Improbably, for a writer of his faith, his locale is traditionally Lutheran Minnesota. The advantage to him of this setting, however, is just that it intensifies the essential contradictions. His fictive Minnesota is a country of interminable flats, vague lakes and woodlands, and slightly hostile natives. It is very far from Rome (traditional Rome) and centuries away from St. John of the Cross. The distance lends a certain unreality to Church Latin, black habits, medieval vows, and dogmatic assumptions; and from this unreality arises some of the severity and much of the hilarity of the whole spectacle of priestly endeavor in Powers's domain. Yet neither the vague unrealities nor the all too raw realities of his Minnesota keep Powers from depicting it with restrained affection: the heart has, apparently, its regions. Nor are his ecclesiatics and their lay followers submitted to the kind of doctrinaire scrutiny which might see them as all of a piece. True, Powers excels at portraying specimens of "the terrible thing a false vocation can be"—irate beer-swilling Fathers whose inner wastelands make a desolation all around them.

But there is always somewhere, portrayed with the same skill, belonging to the same novelistic world, some austerely dedicated cleric to judge the falsifiers. And there is the old Franciscan, Father Didymus, of "Lions, Harts, Leaping Does," who seems to attain authentic holiness, if only when he is at the point of death.

Death, however, is a rare thing in Powers's world, and so is any theological obsession with mortality in general. His characters, both lay and ecclesiastic, are remarkable for their stubborn grasp on life, their fierce little wills, their flat assertive speech, their aggressive actions. They make vivid characters for fiction but have too much character for the good of their souls. And the mortuary solution is withheld from them as, possibly, too easy.

Powers's is a world of the living all too living, and only in such a world can the ethical consideration bear much weight. For the purposes of fiction, he effects a divorce between faith and morals. The question is not whether faith, in the measure his characters have it, makes them greatly better or greatly worse than those outside the fold. The question is whether those inside the fold can sustain the moral life at the level of *average* good will, self-respect and taste. If this approach is necessary to Powers as a moral realist, it is also congenial to him as a storyteller; and his love of narration in all shapes, sizes and degrees of seriousness is obvious. Stories within stories, ranging from rectory-table anecdotes through biblical parables to scraps of radio serials caught from the airwaves, thicken the fictional atmosphere. Each sentence tends to be an event; yet every event, like every firm but fluent sentence, is an open door into the next half-expected, half-shocking encounter. Thus does J. F. Powers coax stories out of the shabby rectories of his not altogether mythical Minnesota.

Morte d'Urban is his supreme fiction so far and its hero, Father Urban, is his largest and gayest embodiment of the old contradiction. "You may be right," is Father Urban's slogan, his favorite formula of moral accommodation. Another Sir Lancelot, brave, beautiful and gracious, he has a weakness for his worldly Guinevere, which in Father Urban's case is several aggressive laymen (and lay-women) headed by an especially alluring and awful Chicago tycoon. (I suspect that the Malory echoes are meant to provide only grace notes to the comic tune of the novel: isn't just about every modern fictional hero required to establish an "ironic" relation with some figure out of mythology?) Actually, Father Urban's too accommodating spirit springs from a certain quality of radiant good will about him, a quality which, far from being evil in itself, is ideally human and generically "American." If the chances of an impoverished childhood had not made a priest of him, Father Urban would be imaginable as a vastly superior Babbitt, a Gatsby whose romance with life is better rewarded than Gatsby's was, an Eisenhower whose golf, like his English, is more expert than that of the recent President. Even as a priest Father Urban keeps his radiance until the temptations of "Guinevere" combine with the envy of his fellow ecclesiastics to bring out the contradiction. Then, to be sure, he gets his come-uppance, in a crescendo of "ordeals" or "trials" as touching as they are ludicrous. Yet, as a reviewer in *The Commonweal* pointed out, these culminate, not in the actual "morte" of the hero but in the demise, so to speak, of his worldliness, an event that apparently makes possible, though it doesn't guarantee, his redemption.

Meanwhile Father Urban, though without a developed spiritual vocation, has a healthy respect for the priesthood considered as a *profession*. As such his role is very dear to him, and he plays it throughout with charm and tact. It is true that his performance during the "ordeals" or "trials" is not in its moral essence superior to that of any self-respecting man belonging to a respected profession. Such a man could be trusted to object, as Father Urban objects, when a brutal hunter tries to drown a helpless deer. Such a man could perhaps even be trusted to resist, as Father Urban does, the drunken provocations of the woman who, in very ominous circumstances, throws off her clothes and invites him to join her in a midnight swim. For the question, again, is one of *average* standards of decency. Yet few men could hope to come through it all with the fine masculine *élan* that Father Urban shows and that makes him such a marvelous literary creation. His fellow priests avoid such scrapes, not because they have the grace of God in them, but because they are merely less enterprising or more prudent than he is.

Father Urban is the central figure in what is—if such labels apply here—a comedy with strong satirical overtones. The point is distinctly made that, according to *Time* magazine, the Catholic Church is second only to Standard Oil among American corporate enterprises. And the satire shows, among other things, to what an extent *Time*'s claim is literally true. The satire shows the earthly church in its guise as an immense if rather antiquated corporate enterprise, its priests mostly job-holders, its upper hierarchy an arbitrary and oppressive bureaucracy. Father Urban's troubles begin when, all too successful as a churchly go-getter in Chicago, he is banished by his jealous Father Provincial to a decrepit mansion on the Minnesota plains which his decrepit order has acquired by gift and which it hopes to convert into a prosperous home for retreatants. Here Father Urban is obliged to labor as a common workman under the command of obscure Father Wilfrid, an excruciatingly comic figure of militant mediocrity. And here, too, *Morte d'Urban* begins clearly to show its hand—or both its hands—and to take on the character of an ecclesiastical satire which is also a satire of American culture. The forlorn circle of clerics at work on the retreat are, from another point of view, just a bunch of fellows on their uppers trying to patch up an old hotel into a paying proposition, buying their supplies from a discount house, getting out cheap brochures, and arousing the suspicions of the natives. And so on, throughout the main body of the narrative—which has been criticized as "episodic" but which is just lucid and well-timed far beyond the average. Successively, Father Urban is juxtaposed to many well-known features of the American cultural scene. One by one, the golf match, the drag race, the McCarthyite journal, the wild party, the dreary lakeside cottage, the dreary lunch-room meal, the TV set, the electrified crèche, insinuate themselves into his destiny. Sustained by Powers's gift for discreetly daring invention, the effect is satire at its most amusing and deadly. Gazing down from a church on a new housing development "whose windows, yards and rooftops were all lit up for Christmas," an elegant Monsignor mutters: "The fires of hell, and in the summertime, with all those barbecue pits going, it smells like Afghanistan." The American Church, caught in its contradictions, is not far from suggesting the same fires and smells, even though the finely managed transition to a more sober conclusion shows, I suppose, the author's essential piety, his eternally springing hope.

As with some thickly peopled and richly developed small country, the size of Powers's work is relative to the delight one feels on discovering it and immersing oneself in its particulars. My own delight in doing so has been great.

1963

Malamud:
The Uses and
Abuses of
Commitment

Looking up Malamud in Leslie Fiedler's capacious *Love and Death in the American Novel* I find that the treatment of him there is surprisingly brief and unenthusiastic. Given Mr. Fiedler's well-known prepossessions I should have expected him to award Malamud high marks. Fiedler is carrying the torch for "mature genital sexuality"—something that he finds deplorably lacking in the erotic life of the American novel. I have myself just read, not only the recent *Idiots First*, but all of Mr. Malamud's work that I can find in print; and it is my impression that the sexual norm of his world is eminently normal, as in fact it would have to be since his people are mostly too busy establishing themselves and their families in an elementally hostile world to feel desire in excessive or distorted forms.

True, they often suffer mildly from an *insufficiency* of sexual fulfillment, especially when they are young. But this suffering is apt to seek relief in the simpler forms of action, namely in going to bed with the opposite sex, or trying to. At worst, the deprivation manifests itself in a sexual curiosity so candid as scarcely to deserve the fancy term "voyeurism." In no other author, surely, are so many pretty girls so sweetly obliging about getting undressed in front of their boy friends. "Would you mind if I peeled and went in for a dip?"

the girl student asks her teacher in "A Choice of Profession," a story in *Idiots First*. "Go ahead," the teacher says happily, and she does. But "A Choice of Profession" is not, as this scene by itself might suggest, one of those steamy romances with a campus setting. The student turns out to have been a call girl in her past life; and the teacher, on her telling him this, recoils from her in fear and disgust even though he is so far from being a lily himself that he has been entertaining furtive designs on her. But he is only a prig, not a creep; and the point as finally voiced by him is that "It's hard to be moral."

In Malamud's novel, *The Assistant*, to be sure, we have in the Italian youth, Frank Alpine, a bad case of distorted sexuality. He is a thief, a peeping Tom and, just once, a rapist. But Frank is by definition an outsider, especially in the Jewish family that shelters him. Even so, he finally atones for everything. He settles down, marries the girl he raped, has himself circumcized and becomes a Jew. The lesson is as clear as the lesson is in *The Golden Bowl*, where James's Anglo-Saxon girl succeeds in reforming *her* beloved Italian, the adulterous Prince Amerigo. Essentially the lesson is the same in both authors. Mature sexuality culminating in marriage is the norm. And so potent a force is the norm that it accomplishes not only the regeneration of the erring ones but their actual or virtual assimilation to another culture. Indeed "assimilation," but with the Jew seeking the moral assimilation of the non-Jew, is a basic principle of Malamud's work. And as concerns sex, the power of the Jew is reinforced by his relative normality.

If Mr. Fiedler fails to credit Malamud with his own sexual values it is because he has other tests that Malamud's work fails to pass. Fiedler is carrying a second torch: for the

"Gothic" strain in American fiction. Gothic fantasy, he believes, "provides a way into not only the magic world of the baseball fan . . . but also into certain areas of our social life where nightmare violence and guilt actually exist." The reference here is to Malamud's first novel, *The Natural*, which is about the heroics and horrors of professional baseball. Influenced, apparently, by Nathanael West's mordant dealings with American folklore, *The Natural*, true to its Westian prototypes, explodes at one point into bloody fantasy. This is what Mr. Fiedler means by "Gothic" and it is what he likes about *The Natural*. And so, while praising that book for its "lovely, absurd madness" he reproaches its author for the "denial of the marvellous" implicit in much of his later work, where, says Fiedler, "he turns back to the muted, drab world of the Depression as remembered two decades later." For Fiedler, "the denial of the marvellous" seems to be the gravest of apostasies, a dereliction of one's duty to be Gothic. But as I see it, the "marvellous" requires of its user the rarest of talents. The mode of it established by one writer seldom survives imitation by another (consider the fate of Kafka's imitators). And the presence in a novel of standardized Gothic machinery—for example the secret staircases and come-alive portraits in Hawthorne—often substitutes for true literary invention. In any case, so irrelevant are Gothic fancies to Malamud's sturdy characters, so little can they afford the luxury of a "lovely, absurd madness," that they are easily imagined as retorting: "So what's lovely about madness that we should play Ophelia?"

All this by way not so much of quizzing Mr. Fiedler, who has his better moments, but of trying to define Malamud, especially his differences from the "Gothic" or "wacky" strain in contemporary novels from *Catch 22* to *Naked Lunch* to *V*.

The differences are notable and tend to align Malamud with such a writer as J. F. Powers rather than with most of the Jewish-American novelists of today to whom he is generally compared. Like Powers, Malamud is a mildly conservative force in writing at present, a fact that he, like Powers, perhaps owes in part to his interest in the short story with its necessary economy and—in old-fashioned parlance—its highly "conscious art." Not for Powers or Malamud, in any case, those specialities of the modern Gothic or wacky novel: the "sick" hero, the "stateless" setting, the general effect of improvised narrative, the marathon sentence which, in its attempt to deliver instantaneously a total physical experience, leaves the reader feeling as if he had been frisked all over by a peculiarly assiduous cop. For the people of Malamud and Powers, Bellevue is out of bounds; they are not *that* sick. Moreover, a distinct localism rules their choice of settings; even when foreign, they are never "stateless" in the sense given to that word by Mary McCarthy in her account of *Naked Lunch*. In addition, neat patterns are traced on the reader's mind by the movement of the "story lines" of a Malamud or a Powers narrative; there is no effect of improvisation. And their prose avails itself of the special authority, so thoroughly exploited by the early Joyce, that is inherent in the short declarative sentence. Norman Podhoretz has noted Malamud's genius for getting the maximum authenticity from the maximum economy of such a statement as, "And there were days when he was sick to death of everything." Here are familiar words and a familiar rhythm for one who is "sick," presumably, in the sadly familiar way of hard-pressed people.

Malamud's ability to persuade us of the reality of his characters—their emotions, deeds, words, surroundings—remains astonishing. In most of the twelve stories that make up *Idiots First,* that ability is quite as evident as it was in *The Magic Barrel,* his earlier short story collection, and in those long stories (*The Assistant, A New Life*) we call his novels. There is no accounting for this elusive gift except by terms so trite as to seem like abstractions. His identification with his people tends to be perfect; and it is perfect because, on the one hand, they are mostly Jews of a certain class, as he is, and on the other (to quote Mr. Podhoretz further), they are "copied not from any models on earth but from an idea in the mind of Bernard Malamud." The idea brings about a grand simplification, or specialization, of historical fact. For one thing, Malamud's Jewish community is chiefly composed of people of East European origin. For another, they tend to retain, morally speaking, their immigrant status. Life is centered in the home and the workshop and remains tough and full of threats. The atmosphere is not that of the 1930's Depression alone, as Fiedler says, but that of the hard times ever immanent in the nature of things. His people may prosper for a while and within limits. But memories and connections continue to bind them to the Old World, in some cases to the world of the Old Testament where Jacob labors for Laban and Job suffers for everyone. Some of them, it is true, progress to the point of acquiring ineffably Anglo-Saxon first names ("Arthur Fidelman," for example). Some are found claiming that all-American privilege of the post-war period, "a year in Italy." But in Italy they become, or fear to become, immigrants all over again, and the old American theme of innocents abroad is updated. Golden Italy so confounds the professor of "The Maid's Shoes" that he dares open his heart to it not at all. The art student Arthur Fidelman is made of different stuff but not of stuff dependable enough to prevail against the glorious menace of golden Italy. In the story about him in *The Magic Barrel,* his first days in Rome were shown to be haunted by a crafty alter-ego (a "refugee from Israel") and Fidelman lost his notes on Giotto, the "Christian artist." In the two stories about him in *Idiots First* he is still being badly hustled in Italy and his few victories are painfully Pyrrhic.

The Fidelman stories are beautifully done and very funny. Something about them, however, suggests the rigors of a punitive expedition on the part of the author and possibly at his own expense. I remember his earlier tales of would-be artists and intellectuals—those dreary youths who lie all day on their rooming house beds trying to concentrate on the reading of *Madame Bovary* or on writing novels themselves. And I suspect that in these cases Malamud's identification with his world is carried beyond the point of perfection to a certain guilt and fear. His people seem to be watching him, rather than he them, to make sure that he doesn't get out of line. And then there is the story ("Black Is My Favorite Color") in which Mr. Malamud tries to motivate the love of a Jewish liquor dealer for a Negro woman by giving the liquor dealer a good deal of wry sensibility. "That was the night she wore a purple dress and I thought to myself, My God, what colors. Who paints that picture paints a masterpiece." This strikes me as a mere stereotype of Second Avenue folksiness. Nor are the author's powers of invention quite equal to the demands of the metaphysical fantasy which serves this volume as title story. Here an old man is pursued by Death until at last he acquires the courage to look Death squarely in the eye, thus winning the desired extension of his borrowed time. Meanwhile each has clarified his position to the other in the artificially racy speech of what sounds like a bull session. Challenged to explain his lack of "responsibility," Death says, "I ain't in the anthropomorphic business." And the old man yells, "You bastard, don't you know what it means human?" Nor does it help that Malamud, humorizing, calls Death "Ginzburg." He sets out, perhaps, to disinfect Kafka's universe of its total tragedy and ends up approximating the whimsical affirmations of Paddy Chayefsky. Such are the occasional failures of a first rate talent bent upon maintaining his "commitment" (in the sloganeering phrase) to his own people and trying to be as positive as possible. In these cases, commitment, that very necessary stage in anyone's development towards freedom of self and imagination, seems to have become an end in itself, a commitment to commitment.

Among the many fine stories in *Idiots First*, two are very fine. One, "The German Refugee," simulates reportage rather than fable—perhaps it *is* reportage—and is the most profound rendering of the refugee theme I know. The other, "The Death of Me," is the epitome of the author's whole matter and manner—his fabling, as distinguished from his reporting, manner. Marcus, a former tailor, has risen to the level of clothier only to be harassed to death by the furious quarrels of his present tailor, a thin bitter hysterical Sicilian, and his presser, a beefy beery sobbing Pole. Their fury flows from their consciousness of old unhappy far-off things in their lives. And the prose in which Malamud renders their deliberate squalor and pain-wrung cries makes their troubles sound like all the troubles that ever were in the world.

To Malamud, Mr. Podhoretz says, "the Jew is humanity seen under the twin aspects of suffering and moral aspiration. Therefore any man who suffers greatly and also longs to be better than he is can be called a Jew." True, and the special appeal of "The Death of Me" comes from its giving the thumbscrew of this theme a decisive turn. Here are two men whose sufferings exceed those of Marcus the Jew until, realizing that they are beyond assimilation by his own ethos, he experiences the supreme suffering of total despair and gives up the ghost. There is true "madness" in this story—the madness not of Fiedler's prescription but of art.

1964

Difficulty
as Style

Although T. S. Eliot's early poems are now fairly intelligible to me, I still remember the trouble they gave me when I first saw them, in the twenties. Even then I felt in Eliot a remarkable pathos and distinction. But the poems as a whole were all the more bewildering because certain of their details and episodes seemed perfectly transparent. There were clear fragments of story, characters with lifelike names, recognizable references to history and literature. But these particulars existed in such strange combinations as to make me suspect even my moments of apparent illumination.

Then I began to study the critics who were explaining Eliot to the general reader, and I discovered that it was a mistake to read him for logical argument or continuous story. What appeared perversely arbitrary in his poems was in fact arbitrary on principle; they had the allusive structure of a dream. And thus in time I began to respond to the poems in such a way that it might be said I "understood" them. Yet this understanding helped me in only a general way to follow Eliot's later work or the work of other "difficult" poets. From poem to poem and poet to poet there was always for me a margin of obscurity which had to be overcome by study be-

This was originally a paper read at a session of The Modern Language Association.

fore I could say to myself that I "understood." Besides, the generation of Eliot was followed by the generation of Auden, and that in turn by the generation of Dylan Thomas; and although beliefs and methods altered considerably from one generation to the next, the factor of difficulty remained fairly constant.

Now much of the writing about modern poetry has of course been polemical and has centered around just this question of its obscurity. As a result, its obscurity has come to be regarded as an accidental feature which could be overcome if the poet were more cooperative or the reader less lazy. A critic like Max Eastman blames the willful snobbishness of poets who could be more lucid if they wished. A critic like Allen Tate replies that the poetry only *appears* difficult, and does so because we have "lost the art of reading" or because we try to read all poetry in the light of habits and expectations formed by a taste for Keats and Shelley. Mr. Tate even maintains that "the complainant does not understand Donne or Marvell any better than he understands Eliot." But it is hard to say whether this latter statement is true or not: so much hinges on the word "understand," to which critics like Mr. Tate, influenced by the intricate nature of modern poetry itself, have given a new and complex meaning. And they have so impressed us with this meaning that even a writer like Sidney Hook, who is not a literary critic, can say (and quite rightly), "The effort to discover what the poet is trying to say contributes to the process of understanding the created whole."

But there is another possible approach to the question of poetic difficulty. Instead of trying to explain it by the failings of individual poets or of individual readers, we may conceive of it as a regular feature of the modern poetic *style*. Many imponderables enter into the formation of any such style, but surely a style is in part determined by the kind of relations that exist between the art and the culture at large, between the artists and the society. From this point of view the lazy reader and the aloof poet must both be taken into account because both are elements in the cultural situation out of which the difficult style of poetry springs.

I am all the more inclined to regard obscurity as a special trait of modern verse because to my knowledge it has never been much of a problem to past critics. They have complained of it but seldom, and then as merely an occasional and superficial blemish. Horace said in the *Ars Poetica,* "Brevis esse labore: obscurus fio"—"I labor to be brief and grow obscure"—implying that obscurity is simply a deplorable by-product of the compressive process of metrical composition. Even the somewhat difficult John Donne seems to have shared, at least in theory, this purely rhetorical view of the problem. He remarks in one of his sermons: "It is true, thou mayst find some dark places in the Scriptures; and *Est silentii species obscuritas.* To speake darkly and obscurely is a kinde of silence, I were as good not be spoken to, as not be made to understand that which is spoken."

Thus for Donne obscurity is "a kinde of silence," or as we would say today, "a failure of communication." In nineteenth-century criticism of Shakespeare, however, critics begin to see in the tangled passages of the later plays a witty and allusive virtue. But it remained for T. S. Eliot, in his influential early essay "The Metaphysical Poets," to characterize obscurity as a positive, one might almost say, a principled, element of modern verse. "We can only say that it appears likely that poets in our civilization, as it exists at present, must be *difficult.* Our civilization comprehends great variety and complexity, and this variety and complexity, playing upon a refined sensibility, must produce various and complex results. The poet must become more and more comprehensive, more allusive, more indirect, in order to force, to dislocate if necessary, language into its meaning."

Since Mr. Eliot's essay is not intended as a formal defense of poetic difficulty, his remark ought not to be taken as a formal argument. Even as a partial explanation, however, it appears to me of limited value. If cultural complexity in a merely quantitative sense were all that was in question here, then it would be possible to argue—indeed it has often been argued—that other ages had witnessed a comparable complexity without exhibiting any such drastic complication of poetic style as we have at present.

Or did Mr. Eliot mean his remark on the complexity of our civilization as more than a description of this civilization—as in fact a *judgment* on it? Strictures on this civilization are extremely common and extremely vehement in Eliot, and also in the work of other poets of the difficult school as far back as Rimbaud, who was one of its founders. May not the difficult style, then, be regarded as a kind of implied *judgment* on modern life, the complexity of which is only one of the terrors it holds for artists? May not this style, with its ambiguity, its allusiveness, its structure of myths derived sometimes from private experience or from relatively new and inaccessible sciences, be another symptom of that "alienated" consciousness which manifests itself in so many ways in modern literature?

I wonder, in short, if a high degree of difficulty is not an aspect of the modern poetic style just as a peculiarly brilliant and aggressive clarity was a stylistic aspect of the school of Pope. We know that by and large the school of Pope was sympathetic towards the society of its age and regarded itself as the champion of accepted values against dunces and out-laws; whereas contemporary poets are the heirs of a century-old tension between artists and society. Of course I do not mean that modern poets *deliberately* obscure their meaning in order to be rude to a world they cannot abide. It is not a question of individual poets and their motives, but of a general style, of which no single poet was the inventor and in which those who participate do so without necessarily having full awareness of its broader cultural implications. Indeed, so prevalent is the style today that poets with only a lesser grievance against the modern world—poets like E. E. Cummings and Wallace Stevens—are no less difficult than Eliot or Rimbaud. And finally, the difficult style is not confined to poetry but is present in painting, in certain works of prose fiction, and in other contemporary arts.

What I have been saying is not intended as a "theory" of diffculty in poetry; and considered as a contribution to the polemics over this issue it certainly begs the question. The opponents of modern poetry will say that if difficulty is inherent in the style, then it is the style that must be assailed or defended. This I happen to think is true. Not the obscurity of the poetry but the poetry itself ought to be the issue, if we assume that by study and experience modern poems can, with whatever tax on our patience, be made to yield up reasonably satisfactory meanings. In short there is no very sensible *a priori* defense of this factor of difficulty; it is defensible only in so far as it is an element in a poetry which can on other counts be shown to be great poetry. For poetry has often had to make its way against common sense: the early reviews of Keats are very persuasive so long as we don't read Keats. Similarly, the obscurity of modern poetry may often seem to be unreasonable, antisocial, even insane; but out of that poetry have come Rimbaud's *Illuminations,* Eliot's *The Waste Land,* Yeats's Byzantine poems, Stevens's *Harmonium*—works which are not, surely, unreasonable or antisocial or insane but are great examples of poetic literature.

1945

The
Muse
as House
Guest

Young America can still be heard singing, by anyone with very sensitive auditory equipment. Writing verse, publishing volumes, giving public readings from their work, winning prizes and fellowships, a lot of young men and women continue to go about the business of being poets. If this is news to most readers, lost as I imagine most readers are in contemplation of "the novel," it is partly because the poems of the young make little clamor. Resourceful leaders are lacking to them, and self-advocacy in the form of critical pronouncements is generally not a part of their business.

Yet the younger poets are not without ample public support, as I gather from the biographical data included in the several recent volumes I have at hand. Honors abound: if a poet is unlucky enough to miss out on one of the Borestone Mountain Awards he may still capture the Glascock Memorial Prize or the less lugubrious-sounding Lamont Poetry Selection, bestowed annually by the Academy of American Poets. Besides this group, a great many lesser societies for the encouragement of verse writing flourish, whether in Atlanta, Worcester, Denver, or New York City. Even the employees of the federal government have one, named The Federal Poets. In some respects, moreover, conditions of publication have become increasingly favorable to the little-known poet. It is true that the more prominent publishers continue to list just about the same judiciously small number of poetry "titles" that they have always listed. But some of the university presses (Michigan, Indiana) now include volumes of verse among their scholarly items. Then the flourishing paperback gets many poets into public circulation, often in an attractive as well as inexpensive format (e.g. the delightful volume Evergreen Books has made out of James Broughton's *True & False Unicorn*).

As for magazines that print respectable poetry, there is always, for the *poème bien fait*—and not too radically original—pre-eminently *The New Yorker*. The small audience magazines that give much space to verse are now more numerous than anyone except the harassed librarian in the periodical room could imagine. *Broom, Blast, Blues* and the other ancestral little magazines have, as it were, multiplied like minks through the subsequent decades. Unfamiliar names crowd the acknowledgment pages of many volumes. For the right to reprint her work, one poet renders thanks to *Spirit, Voices, Quicksilver, The Step Ladder, Kaleidograph, Poetry Digest, The Lyric, Variegation, American Weave, University of Kansas Review, Prairie Schooner, Yankee, The Bronxville Villager, Educational Forum, American Bard,* and *The Fawnlight.*

The younger poets are not only richly honored and thoroughly published, they are distinctly a job-holding generation. A census-taker would have no trouble with them when it came to specifying their occupations. Among the contributors to *New Poems By American Poets 2*, a representative paperback anthology edited by Rolfe Humphries, only oldtimers like E. E. Cummings and Vincent McHugh are listed as unemployed. Nor are the remainder of Humphries' contributors to be found exclusively where one might expect to find them: in university posts. A young poet today may be in anything from occupational therapy to the Catholic priesthood to the U. S. Forest Service. But the classroom certainly claims the majority of them—so many that Robert Frost is at pains to defend them in a foreword to *New Poets of England and America,* declaring that "poetry has been a great concern of schools all down the ages." Such, however, is the eagerness of editors for fresh material that they seek it from poets who are still in the undergraduate stage. One young man whose work occupies a third of a volume with two co-versifiers is advertised as "studying with Robert Lowell at Boston University" while a second is "studying Classics with Dr. Roger Hornsby" (university unnamed).

So far as my data go, the record for continuous recognition and uninterrupted occupation is held by a twenty-seven year old poet whose first volume has recently been given to the world by a university press. The jacket reads in part: "After graduating in 1952 from Amherst College, where he won the Colin Armstrong Poetry Prize, he was employed as a research analyst with the National Security Agency in Washington, D. C. In 1953 he was drafted into the army and served in the Counter Intelligence Corps until his discharge in May, 1955. While in the army, he applied for a Fulbright scholarship to study in England and was awarded one to Worcester College, Oxford." No grass grew under these winged feet, even "while in the army."

No doubt the favorable—if that is the word for it—economic situation of recent years has affected the tone and substance of the poetry written by the young generation. So has the domesticity which is now made easily possible, if it is not actually encouraged, by their job holding status. A verse

writing father and husband is less likely than a muse ridden
bachelor to arrive in the classroom with a hangover and his
papers uncorrected. But marriage is obviously an attractive
as well as advisable state for the young poets, and it provides
them with a large stock of poetic subjects. House, wife, children, parents, pets, gardens, summer resorts, travel *en fa-
mille* make up the unromantic romance of this poetry and
equip the poet with a special kind of consciousness—what it
is I shall try later on to make clear. For this observation there
is not only the internal evidence of the poems but—again—
the evidence supplied by compilers of biographical notes.
The compilers seem to be in love with family happiness these
days and like to name the poet's wife, enumerate his children, and offer other homely details. We learn of one poet
that "while there [in Cambridge, England], he was married,
in 1954, to —— who traveled all the way from Missouri for
the purpose." Missouri *is* a far piece to travel from, for any
purpose; and it is interesting to discover that another poet
bears a different name "in private life" and that "three children and many more dogs share her interest, but she admits
she 'can't communicate with cats.' "

New Poets of England and America assists us in penetrating the apparent anonymity, not to say nonentity, of the
youthful band of men and women who make verse under
these circumstances. The volume has been carefully edited,
probably with some such purpose as this in mind, by three of
the young poets themselves: Donald Hall, Robert Pack, and
Louis Simpson. The editors include work by poets ranging in
age from about twenty-two to about forty. The presence of
some of Robert Lowell's truly impassioned poetry allows us
to see how little impassioned—in any usual sense—the work
of the younger writers is, and so encourages us to look in it

for other qualities. Representatives of the West Coast School (the "Beats") are not, so far as I can make out, included; and while this omission makes for unity in the volume, it also makes for a certain monotony, as well as for an incomplete roster of "the new poets." Nor is Frost's foreword, good as it is in itself, a substitute for the introduction which the editors might better have written for themselves, thereby setting forth, as Frost does not dream of doing, their intentions and claims. Does an anthology of verse have to be sponsored like a television program? If so, Frost's is the best of brand names; and it is noteworthy that the young now acknowledge, as the young did not always do, his mastery. But the relation in this case, as in that of the young generation with other established poets and artists, does not seem to me to be a very active or helpful relation. It is the soothing one of homage eagerly given and complacently received; the atmosphere is that of a congenial party rather than of a working studio. (Indeed, the poem of homage to this or that authority is among the stock subjects.) And for all Frost says of "schools," it was not as a poet in residence or a Brooks and Warren instructor that he learned to write "An Old Man's Winter Night" or "A Servant to Servants."

A bursting rocket photographed against a black sky is on the cover of *New Poets*. Shall we say that the fireworks are all on the cover? It depends on what is meant by fireworks. In the contents of the volume there is little pyrotechnic display in the form of verbal or typographic experiments. The presiding muse here is unassertive, intelligent, amusing, voluble, company-conscious—the perfect guest. The scene tends to be indoors, the mode of communication is conversation, the talk is generally good. If this state of poetic manners excludes shows of unique energy and vision, it does so deliberately rather than furtively. And one of the contributors, Adrienne Rich, seems to allude to the whole situation when she ends "The Celebration in the Plaza" with

> The viceroy of fireworks goes his way,
> Leaving us with a sky so dull and bare
> The crowd thins out: what conjures them to stay?
>
> The road is cold with dew, and by and by
> We see the constellations overhead.
> *But is that all?* some little children cry.
> *All we have left,* their pedagogues reply.

The viceroy of fireworks goes his way; the emperor of ice cream is dead. All we have left is a rueful recollection of their exploits. So say the pedagogues. But their dogmatic gloom is belied by the appeal of the poem itself, which says more than it asserts.

The characteristics of this poem are, generally speaking, the characteristics of all Miss Rich's work and of the best work of her generation. The language is neither systematically colloquial, as Frost's language once tended to be, nor alternately colloquial and conceptual, as Eliot's was in his early poems; nor does it burst into a dazzling spray of fantastication as Stevens's was apt to do. Miss Rich seems to have access to some common style, a language which she and her contemporaries all tend to speak easily, with a minimum of individual inflection. It permits them to retain the "conversational tone," that all but universal idiom of modernist poetry, and yet to sound it without the apparent exercise of any strict selective principle. So too with the structure of the verse, which generally scans but is free enough to allow the musical phrase, as distinguished from the metrical foot, a certain autonomy. But the way of this common style with metaphor is probably its most definitive trait. The proud, self-sufficient "image" or "symbol" of modernist poetry, subduing all local or random figuration to its central purpose, and offering to the reader the allurement of a dark glass turned on an enigmatic universe, is largely gone from this poetry. With it is gone the modernist assertion of the supremacy of imagination and the artist. To claim access to an *anima mundi* or to the omniscience of a Tiresias, in the manner of a Yeats or an Eliot, would occur to none of these poets, if I know them. Indeed, figures of speech are now apt to be announced by a candid "like" or "as"; the homely simile is back; experience is fancified rather than transformed; readers are cordially invited to share in the processes.

The muse as desirable visitor is eminently and happily Miss Rich's muse. A woman in a non-feminist age, an artist in a time that is not *conspicuously* creative, she makes poetry out of a sense of limitations, is equable without the accusing calm of the self-accepting, wise without being a young owl. Her "Living In Sin" describes a studio love affair from the viewpoint of a mildly domestic-minded girl. It is in twenty-seven lines of limpid unrhymed verse and is an admirable work of this poet and this time.

Some of the men poets are more ambitious than Miss Rich but they are not often better. On many of them, too, acute feelings of limitation are patently at work; and the domestic status, in those who have it, is apt to induce the peculiar form of restrictive consciousness on which I remarked above. The poems that express it, in their several ways, are among the most original in the various volumes. This consciousness helps to do duty for the highly developed sense of role which good poets generally have and which does not seem to come

easily to these younger poets. By sense of role I mean the
kind of postures assumed by Whitman when he is being the
cosmic reporter to whom all things are copy, or by Emily
Dickinson when she beautifully queens it in her suffering universe, or by Ezra Pound when he is the Promethean exhorter,
or by Frost and Stevens when they take up opposite but com-
plementary positions toward the world's work, becoming respectively the visionary farmer and the Sunday poet with a
Monday morning conscience. This dramatic conception of
self vis-à-vis the reader and the world is, I suggest, largely
alien to the younger poets, and the absence of it is probably
more damaging to their work than the mere blackout of
modernist fireworks. It is here, possibly, that the security
provided by their common style and material well-being
plays them false. They appear content to be just poets together, indifferent to the histrionic claims that poetry makes
on a culture when poetry is a major art.

In that restrictive consciousness of theirs, however, there
is, in certain cases, something like an emergent sense of role.
It is apt to express itself in a confessional form which has its
antecedents in Yeats, Eliot and Auden. But the confessor is
now increasingly finite and personal. Saying I, he usually
means his literal self in all its literal daily reality. "Mirror,
mirror on the wall, / Who is Donald Andrew Hall?" inquires
Donald Hall; and in another poem (both of them in *New
Poems*) he locates himself still more exactly: "I sit upon a
changing porch and think / ideas about the insubstantial
wood, / that I may make real porches out of ink." Hall has
other subjects and some expert verse; but a certain blunt assertion of self, as of a real poet in a real garden, place and
hour and weather specified, state of mind clarified and moral
drawn, does tend to characterize his performance. He has a

more free-spirited counterpart in W. D. Snodgrass, who also makes poetry out of a very tangible personal relation to children, job, landscape and even to his surname ("Snodgrass is walking through the universe"). Pressure of circumstance makes this poet's consciousness half assertive, half uneasy. Out of the compound comes, now and then, something freshly comic, for this American poet has affinities with the comparable English school of Kingsley Amis, in his poems and novels, and Philip Larkin, in his poems. Divested, like them, of the myths, masks and ideologies of modernism, Mr. Snodgrass inhabits a kind of spiritual nudist colony where, embarrassed in spite of himself, he braves it out with grins, quips and little shivers of pathos. But he is never as indignant, or as funny, as Amis is capable of being; nor does he possess the crepitating moral sensibility that invests Larkin's verse with its faint appealing music. Snodgrass's rhymes and rhythms are unfaltering, and his command of rather bouncy colloquialisms is invincible. *New Poets* contains several selections from *Heart's Needle*, Snodgrass's long poem about a child lost to the poet-father by reason of a divorce. Expressions of grief and guilt here sound with a spare eloquence in stanzas of considerable intricacy and, often, beauty. Everything goes well until the poet, remembering that he is an oddball and funny man, refers to himself as an "absentee bread-winner" or recalls how he and his child once roasted hot dogs on "old coat-hangers." Snodgrass, too, is a university teacher, and in another selection, "April Inventory," he writes: "The sleek expensive girls I teach,/ Younger and pinker every year,/ Bloom gradually out of reach." (Fortunately, one thinks, for the propriety of the classroom.) Again: "I taught myself to name my name,/ To bark back, loosen love with crying,/ To ease my woman so she came."

A pose similar to Snodgrass', though without his unfortunate swagger, is occasionally struck by Howard Nemerov and Reed Whittemore, both represented in *New Poets*. In "The Vacuum" Nemerov writes: "The house is so quiet now/ The vacuum cleaner sulks in the corner closet,/ Its bag limp as a stopped lung, its mouth/ Grinning into the floor, maybe at my/ Slovenly life, my dog-dead youth." In "A Week of Doodles" Whittemore is no less humorously despondent over the failure in him of the poetic afflatus. He is "waiting and waiting and waiting/ For something to say." Meanwhile, what he does produce is "Neither major nor minor but merely (an old kind) doodle." But doodle, he goes on to say, has its uses. "Doodle is waiting raised to a fine art." Maybe.

The role of the academic schlemiel is a slight one at best, and the present tyranny of "light verse" contributes to its further attenuation. It has the painful effect of stifling any emotion beyond what can be experienced while one is being watched by a wife or a child or a class of students or—as it sometimes appears—by the poem one is writing. It produces a nervous intensity of observation, a poverty of vision, and seems to render impossible any connection between poetry and the realm of general ideas.

An historical as opposed to a personal account of the role is given by Louis Simpson, a poet of greater scope than most and of formidable technical skill. I am quoting "The Silent Generation" in *New Poems*. It was his contemporaries, Simpson says, who "put the Devil down" (meaning Hitler) with great enthusiasm—

> But now our occupation
> Is gone, our education
> Is wasted on the town.
> We lack enthusiasm.

Life seems a mystery;
It's like the play a lady
Told me about: "It's not . . .
It doesn't have a plot,"
She said, "It's history."

It probably is just history—the Cold War and all it implies
—that has caused and is causing the impoverishment of the
creative spirit, and not only in poetry and in Mr. Simpson's
generation. Still, single poems may be superior to the general
state of poetry, and individual talents may hold promise of
development. In the volumes at hand there are superior
poems by several writers, including William Jay Smith,
Richard Wilbur, William Meredith, Philip Booth, John Hollander, and Anthony Hecht. In Hollander and Hecht, the
pleasure in wit and musical structure replaces any acute preoccupation with self and history. And then there is W. S.
Merwin, a poet who seems to have arrived on the contemporary scene out of another world. It is not yet a clearly defined
location, and the atmosphere of it can be windy as well as
airy. But Love is there a passion instead of a slogan, and
verse shows an elemental confidence in itself, transcending
jobs, awards, fellowships, history and the other conditions of
its making.

1958

Note

Since the above remarks were written, the poetry scene has
definitely brightened. Robert Lowell has reached a consider-

able public with his *Life Studies* and *For the Union Dead.* John Berryman's *77 Dream Songs,* and the volumes of verse published just before and just after his death by Theodore Roethke, have further liberated the muse. In John Ashbery, Kenneth Koch and others of the so-called "New York School" we have, moreover, a new avant-garde.

1965

The
Battle
of Lowell

When Robert Lowell's first book of poems appeared, about fifteen years ago, it seemed to me and most others that he was the heir of all the poetic ages, at least from Milton to Hart Crane. He could write with the abandon of Crane and yet make immediate sense like Milton. He proved to have a real subject and a real place in the world at just about the moment when Auden, for one, seemed in danger of forfeiting his place and subject and becoming a globe-trotting commentator. Mr. Lowell's subject was of the largest; it had to do with history and the self. And although this was also the subject of some of his great elder fellow-poets, he had special reasons for laying claim to it too. Boston, city of historic battles and embattled selves, was his birthright as well as his birthplace; his family history was in some degree its history. And so the Boston of the old families, with its monuments, its Public Garden, its favorite suburbs and resorts, its own Atlantic Ocean, became the main setting of his poems—his Lake Country, his Yoknapatawpha.

In his early lyrics and monologues Lowell went to work on this faded locale as Faulkner had done on his faded South. He took the city's latter-day unreality to himself, determined to restore to both of them an awareness of their common past, their common position in the universe, their common fall from grace. In his own mind he revived the vehemence of the old wars and controversies which had made Boston Boston. A Lowell and not a Lowell, an escaped Bostonian, a puritan turned Catholic, a Catholic whose puritanism made him continue to worry his new faith, he rejoiced in his contradictions, including the pain of them. The hurtful exhilaration of the experience was written all over the style of his poetry. The muscular verbs, packed epithets, rushing enjambments, fierce play of wit, persistent interplay of heroic and mock-heroic modes made for a bravura medium awesome in its magnificence and a little relentless in its intensity. In this verse Boston was certainly brought alive, but as Boston might be on a Judgment Day presided over by some half-pitying, half-jeering divinity. An atmosphere of extremity and futility prevailed. Jesus walked the waters on Easter Day to ferry Grandfather Winslow to Acheron in a swan boat from the Public Garden. A Concord farmer trying to kiss his wife saw himself growing scales like Eden's serpent. The Atlantic was fouled with dead sailors and itched to possess nuns and other virgins. A man dreamed, only dreamed, of writing the *Aeneid*.

In the apocalyptic climate of the 1940's Robert Lowell became the leading poet of his generation. He wrote as if poetry were still a major art and not merely a venerable pastime which ought to be perpetuated. But there were difficulties in his extreme position and style. Randall Jarrell, an intensely sympathetic critic, once summed them up by speaking of the contagion of violence, the excess of willful effort, in Lowell's work. "As a poet Mr. Lowell sometimes doesn't trust enough in God and tries to do everything for himself." It may be that he didn't trust enough in nature and human life. His native place and chosen setting offered little that appealed to his senses and affections as intimately as, say, the southern

Negroes and poor whites, with their work-worn hands, sun-seasoned shacks and other attributes, appealed to Faulkner. Nor did religion seem to be a substitute for the tempering effects of such immediacies, except as religion was embodied in character—the character, for example, of the proud Mother Superior in his fine monologue, "Mother Marie Therese." Here as in many other poems, like "The Drunken Fisherman" and "Falling Asleep Over the Aeneid," Lowell's corrosively tragic imagination found its form. Elsewhere it tended to run riot very much as Faulkner's rather similar imagination has occasionally done.

A consciousness of these old difficulties seems to be implied in *Life Studies,* a volume made up of new poems together with a few older ones and an autobiographical fragment in prose. The new style is conspicuously barer than the old style, and the poet is more intent now on understanding the causes of his tragic imagination than on flaunting it. He seems no longer to seek support from theology. The opening poem, "Beyond the Alps," about a train journey from Rome to Paris, appears to record his apostasy; and there is further evidence in the absence of religious feeling and imagery from the poems themselves. A frankly de-converted poet is a rarity in these times; but the poetry here is not about the drama—if any—of de-conversion. It is about the aftermath. After such knowledge, what forgiveness? Guilt, remorse, feelings of loss? Not at all. With scarcely a backward glance at all that, Lowell addresses himself to his life studies like a painter or sculptor who wants to ground his art more firmly in the observation of things as they are in the natural world. But the title of the volume has, of course, only limited application. Nature for Lowell is his habitat, heritage and present existence; and his scrutiny of these things is anything but objective. More than his former religious commitments, these things vex his memory and confine his ego. Two poems describe actual incarcerations: in a mental hospital where the poet was a patient, and in a jail where he served a term as a conscientious objector during the last war.

It is still a dark day in Boston even though it is no longer Judgment Day. Hardly anything is what it should be even though the discrepancies now produce more humor and quizzical tenderness than fierce wit. The book abounds in second-class Lowells, in mothers who were unequal to their pretensions when alive and to their black and gold coffins when dead; in fathers who, though naval officers, preferred automobiles to ships and whose "Sunday mornings were given to useful acts such as lettering three new galvanized garbage cans: R.T.S. LOWELL—U.S.N."; and in only sons who had chronic asthma, chronic truculence and got themselves expelled from the Public Garden. Lowell's merciless anatomy of his parents is matched by his merciless account of himself. The volume that begins with "Beyond the Alps" ends with "Skunk Hour," a poem in which he claims affinity with the little scavengers of the title. Does the poet give the impression of being unjust to himself, as well as unfair to skunks?

His persistent refusal of happiness, his constant indulgence of a guilty conscience, would make a monotonous spectacle if it were not for a knowing humor and a distinct poise of style in the self-proclaimed offender. For Lowell is not only the hunger artist practicing an art of famine because he doesn't like food; he *knows* he is something like that and he makes a conscious role of it. The prose memoirs are the most triumphant example of his essential composure. The surface of them is all anecdote and caricature, malign and dazzling;

but the interior is solid analysis of a family, a society, a period; and when completed the work should excel any poet's autobiography since Yeats's. The portraits and memories in verse are exciting in their search for a cadenced as opposed to a strictly metrical medium. Like *Mauberley*, Pound's sequence of satiric scenes and portraits, including self-portraits, from London life, they add up to a marvellous comedy of secular damnation—in, for the most part, Boston.

1959

Kenneth
Koch's
Poetry

Thank You and Other Poems is a selection from Kenneth Koch's shorter poems. The volume includes none of his plays nor any passages from *Ko* or his other more or less lengthy narratives. The omission is perhaps a pity. Mr. Koch's plays have a special appeal: they give a peculiarly succinct expression to his enormously animated conception of things. Yet his better poems convey that conception too, in their own way.

Koch's position in modern poetry is not easy to determine. It may help to begin by pairing him with a long-established older poet to whom his relations are obviously close enough in some respects, and absurdly distant enough in others, to be instructive. In part he is one of those "literalists of the imagination" who are commended by Marianne Moore in a well-known poem and whose principles are exemplified in her own work. Like Miss Moore, Koch is fond of making poetry out of poetry-resistant stuff. Locks, lipsticks, business letterheads, walnuts, lunch and fudge attract him; so do examples of inept slang, silly sentiment, brutal behavior and stereotyped exotica and erotica. Whatever helps him to "exalt the imagination at the expense of its conventional appearances" (Richard Blackmur's formula for Marianne Moore) is welcome, although not to the exclusion of such familiar poetic properties as the sun, the sea, trees and girls.

But Koch never submits either kind of phenomenon to any Moore-like process of minute and patient scrutiny. He is eminently an activist, eagerly participating in, rather than merely observing, the realm of locks and fudge. And if, like Marianne Moore, he is always springing surprises, he does not spring them as if he were handing you a cup of tea. Her finely conscious demureness is not for him. For him, the element of surprise, and the excitement created by it, are primary and absolute. In short, "life" does not present itself to Kenneth Koch as a picture or symbol or collector's item. "Life" talks, sighs, grunts and sometimes sings; it is a drama, largely comic, in which there are parts for everyone and everything, and all the parts are speaking parts.

> Filmed in the morning I am
> A pond. Dreamed of at night I am a silver
> Pond. Who's wading through me? Ugh!

Those pigs! But they have their say elsewhere in the poem called "Farm's Thoughts."

The thirty-one poems in this volume were written during the past ten or twelve years and are very uneven in quality. Some of this unevenness may be the result of a defective sense of proportion, even a defective ear, on the poet's part. Mostly, it seems to spring from a certain abandon inherent in his whole enterprise. Apparently Koch is determined to put the reality back into Joyce's "reality of experience," to restore the newness to Pound's "Make it New," while holding ideas of poetry and of poetic composition that are essentially different from those of the classic modern writers. In his attempt to supersede—or transform—those writers, Koch has drawn upon far-flung sources. They range from Kafka to certain recent French poets (including Surrealists), to Whitman,

Gertrude Stein, William Carlos Williams and others in the native book.

Koch's general aims are made clear—well, *pretty* clear—in a dialogue poem called "On the Great Atlantic Rainway" which starts the present volume off. A T. S. Eliot character is uncomfortably present at the exchange of views: "an old man in shorts, blind, who has lost his way in the filling station." A wise old Yeatsian bird, also on hand, finds occasion to remark: "And that is our modern idea of fittingness." But our poet raises these ghosts only to shoo them away. His own idea of fittingness is to shed all formulas, "to go from the sun/ Into love's sweet disrepair," to await whatever forms of "unsyntactical beauty might leap up" beneath the world's rainways. In other words, he will flee the sunlight of approved poetic practice, staking his poetic chances on whatever wonders may turn up in the wet weather ("rainways") of *unapproved* poetic practice. He will talk to himself, improvise, consult his dreams, cherish the *trouvaille,* and misprize the well-wrought poem.

Such, as I make it out, is Kenneth Koch's unprogrammatic program (or a part of it), and the calamitous possibilities in it are obvious. Like the similar program of certain of the Beats, it could turn the writing of poetry into a form of hygiene. It could and does: some of Koch's efforts, like many of theirs, suggest the breathing exercises of a particularly deep-breasted individual. "Fresh Air," his most overt attack on the poetic Establishment, is half a witty skirmish, half an interminable harangue. The Unconscious, moreover, is not the dependable innovator it is often alleged to be. It really dotes on clichés; and those unsyntactical beauties supposedly lurking beneath Koch's rainway sometimes turn out to be discarded umbrellas. Consulting the sybil of the unconscious, he occasionally gets stuck with large mouthfuls of predigested images and with lines of verse that make no known kind of music. "I want spring. I want to turn like a mobile / In a new fresh air." Spring? Mobiles? Fresh air? He might start by freshening up his allusions. "I love you as a sheriff searches for a walnut / That will solve a murder case unsolved for years. . . ." Back to the Varsity Show with him. And if his verse is sometimes lacking in the delights of a reliable style, it also offers few of the conveniences of a consistent lucidity. To me his idiom is often a Linear B that remains to be cracked.

But having deciphered quite a lot of it, I feel hopeful that the rest will come clear in time. And for the silly sheriff and the boring mobile there are compensations. There is "a wind that blows from / The big blue sea, so shiny so deep and so unlike us." Marvelous. And there is the strange excitement aroused by this beginning of a poem called "Summery Weather."

> One earring's smile
> Near the drawer
> And at night we gambling
> At that night the yacht on Venice
> Glorious too, oh my heavens
> See how her blouse was starched up

"Summery Weather" is a poem of only twenty-five lines in which is concentrated much of the romance of travel as well as much of the banality of that romance. No wonder the earring smiles.

There are several poems of greater length in the volume, two of the best of them being "The Artist" and "The Railway Stationery." Both can be read as portraits of the artist, possibly as fanciful self-portraits of Koch himself in two of his guises. The first is about a sort of mad Action Painter or Constructivist Sculptor who uses the American landscape as his canvas or showroom. A man of inexhaustible creative powers and many commissions, he consults only his sybil, coming up with a series of colossi which are, it appears, neither artifacts nor art objects. And all the time he records in his journals various Gide-like reflections on the ecstasies and pangs of the creative life. "May 16th. With what an intense joy I watched the installation of the *Magician of Cincinnati* today, in the Ohio River, where it belongs, and which is so much a part of my original scheme." The *Magician of Cincinnati*, a contraption of heroic size, happens to render navigation on the Ohio impossible. But never mind. The Artist will soon attempt something quite different. A good modernist, he never repeats himself—thank God.

"The Railway Stationery" is about a sheet of company letterhead. Engraved on it is a half-inch locomotive which, when the paper is looked at from the reverse side, seems to be backing up; and there is a railway clerk who writes on the stationery, very carefully, a letter beginning "Dear Mary." This poem, composed in blank verse as transparent as the stationery, as touchingly flat as the salutation, may be Kenneth Koch's offering to the artist (lower case) in everyone and everything.

1963

Leavis
and
Lawrence

F. R. Leavis is an influential English scholar and critic, and how provocative he can be on the subject of prose fiction we already know from *The Great Tradition,* his widely read study of the English novel. The present volume has the advantage of forming a sort of sequel to that one, and in Lawrence considered as a novelist Mr. Leavis has a little-explored subject—one, moreover, which he knows thoroughly and for which he has enormous enthusiasm. Yet his enthusiasm does not prove to be contagious, for *D. H. Lawrence: Novelist,* with all its promise and its undoubted virtues, is in many ways a tedious and unconvincing performance. The reasons for this are fairly obvious, and before considering them we had better make a brief accounting of the virtues.

These consist in Leavis' comprehensive feeling for Lawrence's greatness and his willingness to demonstrate it by a minute examination of Lawrence's performance in the novel, the genre on which that writer set most store. It is Leavis' opinion that Lawrence excelled at the long narrative but this is not the more general opinion. T. S. Eliot, as Leavis never tires of reminding us, has admitted Lawrence's genius but refused to credit him with the very qualities which would make that genius effective in the larger forms of literature. He has denied him intelligence, culture, humor and art; and a similarly invidious view has prevailed widely in criticism. The view may not be so entrenched as Leavis thinks, nor owe what currency it has to the sort of Eliotish conspiracy he conjures up. Yet the denigration of Lawrence has been common enough to justify the defense of him, and it is just on those disputed points that Leavis' defense is centered.

Where Lawrence has been charged with cultural barbarism, Leavis claims for him "a marvelous intelligence" and "an astringent delicacy" of feeling for human relationships; and these qualities, he maintains, were fostered by the strictly English traditions in which Lawrence was reared. As opposed to the assertion that he was only intermittently an artist, Leavis acclaims his "marvelous rendering of the movement of life"; and if he never quite says what this rendering of life may be as distinguished from what he calls "the mere pondering of experience" (pondering seems not to be a part of life for him), he does insist with much cogency that Lawrence's power of art rested on conscious principles which were effectively present in all his major fiction, long as well as short.

This may be described—fairly, it is hoped—as the minimum intention of *D. H. Lawrence: Novelist;* and allowing for Leavis' exaggerations, the intention was altogether worth carrying out. To be sure, his estimate of *The Rainbow* and *Women in Love*, the two most ambitious novels, may seem unduly high. Yet he makes clear Lawrence's purposes in them, points out their indubitably fine moments, and is generally more interesting on the subject than those who merely repeat: "Lawrence was not a novelist." And the same probably holds for his inordinate, as it seems to me, evaluation of that writer in relation to his contemporaries. Not content to reclaim him from partial neglect, Leavis contends that Lawrence is "incomparably the greatest writer in English of our time," excelling everyone else as a novelist, a master of the short story, and even as a critic. Yet if a writer is as remarkable as Lawrence certainly was, this exaltation of him is not in itself harmful. No doubt it is better than the not infrequent practice of malice or condescension toward him.

In exalting Lawrence, however, Leavis also debases other writers of Lawrence's and our time, notably Eliot and James Joyce. He persecutes those whom he conceives to have been the persecutors of Lawrence, and it is this violence which makes his pages acrid with the smoke of old feuds and goes far toward spoiling his whole enterprise. So extravagant are his claims and charges that what appears to have been planned as a grand offensive—like Shaw's in favor of Ibsen, or Ruskin's for Gothic architecture—turns into a protracted and wearisome campaign of defense. Between struggling to put his subject in the best light, and contending with his own enemies, Leavis gets between Lawrence and ourselves and is seldom at ease with either.

These are "tactical" exertions, as he calls them, and they are one thing. More serious is the way that, in his own irascible consciousness of isolation, he isolates Lawrence from the genius of modernity which helped to ignite his flame just as it did that of Eliot and Joyce, a "tradition" in itself, what was, after all, thus constituting the tradition of modernity. For Leavis, the tracing of traditions is a means not of clarifying literary relationships and indicating preferences but of drawing the line in blood between creative minds. He insists that if you admire Lawrence, who was all life-enhancing "art", you cannot admire Joyce, who was all life-denying "contrivances." What arrogant nonsense, one is tempted to say, while at the same time remarking on the amazing persistence and tortuous transformations of the philistine spirit in English letters.

The only sympathetic literary relationship Leavis allows Lawrence is one with George Eliot. But surely Lawrence had as much in common with, say, Tolstoy and Nietzsche, as he had with the author of *Middlemarch*. Nor would a reader guess from these lonely embattled pages that anyone besides Leavis had ever written warmly or well about D. H. Lawrence. For all such—and they have been in fact quite numerous—he has one of his small but deadly grenades: "One's tips have been taken up," he writes—meaning, I am afraid, *his* tips—"and have been stultified in the application." In large part, Leavis' own book is stultified by his attempt to appropriate Lawrence for the traditions of "Little England" and for himself as their spokesman.

1956

England Now–
Ariel
or Caliban

Dylan Thomas's radio play, *Under Milk Wood,* is a liquefied Welsh version of Joyce's Dublin Nighttown, with the tears flowing freely and the laughter running over. All of Joyce's buried sentiment, all of his ultimate acquiescence in the lifeness of life, briskly surfaces in *Under Milk Wood,* disports itself in abandon, and cries with Polly Garter, the town fancy-woman of the play, "Oh, isn't life a terrible thing, thank God." No anomalies or contradictions in this Welsh dream-village, no heartbroken mothers, spoiled priests or wandering Jews. Where Joyce, Yeats and others of the older generation had been intense, haunted and hard-working, Thomas was sportive, protean, defiantly untragic. He was Glendower to their Hotspur and could call spirits from the vasty deep by simply raising his voice. Where his elders had strained, he relaxed, although he did so in a medium of language and fancy which they had helped to renew—as it were, for his pleasure. He made a playground of their time-defying and nature-resistant monuments of the literary art, climbing all over those obdurate surfaces and cheerfully defiling them. He was "the artist as a young dog," according to the title of his volume of autobiographic sketches.

In his radio play, the young dog's tricks include some striking impersonations of his master. *Under Milk Wood* is often slavishly Joycean. "From Beynon Butchers in Coronation Street, the smell of fried liver sidles out with onions on its breath. And listen! In the breakfast room behind the shop, Mr. and Mrs. Beynon, waited upon by their treasure, enjoy, between bites, their everymorning hullabaloo, and Mrs. Beynon slips the gristly bits under the tasseled tablecloth to her fat cat." But Thomas's mimicry here tends to advertise his differences from Joyce. These consist not only in the broader humor of "liver with onions on its breath" and similar flights, but in the charmed ease with which the potential anomalies of existence are turned into jests: Mr. Pugh the would-be wife-poisoner; Mrs. Ogmore-Pritchard with her two husbands, both of them dead; Mrs. Willy-Nilly the postman's wife, "full of tea to her double-chinned brim . . . and always ready to steam open the mail." Then there is the radical loosening of Joyce's austere form, the musical interweaving of the many voices, which transform the sleeping inhabitants of Thomas's Welsh village into pure spirit—or whatever their insubstantial substance is.

Performed by disembodied voices on radio or records, *Under Milk Wood* is all that it sets out to be. The spirits do really come at the poet's call, the act of levitation takes place before the mind's eye. But to stage the work in the regular way—with curtains, costumes and other props—is to risk alerting the doubting Hotspur in a spectator. This an English company recently did in a production of *Under Milk Wood* imported from London to New York. Some fifty players bounced, gestured and hallooed their way through the text, each of them determined to make the most of the brief moments allotted to him on stage. In their efforts to look evanescent they merely succeeded in falling over one another on a set which, with its numerous levels and compartments, was an elaborate trap. The London production brought out the least endearing aspects of the play. Its vapors tended to collect, settle and condense into moist banalities—something that doesn't happen in Thomas's best poems.

Poetry appears to remain Britain's most dependable literary export, for Dylan Thomas has had a greater reputation and influence, in America at least, than any other British-born writer since Auden. The novelists and playwrights of that country get only a passing celebrity here, despite the eagerness of many Americans to enjoy and learn from them. The women come and go talking of C. P. Snow—or Henry Green or Graham Greene or Joyce Cary or Christopher Fry —but not for long. Perhaps Kingsley Amis, John Wain, John Osborne and others of the younger English generation will prove more infectious. They are prose writers, for the most part; they aim to represent what they believe is a more central and more enduring Britain than Thomas represented: the Britain of factories, small shops and provincial universities; and as a group they are said to hold Thomas in some disdain.

Osborne's play, *Look Back in Anger*, while it is famously of this school, seems inferior of its kind to Amis' novel, *Lucky Jim*. Amis' inventiveness in the department of action is not shared by Osborne. What Osborne gives us is only a full-length portrait, quite ambiguous in its implications, of a man raging in the abstract dark of his largely self-spun universe. *Look Back in Anger* is nevertheless well worth contemplating, especially in the excellent production it is getting in New York, where the original London cast is mostly present.

The New York critics were friendly to *Look Back in Anger*, but they did in some cases object that the hero's anger is in sufficiently motivated. It is—by intention, I assume.

Jimmy Porter, as he is called, is that somewhat depressing figure with which certain American movies and novels, as well as certain young writers who contribute to symposia on the problems of their generation, have made us familiar over here: the rebel without a cause. This creature is more interesting in his English shape. Having wit and rhetoric, Jimmy makes something, dramatically speaking, of his baseless revolt, his career of gratuitous inaction. For his wit and rhetoric, he is able to draw on a long line of British moral bullies and railers, from Hamlet to D. H. Lawrence. Politically impotent though he is, Jimmy Porter can at least blow his jazz trumpet and search the newspapers for gratifying instances of scandal and fatuity in caste-bound Britain. Mainly, he is free to abuse his wife, her family, her social class, her England. Porter is of working-class origins while Alison, his wife, belongs to the upper sections of society. As his "hostage"—her word for it—she helplessly submits to his accusing tirades. *He* knows things undreamt of in *her* philosophy; *he* has seen, as *she* hasn't, men suffer and die; in short, *he's* spiritually alive and *she's* spiritually dead.

Jimmy Porter has Labour Party posters on his wall but doesn't really envision a changed social order. Failing this, he tries to make a blood sacrifice of his wife—all his fantasies are of blood-letting. The trouble, as he sees it, is with his class enemies even more than with himself. They are all empty do-nothings like his wife, whom he calls "the Lady Pusillanimous," and do not even put up a fight. Jimmy rails, Alison quails; and between them they enact an endless ritual of mutual damnation in their dreary Midlands flat. Their windows open on a covered areaway; their door gives on a hall, a much used bathroom and the quarters of a landlady who may throw them out at any moment. The furnishings look provisional, as if waiting for the landlady's ire or a bomb to finish them. Two friends share the Porters' lives for a while without in the long run loosening the pair's mortal embrace. Amid all that is insubstantial in their lives, this grim association alone persists. Meanwhile, Jimmy finds his ideal opponent in his mother-in-law, who never appears in the play. On her imagined presence, embodied in a gas burner downstage, he lavishes his finest flights of abuse, drawing enthusiastically on Hamlet's wit of worms and corpses. Jimmy Porter is often a detestable character from any point of view, including—at moments—the author's. With all its monotony of structure, its false starts into domestic melodrama or screwball comedy, *Look Back in Anger* has the courage of its author's talent for relentless portraiture. There's nothing wrong with Jimmy Porter that a good revolution wouldn't cure, if a good revolution were conceivable by him or anyone else connected with the play. But it isn't. And so a potentially political play becomes—again, I suppose, intentionally—a private lives play of the most suffocating kind. Of such proportions, presumably, is the social stalemate in Great Britain at present that Dylan Thomas can portray an entire community by the simple device of disembodying its inhabitants, whereas John Osborne, for all his socialist concerns, is stuck with a ménage—and *such* a ménage—*à deux.*

1958

Pieces
of the
Hour

Known to professors as essays, to members of the public as articles, and to writers as pieces, works of the kind collected in these three volumes* flourish in the periodicals, big and little, new and old, at the present time. Making us all frenetically magazine-minded, they keep us thumbing through an ever expanding array of publications. When may we expect the piece of the hour in *Organic Gardening*, the indispensable article in *The Yale Review?* And having first enriched the magazine world, many of them achieve a second existence in omnibus volumes such as those at hand. Mr. Vidal's volume is comparatively small. But its acknowledgments page reveals a range of magazine publication which could scarcely be bettered, extending as it does from *Life* to *Zero* The ranges of Mr. Gold and Mr. Swados are pretty impressive too. Roughly averaged, they stretch from *The Hudson Review* to *Playboy*.

Of the three, all in some degree novelists by profession, Gold is the only one who brings to essay writing anything like his full equipment as a writer of novels. Where Swados and Vidal compose essays to persuade us of the validity of their ideas, Gold composes them to show us the meaning of his personal experience.

---

* *Rocking the Boat* by Gore Vidal; *The Age of Happy Problems* by Herbert Gold; *A Radical's America* by Harvey Swados.

Neither effort need exclude the other, of course, and *The Age of Happy Problems* contains several essays that advance ideas on manners and conduct. But even in these reflective pieces Gold draws on memories of dilemmas faced by himself ("Divorce as a Moral Act," "How to Be an Artist's Wife,"), and he writes in a style vaguely suggesting the nervous rhythms of dramatic monologue. But if he tends, as I think, to extract the sweetest wisdom from the bitterest experiences, this is probably a consequence, not of his novelistic approach but of some unworkable partnership between the two chief aspects of his literary personality. One half of him is trying to be a good citizen, a modest hero of moral "commitment." The other half remains a wanderer in the underworld of disgust and despair, doomed to circle back and back over his past as if no moral problem he has encountered was really capable of solution, no city he has visited was ever really strange, and nothing in life was ever quite finished. God knows we are most of us halved in this way, and Gold would be an exemplary essayist if only the citizen and the wanderer were franker with each other and could agree on a common style of writing. As it is, they seem to be involved in a process of mutual intimidation, with the result that one of them sounds compulsively miserable, the other primly sentimental. Neither has a good time; and between the partner who goes in for the fanciest of mandarin prose ("Still, we are not blithe spirits; birds we are not,") and the partner who produces the bleakest of gut prose ("good belly luck," "my battery," meaning his creative energy, "forking up eggs," "I ogle the oglers,") the reader himself has a rough time too.

The best pieces in the book are the portraits of cities that Gold has lived in or visited at some length. His feeling for the modern city and for the oppressed or corrupted lives lived therein is strong. So is his talent for objective reportage—as long as he sticks to it. But as a rule he doesn't stick to it; the inner moodiness takes over. Read in sequence, his metropolitan studies show a certain monotony of grayness in the emotional weather. Scrutinizing his native Cleveland he observes an "acrid pall" hanging above one section of the city. This pall seems to follow the traveler everywhere like a bad conscience. It even trails him to Paris, forbidding him so much as a provisional indulgence in the simple pleasures of escapism. "Death in Miami Beach" is the most brilliant performance in the book. A highly wrought essay-parable, it calls upon all the brutality and vulgarity of the Florida resort city to testify to its theme: the peculiar grimness of death in a mass society. The theme is urgent and Gold tracks it down with a fury of irony that seems more urgent still, sometimes inventing gratuitous horrors. A "nude in plaster" glimpsed briefly outside a resort hotel is imagined to be beckoning obscenely to the crowd and saying, "All aboard, you masturbators." I suggest that if the statue is saying anything it is asking humbly that words not be put in its mouth.

Unable to settle their differences, the moralist and the emotionalist in Gold resort to a kind of obfuscating irony. This irony is the last refuge of the divided soul and it is as familiar today as the divided soul itself is. Considered as a feature of the rhetoric of social criticism, it represents a stock response to the stock properties and catchwords of popular culture. (From "soap operas" to "package deals," the properties and phrases of popculture are just about all accounted for in *The Age of Happy Problems*. Gold's title itself is a sardonic reference to that culture: he remarks that a certain television producer demanded "happy stories about happy people with happy problems.") But the triumph of sentimental irony ensures, I suspect, the defeat of social criticism. The sentimental ironist immobilizes himself along with the abuses he is deploring and makes sad war on sitting ducks. Everything tends to become part of the package deal.

If the chief fault of Herbert Gold's essays is easy ironizing, the *occasional* fault of Harvey Swados's essays is the equally easy rhetoric of sociological expertise. In this, Swados abuses the peculiar authority enjoyed by criticism today through its alliance—or what many suppose to be its alliance—with the social sciences and their techniques of the poll and the survey. Swados writes that it is not "accidental that the only civilized TV programs are presented on Sundays when the average viewer is either sleeping it off or visiting relatives . . ." His point is that the television industry, or at least the capitalist spirit embodied in that industry, is deliberately "degrading" the worker (which is what "average viewer" means in the context) by withholding from him its best programs. But Swados's clairvoyance regarding the worker's Sunday habits seems to me to visit upon the worker a different kind of degradation. Has the worker no alternative to sleeping it off or visiting relatives? Can't he go fishing? Are working class hangovers so much worse than other hangovers that they keep a man in bed all Sunday afternoon and on into the evening, thus depriving him of the civilized programs also available at those times of the day? Has Swados access to some statistical study that he is so knowing? Probably not. Probably he is only going through the motions of the sociological expert.

His regard for logic is rarely as much in doubt as it is in this instance. And his regard for the worker in society, for the meaning of work in general, gives his book its special author-

ity. A professed socialist, he is not very good as a defender of
Marxist theory. The essays written from a dogmatic angle for
the party press are stunningly innocent of any serious doubts
as to the potential rationality of human society. On most
other subjects Swados is persuasive. He is good when he is
contending against the complacent economics of affluence.
His proofs that an authentic working class still exists and
suffers are definitive. So are his studies in the malaise conse-
quent upon non-working. As a critic of the intellectual life of
America today he manages to be impressively monitory
without sounding like a common scold. He doesn't cry "No in
Thunder" like Leslie Fiedler and Jove. He is especially good
at pointing to the historical roots of "anger," "guilt," "sex,"
and "self-advertisement" considered as literary staples.

"The Cult of Personality" is his phrase for the self-
promoters, and it is a pretty dim phrase at that. Any intellectual tendency can be, and usually is, dismissed as a "cult" by
somebody; and what is a "culture" but the sum of its "cults"?
Swados's capacity to shape an argument is greater than his
capacity to turn a phrase. His words seldom sound as if they
belonged to anyone in particular. Perhaps he should join that
cult of personality himself. At most he sometimes sounds like
a youngish socialist imitating an old socialist who finds himself in polite literary company. "It may be accounted cause
for optimism that this play has found an audience"—that
sort of thing. But his "Robinson Crusoe—the Man Alone"
would be a fine performance in any company. Devoted to
demonstrating Defoe's practical humanism, "his ability to
normalize the abnormal," the essay also testifies to Swados's
similar humanism and abilities.

Gore Vidal would probably be the Third Man in any trio of

modern American writers. We learn why from *Rocking the Boat*, which, like the other two books, is frequently autobiographical. As a youth the writer was exposed to some wealth and much Washington senatorial society; and in his guise as an essayist, just as in his social background, there is a mixture—sometimes disturbing, generally engaging—of dazzle and duty.

Vidal's role is that of the free spirit; and through his devotion to writing and to ideas he has made this risky attitude effectively his own, as distinct from merely owing it to his background. Only occasionally does he appear to be under the necessity of reminding a possibly forgetful world of his privileged state. Then he is apt to sound like some member of Proust's ducal family, the Guermantes. One of the first-rate things in *Rocking the Boat* is a sketch of President Kennedy done from the life and enriched with personal observation. It is "good journalism" with a touch of Plutarchian stateliness. Quite in the Guermantes spirit of self-advertising humility, however, is Vidal's remark apropos the White House: "I am happy to say that I have no influence."

So much for the dazzle; the duty comes out in his attacks on dullness, demagogy, and the injustices done to individuals through the abuse of power by statesmen, literary critics, and cops. Indeed power is Vidal's chief subject, just as work is Swados's. The enjoyment of power interests him as much as does the abuse of it, and in several of his best essays he explores the ways in which possessing it or wanting it have modified the fate of individuals from the Twelve Caesars to Senator Goldwater. His friendly essay on Norman Mailer reminds Mailer that there are some people for whom "the preoccupation with power is a great waste of time."

I don't mean to suggest that power is the sole subject of

Rocking the Boat. A professed satirist just as Mr. Swados is a professed socialist, Vidal fires away at numerous features of American life and letters. Some (but not all) of his best stuff is satirical; for example, his brilliant critique of the slogan-eering use made of love and psychoanalysis on Broadway; or his feud with those writers who have converted the American vernacular into an official literary mode, a "national style." *Rocking the Boat* is even more of a miscellany than *A Radical's America* or *Happy Problems*. It includes things that Vidal has written over the past ten or twelve years while pursuing his various careers as a novelist, a writer for television, the movies, and the stage, and a candidate for political office. His many subjects are touched upon with sharply varying degrees of thoroughness. The book does nevertheless have, besides the recurring concern with power, a distinct unity of tone. And this tone, one of its great attractions, clearly reflects a certain style of being and doing in the author. It arises from an unusual (in our time) conjunction in him of audacity, wit, and pure if spasmodic intelligence. That boat Vidal is cheerfully rocking is a small-scale ship of state. He is testing its ability to float, not all culture and "the family" too, but only a single, separate, rather exacting person like himself. There are, he plainly implies, *other* free spirits besides Gore Vidal. *Rocking the Boat* is further distinguished by a remarkable literary style: clear, unmannered, lively, at times dazzling but never unmindful of its duty to be prose. He prefers to call the writings in *Rocking the Boat* neither essays nor articles nor pieces but "comments."

1962

James
Baldwin and
"The Man"

As a writer of polemical essays on the Negro question James Baldwin has no equals. He probably has, in fact, no real competitors. The literary role he has taken on so deliberately and played with so agile an intelligence is one that no white writer could possibly imitate and that few Negroes, I imagine, would wish to embrace as a whole. Mr. Baldwin is the Negro *in extremis,* a virtuoso of ethnic suffering, defiance and aspiration. His role is that of the man whose complexion constitutes his fate, and not only in a society poisoned by prejudice but, it sometimes seems, in general. For he appears to have received a heavy dose of existentialism; he is at least half-inclined to see the Negro question in the light of the Human Condition. So he wears his color as Hester Prynne did her scarlet letter, proudly. And like her he converts this thing, in itself so absurdly material, into a form of consciousness, a condition of spirit. Believing himself to have been branded as different from and inferior to the white majority, he will make a virtue of his situation. He will *be* different and in his own way be better.

His major essays—for example, those collected in *Notes of a Native Son*—show the extent to which he is able to be different and in his own way better. Most of them were written, as other such pieces generally are, for the magazines, some obviously on assignment. And their subjects—a book, a person, a locale, an encounter—are the inevitable subjects of magazine essays. But Mr. Baldwin's way with them is far from inevitable. To apply criticism "in depth" to *Uncle Tom's Cabin* is, for him, to illuminate not only a book, an author, an age, but a whole strain in the country's culture. Similarly with those routine themes, the Paris expatriate and Life With Father, which he treats in "Equal In Paris" and the title piece of *Notes of a Native Son*, and which he wholly transfigures. Of course the transfiguring process in Baldwin's essays owes something to the fact that the point of view is a Negro's, an outsider's, just as the satire of American manners in *Lolita* and *Morte d'Urban* depends on their being written from the angle of, respectively, a foreign-born creep and a Catholic priest of American birth. But Baldwin's point of view in his essays is not merely that of the generic Negro. It is, as I have said, that of a highly stylized Negro whose language is distinguished by clarity, brevity, and a certain formal elegance. He is in love with syntax, with sentences that mount through clearly articulated stages to a resounding and clarifying climax and then gracefully subside. For instance this one, from *The Fire Next Time:*

> Girls, only slightly older than I was, who sang in the choir or taught Sunday school, the children of holy parents, underwent, before my eyes, their incredible metamorphosis, of which the most bewildering aspect was not their budding breasts or their rounding behinds but something deeper and more subtle, in their eyes, their heat, their odor, and the inflection of their voices.

Nobody else in democratic America writes sentences quite like this anymore. They suggest the ideal prose of an ideal literary community, some aristocratic France of one's dreams. This former Harlem boy has undergone his own incredible metamorphosis.

His latest book, *The Fire Next Time,* differs in important ways from his earlier work in the essay. Its subjects are less concrete, less clearly defined; to a considerable extent he has exchanged criticism for prophecy, analysis for exhortation and the results for his mind and style are in part disturbing. *The Fire Next Time* gets its title from a slave song: "God gave Noah the rainbow sign,/ No more water, the fire next time." But this small book with the incendiary title consists of two independent essays, both in the form of letters. One is a brief affair entitled "My Dungeon Shook" and addressed to "My Nephew on the One Hundredth Anniversary of the Emancipation." The ominous promise of this title is fulfilled in the text. Between the hundred-year-old anniversary and the fifteen-year-old nephew the disparity is too great even for a writer of Baldwin's rhetorical powers. The essay reads like some specimen of "public speech" as practiced by MacLeish or Norman Corwin. It is not good Baldwin.

The other, much longer, much more significant essay appeared first in a pre-Christmas number of *The New Yorker,* where it made, understandably, a sensation. It is called "Down At the Cross: Letter From a Region of My Mind." The subtitle should be noted. Evidently the essay is to be taken as only a partial or provisional declaration on Mr. Baldwin's part, a single piece of his mind. Much of it, however, requires no such appeal for caution on the reader's part. Much of it is unexceptionably first-rate. For example, the reminiscences of the writer's boyhood, which form the lengthy introduction. Other of Baldwin's writings have made us familiar with certain aspects of his Harlem past. Here he concentrates on quite different things: the boy's increasing awareness of the abysmally narrow world of choice he inhabits as a Negro, his attempt to escape a criminal existence by undergoing a religious conversion and becoming at fifteen a revivalist preacher, his discovery that he must learn to "inspire fear" if he hopes to survive the fear inspired in him by "the man"—the white man.

In these pages we come close to understanding why he eventually assumed his rather specialized literary role. It seems to have grown naturally out of his experience of New York City. As distinct from a rural or small-town Negro boy, who is early and firmly taught "his place", young Baldwin knew the treacherous fluidity and anonymity of the metropolis where hidden taboos and unpredictable animosities lay in wait for him and a trip to the 42nd Street Library could be a grim adventure. All this part of the book is perfect; and when Baldwin finally gets to what is his ostensible subject, the Black Muslims or Nation of Islam movement, he is very good too. As good, that is, as possible considering that his relations with the movement seem to have been slight. He once shared a television program with Malcolm X, "the movement's second-in-command," and he paid a brief and inconclusive visit to the first-in-command, the Honorable Elijah Muhammad and his entourage at the party's headquarters in Chicago. (Muhammad ranks as a prophet; to him the Black Muslim doctrines were "revealed by Allah Himself.") Baldwin reports the Chicago encounter in charming detail and with what looks like complete honesty. On his leaving the party's rather grand quarters, the leader insisted on providing him with a car and driver to protect him "from the white devils until he gets wherever it is he is going." Baldwin accepted, he tells us, adding wryly: "I was, in fact, going to have a drink with several white devils on the other side of town."

He offers some data on the Black Muslim movement, its aims and finances. But he did a minimum of homework here. Had he done more he might at least have provided a solid base for the speculative fireworks the book abounds in. To cope thoroughly with the fireworks in short space, or perhaps any space, seems impossible. Ideas shoot from the book's pages as the sparks fly upward, in bewildering quantity and at random. I don't mean that it is all fireworks. On the cruel paradoxes of the Negro's life, the failures of Christianity, the relations of Negro and Jew, Baldwin is superb. But a lot of damage is done to his argument by his indiscriminate raids on Freud, Lawrence, Sartre, Genet and other psychologists, metaphysicians and melodramatists. Still more damage is done by his refusal to draw on anyone so humble as Martin Luther King and his fellow-practitioners of non-violent struggle.

For example: "White Americans do not believe in death, and this is why the darkness of my skin so intimidates them." But suppose one or two white Americans are *not* intimidated. Suppose someone coolly asks what it means to "believe in death." Again: "Do I really *want* to be integrated into a burning house?" Since you have no other, yes; and the better-disposed firemen will welcome your assistance. Again: "A vast amount of the energy that goes into what we call the Negro problem is produced by the white man's profound desire not to be judged by those who are not white." You exaggerate the white man's consciousness of the Negro. Again: "The real reason that non-violence is considered to be a virtue in Negroes . . . is that white men do not want their lives, their self-image, or their property threatened." Of course they don't, especially their lives. Moreover, this imputing of "real reasons" for the behavior of entire populations is self-defeating, to put it mildly. One last quotation, this time a regular apocalypse:

> In order to survive as a human, moving, moral weight in the world, America and all the Western nations will be forced to re-examine themselves and release themselves from many things that are now taken to be sacred, and to discard nearly all the assumptions that have been used to justify their lives and their anguish and their crimes so long.

Since whole cultures have never been known to "discard nearly all their assumptions" and yet remain intact, this amounts to saying that any essential improvement in Negro-white relations, and thus in the quality of American life, is unlikely.

So much for the fireworks. What damage, as I called it, do they do to the writer and his cause—which is also the concern of plenty of others? When Baldwin replaces criticism with prophecy, he manifestly weakens his grasp of his role, his style, and his great theme itself. And to what end? Who is likely to be moved by such arguments, unless it is the more literate Black Muslims, whose program Baldwin specifically rejects as both vindictive and unworkable. And with the situation as it is in Mississippi and elsewhere—dangerous, that is, to the Negro struggle and the whole social order—is not a writer of Baldwin's standing obliged to submit his assertions to some kind of pragmatic test, some process whereby their truth or untruth will be gauged according to their social utility? He writes: "The Negroes of this country may never be able to rise to power, but they are very well placed indeed to precipitate chaos and ring down the curtain on the American dream." I should think that the anti-Negro extremists were even better placed than the Negroes to precipitate chaos, or at least to cause a lot of trouble; and it is unclear to me how *The Fire Next Time,* in its madder moments, can do anything except inflame the former and confuse the latter.

1963

Later
Portraits
and Comment

Henry James
and
The Wings of the Dove

I

Chapter 30 affords us one of the most memorable scenes in *The Wings of the Dove*. We remark in it the kind of vision which, apprehending all things in their likenesses as well as their differences, gives the novel its peculiar scope and power.

Densher stands with Eugenio on the water steps of Milly Theale's rented palace alongside the Grand Canal in Venice. Eugenio, her majordomo, has just let Densher know that her door is now shut to him. The lady is a "leetle" fatigued, says Eugenio; but his smug smile tells Densher that there has been "a rupture of peace" between Milly and himself. He suspects that she is greatly disaffected where he is concerned, and that if she is fatigued, it is because she is, in all probability, mortally ill. Realizing all that he has done to hasten, or at least embitter, her end, Densher feels the furies of remorse begin to stir in him—they have lurked there all the time. And just as the furies stir within Densher, so the bad autumn weather rages around the two men on the water step.

> It was a Venice all of evil that had broken out for them alike, so that they were together in their anxiety, if they really could have met on it; a Venice of cold, lashing rain from a low black

sky, of wicked wind raging through narrow passes, of general arrest and interruption, with the people engaged in all the water-life huddled, stranded and wageless, bored and cynical, under archways and bridges.

Disconsolately Densher wanders away into the piazza San Marco. Like the rest of Venice, this great public square, open at one corner to the lagoon, seems threatened by the elements.

There were stretches of the gallery paved with squares of red marble, greasy now with the salt spray; and the whole place, in its huge elegance, the grace of its conception and the beauty of its detail, was more than ever like a great drawing-room, the drawing-room of Europe, profaned and bewildered by some reverse of fortune.

So far the scene has consisted of the impressions made upon Densher's agitated mind by his encounter with Eugenio and by the spectacle of stormy Venice. But now, in the piazza, the scene is brought to a sudden climax by his encounter with another and more fateful individual than Eugenio. Behind the window of Florian's cafe, reading the *Figaro*, sits Lord Mark, who feels Densher's eyes on him and stares rudely back. Lord Mark's presence in this city at this unfashionable time of year can mean only one thing. He has come to inform Milly of Densher's secret engagement to Kate Croy, thus making known to her, incidentally, the conspiracy against her heart and fortune originated by Kate and carried out, with whatever reluctance, by Densher. No wonder Milly's door was closed to him. His worst fears, for her and for his own sense of honor, are confirmed, and he assumes all the responsibility for his actions. In his distress, however, his consciousness has been expanding to include, and to color with its own dark hues, whatever he has seen: people, storm, Venice. Thus the Venetian servant, the English nobleman and the English gentleman (Densher) are all felt by him to be "together in their anxiety, if they really could have met on it." All have entertained designs on Milly's money, in their different fashions and degrees. And the glances Densher has exchanged with them have conveyed his sense of their mutual complicity.

Similarly with the storm in Venice. It is no cosmic shake-up, like the storm on the heath in *King Lear.* It is only the mistral, the penalty for staying on in Venice too late into the autumn. Its significance is relative to the place it occurs in and the man who observes it. The place is this unique city, a product of the combined forces of man and nature. Venice, rearing the delicate monuments of its elaborate civilization from the mud of several small islands in the sea, has long defied the elements. It has thus tempted others besides Densher (and James) to see it as a symbol of all civilization, so heroic and so precarious. More than that, generations of tourists have noted, as Densher notes, that the piazza San Marco has something about it of an elegant interior. The piazza is wet now with spray from the lagoon and to Densher's expansive consciousness it is "the drawing-room of Europe, profaned and bewildered by some reverse of fortune." Nothing in the whole chapter fixes the scene more securely in Densher's mind—and incidentally, in James's vision—than this image. It was in Milly's Venetian drawing room that the plot against her was proposed to Densher by Kate Croy. It is the drawing room in general which is the human center of James's vision as a novelist. What happens in the drawing room is for him the index of the state of morals and manners in society at large. And if Densher's image proliferates extravagantly to include "Europe," that fact too has its natural causes. He is a journalist whose specialty, it appears, is reporting on international manners for his London paper. Having first known Milly while he was on duty in New York, he is uniquely conscious of her nationality and the differences in outlook it implies to the English. If Lord Mark reads the *Figaro*, as Densher notes, Densher himself is capable of converting the stormbound piazza from a symbol into a subject for gloomy editorializing. Will all of Europe experience the fate of Venice, once the capital of a vast maritime empire, now chiefly a showplace for visitors?

The question is no less important because it is Densher's and is tacit. James has written the entire scene in such a way as to combine a sense of the differences of things with a sense of the likenesses; and while entering deeply into the processes of Densher's mind, he has preserved the distinction between subjective and objective phenomena. The things Densher has observed are not simply projections of his agitated consciousness. He is not Gerontion: the universe, far from being devoured by his subjectivity, remains intact, solid, capable of accusing him and making him humble. According to James's lights, extreme subjectivity is the ego's last stand, its most desperate and at the same time most effective maneuver. Densher's distress, the basis of his future repentance, would be invalidated if he should seek to devour or be devoured by the universe. That is just what Gerontion does when, "a dull head among windy spaces," he dreams of the wind conveying him and all his acquaintances to a blissful annihilation.

> . . . De Bailhache, Fresca, Mrs. Cammel, whirled
> Beyond the circuit of the shuddering Bear
> In fractured atoms.*

---

* T. S. Eliot, *Collected Poems 1909–1962* (Harcourt, Brace & World, Inc., 1963).

It is essential to James's art and mind that Densher should seek redemption rather than annihilation.

II

Spelling out in this way some of the meanings in a great passage of *The Wings of the Dove* is not, I hope, superfluous. James's prose, here as in the two other novels of his last great period, *The Ambassadors* and *The Golden Bowl*, invites such attentions. While retaining the rhythms of prose, his language has the dense suggestive power of poetry. It is a true *medium* in the dictionary sense: "a substance through which a force acts and an effect is produced." The force, James's creative vision, unifies things even while it discriminates among them. He had always sought to do this in his work; he does it with supreme confidence in the trio of last novels. Like the others, *The Wings of the Dove* has its faults. It is "perhaps vitiated by the effort to comprehend more than it contains," as James himself said about another of his late works. He can be, at times, as tiresomely solicitous of his story as Milly's physician, the ineffable Sir Luke Strett, is of Milly. The "effort to comprehend" is nevertheless abundantly rewarded in the late novels. They comprehend much more of things, from storms in Venetian exteriors to sex in Venetian bedrooms, than his earlier work had done. And with all that, James remains faithful to his original conception of the novel, as taught him above all by Balzac. Balzac's principal subject, *les splendeurs et les misères du monde*, remains James's principal subject; and nowhere in his work is the World, its beauty and terror, better presented than in *The Wings of the Dove*.

To be sure, the book comes to us trailing clouds of firsthand documentation that suggests a variety of possible readings.

The documentation includes entries in his notebooks, letters to friends, a preface, and a pregnant allusion in his auto-biography, all bearing on the origins and aims of *The Wings of the Dove* as James saw them. It is a useful body of data but it can be misleading. Taken literally, it leaves large parts of the actual novel insufficiently accounted for, especially the role of Kate Croy. Taken sentimentally, it makes *The Wings of the Dove* a contribution to the literature not of the novel but of the personal elegy.

The idea for the book unquestionably originated in an elegiac impulse on James's part. He tells the story in the moving final chapter of *Notes of a Son and Brother* (1914), the second installment of his autobiography. The fate that was to be Milly Theale's was suggested to him by the actual death, in 1870, of a beloved young cousin, Minny Temple. Minny Temple succumbed to tuberculosis after a protracted strug-gle, remaining throughout as eager for life as she was talented for it. Lively, intelligent, affectionate, she kept to the end that quality of goodwill, that habit of thinking well of life, whatever it brought, which for James typified American "innocence" and which he would attribute to many of the American girls portrayed in his fiction. Yet "death, at the last, was dreadful to her; she would have given anything to live," he wrote; and for him and his brother William her extinction had meant "the end of our youth." So far as James's emotions were concerned, however, it was not the end of Minny Temple. The image of her premature death "was long to remain with me." It "ap-peared so of the essence of tragedy that I was in the far-off aftertime to seek to lay the ghost by wrapping it, a particular occasion aiding, in the beauty and dignity of art." He doesn't name the occasion but it could only have been the writing of *The Wings of The Dove*.

But James makes clear that it was Minny Temple's "situation," her living under mortal sentence, that inspired Milly Theale. As personalities, the real girl and the fictional one have little in common. Milly has less intellectual curiosity and homely humor than Minny, and she has much more money. What did evidently survive in the novel, besides the "situation," was the complex of feelings stirred in James by his cousin and her death. These feelings, which he communicated in his letters of the time with unusual abandon, combined grief and guilt, a sense of identification with the dead and sense of detachment from her. It may have been these emotions, rather than Minny herself, that constituted the "ghost" he sought to lay by writing the book. Read as an allegory of James's psychic life, in respect to other women he had known as well as to Minny, the book would yield a lush picture of contradictory and compensatory passions, with Densher very much in the foreground.

But *The Wings of the Dove* is not a psychic allegory any more than it is a work of the graveyard school of fiction. Whoever or whatever the ghost was, James really exorcised it, really wrapped it in the beauty and dignity of art. He entered fully into the passions of all the principals, and not least into those of Kate Croy, whose commanding presence in the novel, corrupted though she is, is one guarantee of its objectivity. Milly Theale, it is true, is wrapped in a peculiar piety. James's preface asserts that her situation is primary and that the other situation, Kate's and Densher's, came to him as a result of his search for a "dramatic action" which would bring out the "values" in the primary one. Two notebook entries for 1894, at which date he first sketched the plot of the future book, document this search in detail. By reason of her illness, he says, his heroine is peculiarly vulnerable. The dramatic action can only consist, then, in her falling into some kind of serious, possibly fatal, entrapment. What he doesn't say, but seems to mean, is that this entrapment should reproduce in human terms the harsh, impersonal, and arbitrary fate under which she labors in her illness. He does say, however, that the dramatic action must be such as to allow her to live significantly while awaiting death. In other words, she must be able to love and be loved, thus playing a decisive part, however briefly, in a representative community, however selective, of men and women. In thus seeking an appropriate action, James arrives at the *other* principal situation of the novel, the liaison of Densher and Kate and *their* fatal disability, the need of money.

He may seem to have stacked the cards still more in Milly's favor by making her enormously rich as well as good and charming. And his remarks in the preface on the subject of Milly's part in the disaster are not illuminating. "I saw the main dramatic complication much more prepared *for* my vessel of sensibility (Milly) than by her—the work of other hands (though with hers imbrued too, after all, in the measure of their never not being, in some direction, generous and extravagant, and thereby provoking)." But "generous" and "extravagant" don't mean the same thing, and there remains the question of how much and in what way Milly's use of her wealth is "provoking." The "poor little rich girl" of reality, as distinct from romance, is, one thinks, as likely as not to hang onto her wealth, with a grip all the tighter, perhaps, because she hasn't earned it. Indeed Milly's wealth is presented—deliberately, no doubt—as being of a peculiarly American kind: vast beyond all common deserts or expectations, dazzlingly gratuitous, a windfall from the benign tree of American plenty. And is it not just this kind of wealth which, perversely, is apt to beget in its possessors a heightened fear of losing it, as if to do so were tantamount to forfeiting God's grace and one's position among the elect? To reason in this way, however, is to arrive at another and equally untenable idea: that the rich are necessarily in the wrong simply by being rich. Implicitly, James is always attacking this idea—which is not uncommon among the non-rich!—just as he attacks the assumption that Americans are innocent by birthright. In any case, Milly's windfall, much as it tempts Kate Croy to do her wrong, ought not to lead the reader into doing likewise. Indeed Milly's goodness, even unto and after death, little though it may accord with one's ideas of the social "realities," is to be understood in the light of James's general moral assumptions.

These belong, as he repeatedly implied, to the realm of the ideal as much as to the realm of the real. And it is toward the ideal realm of conduct that *The Wings of the Dove*, like other of his more elaborate writings, inevitably moves. Ultimately, he is no ironic observer of the spectacle presented by the miseries and splendors of the World. A story must have a denouement; a dramatic situation must work itself out in a morally meaningful way. Existence in the World must transcend itself, not through any appeal to religion or philosophy but through the capacity of single, rare individuals to reflect and to act in such a way that the best elements of existence are separated from the worst. It is a hard process and is usually confirmed by the forfeiting of some material or egotistical advantage, such as revenge (Milly) or money (Densher). Thus James, severe moralist though he is, remains within what he conceives to be the true locale of the novel, namely the World. His "saints" are to be found, not in the monastery or on the land or among the working classes—or in any of the other purlieus of sanctity offered by other novelists—but in the drawing room.

III

The World and its ways provide *The Wings of the Dove* with a large part of its interest. While Milly Theale wins a well-deserved moral victory over the other characters (after her death!), most of them stoutly hold their own as dramatic creations. They do so, as exemplified in the Venetian storm scene, by being shown in all the intricacy of their relations—with one another and with the cities, houses, streets, parks, and museums which make up their various milieus. And if Densher remains comparatively dim until the crisis in Venice, failing to show even the courage of his weakness, and forcing James into surreptitious apologies and explanations for his hero's conduct (Densher, one thinks, is a modern "anti-hero" without knowing it), it is because he has no moral counterpart, or foil, among the other characters. Lord Mark, a possible candidate for that role, is too insubstantial to fill it.

But Mrs. Lowder and Mrs. Stringham make a perfect pair. Old school friends, reunited after these many years, the insensitive British hostess and the susceptible New England lady novelist, both widows, begin by suggesting a study in black and white. But gray comes to be the predominating color scheme when we know them well. Mrs. Lowder has the advantage of being exactly what she seems to be. No part of her, including her taste for bulky furniture, is at odds with the other parts. Thus she can be coped with by her antagonists, even as she copes with them. Like the net on the tennis court, she is essential to the exertions and pleasures of the game. The queer friendship between Mrs. Lowder and Densher, who might well be her "pet young man" if he were not so dangerous, is one of the rewards, for the reader, of her candid Britannic effrontery. But Susan Shepherd Stringham, who is much more high-minded, is for just that reason more problematic. She is Milly's thoroughly kind and solicitous companion and friend, wanting, and apparently getting, nothing for herself in the way of large material benefits. She is nevertheless a refined example of the insidious workings of mixed motives. These are probably implicit in her very position as companion to an indulgent American heiress—one, moreover, who, described as succeeding to the title of "heir of all the ages" formerly held by the young Englishman of "Locksley Hall," seems to her to be enacting a role positively heroic. But Mrs. Stringham also belongs to a long line of Jamesian "romantics," people whose expectations of life have been formed by literature and who, unable to realize those expectations for themselves, tend to live vicariously off the exploits of others. A writer of stories, Susan Stringham is said to have the distinction that she has "taken New England out of the kitchen"—taken it, presumably, into the parlor. Thanks to Milly, she is able to establish herself in the best drawing rooms of London. Thanks, too, to her own efforts. For it is she, presumably, who has informed Mrs. Lowder by letter of her companion's wealth, thus assuring Milly and herself of the overwhelming welcome extended to them by the London lady and her niece on their arrival in that city. It is Mrs. Stringham's exuberant fancy, too, which envelops Milly in all the panoply, so cruelly ironic in the circumstances, of a "princess"; and the princess, it is to be noted, confides in her companion less and less as time goes on. Meanwhile, Mrs. Stringham finds other confidants. Above all Densher, whose advances to Milly she encourages even after she is aware of his real intentions. All this she does from the best motives, of course, believing that love, even pretended love, may save Milly. Thus she really has as little true knowledge of love as Kate Croy has. To the New England novelist, love is a simple medicament of the soul. To the London girl it is a kind of venture capital to be risked in the expectation of enormous future profits.*

"Did he who made the Lamb make thee?" inquires Blake in "The Tyger." The answer for James as for the poet is yes, although it is not expressed in religious terms. Milly, the lamb (or in James's symbolism, the dove), is the necessary counterpart of Kate, who is envisioned by Milly as having the strength and beauty of a tigress. The two are inevitable counterparts in the social creation, even though, individually, each is morally responsible for her actions. The essential differences between them are given prominence by the fact that the two girls have much in common, including their mutual affection and admiration. Each in her own way enjoys a "talent for life"; both love the same man; and just as one kind of curse hangs over Milly, so another kind hangs over Kate. The product of a society that holds the possession of riches to be a necessity, Kate is without real funds; and her sense of deprivation is made worse by the spectacle of her father and sister and their "failure of fortune and of honor." The awesome irony of Kate's career is, of course, that she too will undergo a similar failure through her very efforts to escape it, forfeiting the love of Densher into the

---

* See Sister M. Corona Sharp, *The Confidante in Henry James*, for a discerning study of Mrs. Stringham.

bargain. Meanwhile, she has been portrayed by James with infinite fascination and understanding, the kind of understanding which leads, not to forgiveness—there's no question of that—but to pity and, as I say, a certain awe.

Kate, more than Milly, is the tragic protagonist of *The Wings of the Dove*. Her tragedy consists not only in the loss of certain tangible advantages but in the destruction of her superior character. How remarkable her character originally is appears in her refusal of an easy success by way of marriage to Lord Mark, in her determination to have money *and* love, in her appreciation of Densher's fineness of mind, in her almost clairvoyant insight into other people's motives. And these qualities are reflected in her personal beauty and poise. But she has too much imagination to play the exclusively social part for which, in other respects, she seems admirably cut out. Kate, too, is a "romantic," determined to create her own role according to her own ideas of greatness rather than enact the one put in her way by convention and Mrs. Lowder. Thus she is intensely active in the pursuit of her destiny, and begins by trying to come to terms with Lionel Croy in the first scene of the novel. But her repeated cries of "Father!" by which she tries to seize his attention only provoke the most unpaternal cynicism from this brilliant portrait of total perversity. From the scene between father and daughter stems the desperation that undermines Kate's character. Her hunger for success on her own terms will turn more and more into a subtle, thoroughly intelligible but nevertheless tigerish, hunt for prey. Just as her father has insisted on lending her to Mrs. Lowder for his advantage, so she will seek to traffic in the affections of Densher and Milly for the profit of Densher and herself. And Kate, who has been urging Densher throughout to "leave things to her," must finally leave to him the hardest task, that of making the decisions and sacrifices by which life in the World is enabled to transcend itself. Thus her extraordinary qualities have been perverted and her very clairvoyance has come to serve the ends of intrigue. To Kate, however, are given not only the first words in the book but the last ones, spoken to Densher: "We shall never be again as we were." Kate, who has always been clarifying things for him, here shows herself capable of clarifying the final situation between the two of them, at whatever terrible cost to her future. It is her proudest and saddest moment, the ultimate fusion of the splendor and misery of the World.

1964

Samuel Butler
and
The Way of All Flesh

The Way of All Flesh is one of those books that come down to us trailing a legend. In this case the legend has a real bearing on the nature of the book. One of the features of the legend has to do with the manner of the book's composition and belated appearance in print. *The Way of All Flesh* was written in spurts during the years 1873–84. It was not published until 1903, the year following its author's death at the age of sixty-seven. Once in print *The Way of All Flesh* was pronounced by Bernard Shaw "a great book." Alive, Samuel Butler had been known, insofar as he was known at all, as a sort of curiosity-about-town (the town of London). The deceased now became abruptly famous.

In all the English speaking countries (the book has had no great reputation elsewhere), advanced young men and women devoured *The Way of All Flesh*. Certain of them went on to write their own novels of adolescence. These novels were mostly inferior imitations of Butler. Only in *Sons and Lovers* and more directly in *A Portrait of the Artist as a Young Man* were Butler's materials—religion and family, repression and freedom—made into finer stuff. These greater books did not "supersede" *The Way of All Flesh:* supersession is rare in literature, which is ideally made up of entities unique and hence by definition irreplaceable. Butler's book thrived on what V. S. Pritchett has called the "parricidal fury" released by the First World War, and its fame continued on into the early 1920s. After that, as I make out, *The Way of All Flesh* faded somewhat. Fatigued by so much attention, it became a book with a past. It was retired to the sanctuary reserved for minor classics. More complex novels, such as those by Joyce and Lawrence mentioned above, captured the estimation of advanced people. Butler himself, formerly admired for his cranky independence of mind, fell victim to the new tyranny of "tradition," Marxist or Eliotist.

By the mid-1930s Butler and his works were carrion for the debunker, who appeared in the person of the English writer, Malcolm Muggeridge. Mr. Muggeridge's biography of Butler, *The Earnest Atheist*, made of its subject a dreary fool. Butler's sufferings, which had been extreme, were made to look painfully absurd, like those of some clown, Malvolio or Caliban, whose sensibility exceeds the requirements of his station; while the scandal, as it then was, of Butler's probable homosexuality was summed up in the image of two gray beards wagging under a single sheet. *The Earnest Atheist* carried debunking so far that it ended by debunking itself. It excited more disbelief than indignation. For the knowing, moreover, the book concealed an inside joke of some positive consequence for Butler's standing: the author of *The Earnest Atheist* was *himself* in the line of descent from Butler—the Butler, for example, of that remarkable conjuring act, *The Authoress of the Odyssey*. In both writers was the same relentless hunting instinct, the same mischievous rapture in revealing some awful truth, the same skillfully hewn and hyper-confident prose. *The Authoress of the Odyssey* is one of the books in the Butler canon that most excites ridicule; and the discipleship of a Muggeridge was not in itself a boon to

Butler's reputation. Readers of *The Earnest Atheist* were nevertheless reminded of how pervasive the influence of Butler had once been and still was. Traces of his mind and manner could be found in such writers as Shaw himself, Lytton Strachey, H. L. Mencken, Norman Douglas, Robert Graves, and, in certain moods, Edmund Wilson. Butler, it was seen, had himself helped to father a "tradition" in twentieth-century writing, the tradition of ironic iconoclasm.

Thus began the gradual and partial rehabilitation of Samuel Butler and his writings. The recent critical literature devoted to him is extensive and much of it is good, taking the author on his own terms and clarifying those terms in such a way as to make them interesting in themselves. Rarely does one encounter in the Butler criticism those methods of instant modernization which have been used on Dickens and other Victorians. Once only, so far as I know, has the method been tried on Butler. Ernest Pontifex has been called by someone a precursor of our contemporary anti-hero.

If true of Ernest, the designation of anti-hero applies equally to Butler. He was by turns, or in perpetual combination, a hero and an ass. But he was a much more formidable figure than Muggeridge makes him out to be, formidable even in his foolishness. And some account of his life and personality is now due here. In Butler's case a bit of biography can be really useful.

The legend of *The Way of All Flesh* includes the following considerations: how Butler came to write the book in the first place; why the writing of it was stretched out over so many years; why, having at last finished off the final third of it in haste and apparently with distaste, he left that part unrevised and also left the whole manuscript to be edited and published after his death by a literary executor; and finally, why the story undergoes such violent changes of substance and quality in the course of its telling. In all this we have one of those mysteries, or cases of deliberate mystification, which in Butler as in other Victorians have aroused the hunting instinct of posterity. With Butler though, the underlying, the essential, mystery concerns the *general* relationship of the man Butler to his work and to his very vocation as a writer. Such relationships are proverbially complex. In Butler, the man and the writer were entangled as the drowning man is entangled with his rescuer, that is, with an urgency far beyond the average. And a few, at least, of the reasons for this extreme interdependency can be suggested here in simplified form.

Butler tried to be three different things at once: first, a critical continuator of the clerical tradition embodied in his father and grandfather, distinguished clergymen of the Church of England; second, a get-rich-quick operator; and third, an artist (painter, composer of music, writer). Each of these functions—the clerical, the financial, the artistic—had, we know, a secure existence within the fabric of Victorian society. Butler wasn't, like such contemporaries as Sir Richard Burton, seeking to create for himself new and *outré* roles. His oddness consisted in his determination to combine in his own person three established ways of life which, given the increasing tensions in late Victorian society, were becoming mutually incompatible, even antagonistic. Behind Butler's ambition to excel in these three occupations was his extravagant ambition to excel in general. Just whom, and what, he sought to excel are much in evidence in *The Way of All Flesh*. They were, of course, his parents, in particular his father, and their entire mode of life.

Especially gratifying to the reader and persumably to the author of the novel are those occasions on which Theobald

Pontifex is put down, whether by the headmaster of Roughborough School in whose affairs Theobald tries to interfere, or,
eventually, by Ernest himself as he emerges from prison. For
Butler's reaction against his oppressive upbringing was
intensified by the fact that his chief oppressor was a very
limited man. Like Theobald, Canon Butler was a zealous au-
thoritarian who proved rather obtuse when it came to exercising his authority.* That a man could be equally bossy but
more imaginative, humorous, and flexible about it is shown,
in *The Way of All Flesh*, by the figure of the Roughborough
headmaster, Dr. Skinner, who with his flagrant yet disarming
vanity is one of Butler's triumphs of characterization: the Victorian Public Man, educator and author *in excelsis*.

Unlike the tortured Theobald and—we assume—the tortured Canon Butler, Dr. Skinner is a man *blessed* in his responsibilities. He luxuriates in them and in the attendant
habit of giving profound and conspicuous thought to decisions
big and little. " 'What will you take for supper, Dr. Skinner?'
said Mrs. Skinner in a silvery voice. He made no answer for
some time, but at last in a tone of almost superhuman solemnity, he said, first, 'Nothing,' and then 'Nothing whatever.' "
But a mind so active as Dr. Skinner's mind is unable to rest
with this initial decision, impressively Spartan though it is. He
goes on to apply the whole of his great soul to the question of
supper and at length comes up with a qualification, "Stay—"
he says to Mrs. Skinner, "I may presently take a glass of cold
water—and a small piece of bread and butter." And of
course—the situation is familiar in comedy as in life—he ends
by consuming several substantial dishes and then calling for

---

* Butler's correspondence with his father, much of which survives, shows Canon
Butler to have been distinctly lacking in affection but generally more patient and
reasonable than his embattled son realized.

hot water and gin. Dr. Skinner's jaunty mastery of life is the despair of Theobald.

The heritage of his family experience was a riot of contradictory impulses on Butler's part. The authority he detested in his father he also coveted for himself. His distrust of sex and of love was matched by his hunger for sex and love, his hope of success by his anxiety lest success fail to materialize. In the guerrilla warfare that was his life, therefore, strategies of offense mingled curiously with those of defense and simple evasion. He was at once truculent and timid, tender and nasty, furtively feminine and aggressively masculine, brilliant and foolish. The harsher the conflicts in his soul, the more he was driven to resolve them into Ideas. Ideas were manageable as feelings were not. Ideas could be bisected into opposing principles and played off against one another, divided and ruled. In the best parts of *The Way of All Flesh* such dualities make for more or less realistic drama: Old Pontifex versus his descendants, Theobald versus Dr. Skinner. In the later stretches of the novel the pairing tendency becomes mechanical. The relations of Towneley to Pryer, of Miss Maitland to Miss Snow are those of Morality figures, and the last third of the novel is chiefly parable or didactic allegory.

To see Butler's situation in this way is to overintellectualize it. Butler suffered. For much of his life he was in Hell, the peculiarly atrocious kind of Hell that we partly make for ourselves. His evasive maneuvers render him at times ridiculous. His torments nevertheless refuse to be scoffed away. So do his very evasions and compromises, even though he did invite the derision of future biographers by giving those maneuvers the Darwin-derived term of "adaptations," thus transferring them from the realm of morals and aesthetics to that of biological necessity.

In certain critical situations he *was* the hero. He performed what Henry James would have called, with appropriate solemnity, "acts of life." I shall here deal briefly with two such acts, and with a third that seems to me a caricature of the whole procedure. They are, first, his flight from England and its consequences on his return; second, his writing of *The Way of All Flesh;* and third, his preoccupation in later years with what he expected to be his postmortem fame.

These acts seem each to have followed upon years of highly charged but heavily controlled emotion on his part. The preparation for the first of them lasted longest. It embraced his whole, largely passive, boyhood and youth, spent either with his parents at Langar Rectory in Nottinghamshire or at Shrewsbury School and Cambridge. *The Way of All Flesh* is a prolonged demonstration of how children are made capable of suffering without quite knowing it. The elder Pontifexes, and probably the Canon Butlers, were just as repressive of themselves as of their children. Such parents develop peculiar powers of which they are likely to remain unconscious. Their children's feelings can be manipulated to the point where potential resentment is turned into "harmless" states of guilt, resignation, or numb acquiescence. Young Butler's feelings seem to have hovered among these alternatives. They exploded into full consciousness only when Butler, who had been prepared for ordination and a church career at his father's dictation, defied his father and refused ordination. Strong persuasion was applied by that unfortunate gentleman and countered in kind by his son. Young Butler admitted to having lost his faith in dogmatic Christianity. He proposed, moreover, to leave England, settle in New Zealand, and become a sheep rancher. From his shocked father he got a reluctant consent and even some preliminary financial assistance.

Butler's stay in New Zealand lasted nearly five years—long enough to fill his existence there with the hardships, tediums, and satisfactions of existence anywhere. Essentially, though, his New Zealand life was, and remained for him in memory, an extraordinary adventure in freedom. An idealized representation of it, with rapture predominating over hardship, is found in *Erewhon*, especially in the wonderful opening chapters of this satirical romance: the narrator's tough but enchanting journey through lush mountain forests, his first sight of the mysterious Erewhon (meaning Nowhere) from afar, his arrival at the ring of musical statues (their music suggests that of Butler's favorite composer, Handel) on the country's frontier. There follows his gradual immersion in the civilization of Erewhon, where the more detestable English middle-class values of his time are found to be neatly inverted. Meanwhile, in actual New Zealand, Butler succeeded in the unlikely accomplishment of being the proper young Englishman in the Colonies while at the same time going—in a very special sense—native. He proved a shrewd, hard-working developer and exploiter of colonial resources. He also discovered where his true sexual interests lay. Returning to England, he took back with him a considerable fortune and a handsome young man named Charles Paine Pauli. With Pauli, his companion for many years, he shared his fortune (to the extent of a large yearly allowance) and his heart. Presently, too, the New Zealand adventure brought him some public fame as the author of *Erewhon* (1870), a story whose delightfulness is not seriously impaired by the blend in it of Swift and Jules Verne.

This, his first act of life, was to be compromised, though not really canceled out, by various troubles. Butler loved Pauli and for a time believed himself to be loved in return. Eventually there was a calculating coldness on Pauli's part; and on

Butler's there were acute suffering and lasting regret. If homosexuality is the extension of self-love into the physical sphere, the usual problems of the homosexual are worsened when the loved one is made to assume the character of the lover's ideal alter ego. The tyranny of the ideal helped to make havoc of Butler's relations with Pauli. It long blinded him to the fact that he was being ruthlessly exploited by Pauli, who, as he was to suspect after Pauli's death, in 1897, exploited other susceptible men. For Butler, his friend embodied the perfection of manly poise and worldly elegance—qualities which the prickly, inept, unlovely Butler significantly lacked. In *The Way of All Flesh* the Pauli affair came to be represented in the paired characters of Towneley, the perfect gentleman, and Pryer, the priestly satanist and—it is coyly insinuated—the homosexual (Butler coy is Butler at his worst). He was to have other protégés, and presumably more manageable ones, but he seems to have loved Pauli to the end. A sonnet Butler wrote during the year of his own death which is generally thought to be about Pauli has much pathos despite its Petrarchan artifices. The sonnet begins: *"We were two lovers standing sadly by / While our two loves lay dead upon the ground."* But the implication of the whole poem is that Butler's love is *not* dead. And other misfortunes accompanied the Pauli affair. While trying to enlarge his fortune Butler made bad investments and lost most of it. He was again partly dependent on his capricious "will-shaking" father. Nevertheless his spiritual gains remained intact. He had had New Zealand, Pauli, the satisfaction of writing *Erewhon* and of seeing it delight or outrage many readers. The year after *Erewhon* he was to publish *The Fair Haven*, an ironic attack on the Christian cult of miracles. *The Fair Haven* is introduced by a mock biography of its alleged author. This forty-page "Memoir of John

Pickard Owen" is probably Butler's most perfect single performance.

In retrospect, the "Memoir" looks like a preliminary sketch for *The Way of All Flesh*. Butler had decided to attempt a novel and was casting about for a subject. Unknowingly, he was also approaching the hour of his second large victory, or partial victory, over his father, his society, and the elements of contention in his own soul. His writing thus far had already antagonized his parents. After *Erewhon* his father had literally shown him the door. Now in 1873 his mother died. Loving, in his divided way, both parents and especially his mother, Butler traveled to the scene. But Canon Butler's mood was bitterly unforgiving. Annoyed by his son's presence, he resorted to one of those absurdly all-inclusive charges peculiar to the angrier participants in family quarrels at their angriest. He accused Butler of having killed his mother with his writings. We know Butler to have been almost as divided about his writer's vocation as he was about his parents. The father had thus dealt the son a double blow and the son again recoiled in kind. Within weeks he had affirmed the worth of his vocation by deciding upon a subject for his projected novel. The subject would be the somewhat stylized history of his family and himself. With serio-comic logic, Canon Butler had shown that the essence of the family situation, as he knew it, was a mutual hostility verging on the murderous. Butler need have no scruples about writing his father's revelation into his serio-comic novel. This he proceeded to do.

For nearly a year he worked at what was to be *The Way of All Flesh*, completing a first draft of—roughly speaking—the first thirty chapters. The next thirty or so chapters were not written until five years later, and the concluding chapters had to wait several more years (till 1883–84) before he was in a position or in a mood to finish them off. Then followed the mystifying entombment of the manuscript.

What interrupted his work on the novel during those periods of neglect? Business trips, worry over business losses, concern with other literary projects, and inertia born of doubt concerning his powers as a novelist. And why the final entombment? He had been more or less reconciled with his father but still had reason to dread his father's anger and, with it, possible retaliation by way of disinheritance. But his father died in 1886, Butler came at last into a large part of the considerable family fortune, and still there was no exhumation of the novel. Yet Hardy and others were then creating an audience for a deadlier realism in the English novel, and to that audience *The Way of All Flesh* could scarcely have failed to appeal.

The truth seems to be that the later Butler was a changed man—changed as only a man so susceptible to the attraction of opposites could have been. Having his father's money was one thing. The fact that he owed it to the persistence of the paternal instinct in his father, despite all their differences, was another and, emotionally, more impressive consideration. Other evidence exists—we needn't go into it here—of the workings in the later Butler of sentiments reborn and of old values released from the depths of his being. And no human force is stronger than that contained in the reawakened pieties of the aging. Besides, with a good income, a servant, and faithful younger companions he had other things to do than labor at an old manuscript. He could indulge his generosity toward the faithful, his pleasure in sharing with a young companion the services of a genteel prostitute, his love of travel, his detective's zest for hunting down the truth about, for example, the subject of Shakespeare's sonnets or the authorship and the locale of the *Odyssey*. The books that came out of these and other similar quests are often called brilliant, or provocative, or simply Good Fun. To paraphrase Max Beerbohm, they are the kind of books that people like who like that kind of book. Butler's concerns in them seem to me disturbing. They are the concerns, generally speaking, of hangers-on of the arts, people who haven't themselves made it as artists, or who fear they can't, and who therefore turn with added zeal to the scrutiny of the *makers* of art, searching them for instances of plagiarism and forgery, for coded messages to posterity, and above all for false claims of authorship. To such people, artists are at best mystifiers, at worst impostors. As I see it, Butler could not have joined such circles unless he had come to feel, rather deeply, the after-effects of some grand opportunity bungled, something lost in the shuffle of life or refused out of fear, perversity, or whatever. Whether this something was the buried *Way of All Flesh* itself, or, more broadly, the feelings, convictions, and powers implicit in that novel, is probably an academic question.

If he had lost something important, he had hit upon a sort of replacement. This was his ever-deepening conviction of postmortem fame. His *Notebooks* and other literary remains are occasionally eloquent on the subject. He lived with this conviction as he had once lived with his "prospects"— inheritance of the Butler money—although there was now less worrying. At his most confident, this fame was for him a large substantial fact, like some actual mausoleum designed by himself and built at his orders. He could visit the thing at will and walk all around it, admiring, criticizing. It is not too extravagant to say that the projection of himself into the future, grotesque as it looks, was the last of his acts of life.

In performing the act he had the advantage of a substantial body of precedents. Literature since the Renaissance had been greatly modified by the resurrectionary principle—modified alike in spirit and substance. Remarkable works—original, germinating—had been added to the known territory of literature by writers who in their lifetimes had been neglected or wholly unknown. Blake, Stendhal, and the rest, these great resurrected Lazaruses or small unmuted Miltons, had come to constitute a significant phenomenon, almost an institution, of the literary life. To obscure writers, this phenomenon or institution held out the dream of eventual recognition, to readers, the expectation of buried treasure. What may have excited Butler most was the impact of the whole thing on literary officialdom, whose authority it was always tending to undermine. It helped to show up the precariousness of established critical standards and of sanctified reputations. It revealed the folly of those attempts by officialdom to organize literary history according to arbitrary conceptions of *Zeitgeist:* of what constituted the peculiar identity of a given cultural "age," past or present, and therefore (in Ezra Pound's words) of what "the age demanded" of its writers. For Butler the single talent counted for more than the collectivity of talents, just as in biology the occurrence of the "sport" signified more than the existence of species.

As usual, however, he made something uniquely, even absurdly, his own out of the common dream of literary resurrection. In this situation, just as in others, his mental processes combined wild fantasy with stringent logic. He literalized the fantastic or fantasticated the literal. These mental processes have made him peculiarly vulnerable to ridicule. To write about him without irony has never been easy. But the same

mentality kept him going while he lived and has since fascinated both his sympathetic and his hostile critics—all but
the merely churlish ones (Muggeridge was vicious but not
churlish).

He was as vigilant of his future fame as he was of his investments in those railway securities which he believed were
bound to boom. Or to put it another way: he treated the
prospective members of that alleged audience as Victorian
Volpones treated their hopeful heirs. He teased them, indulged in what we might call "reputation shaking," subjected
them to the divide-and-rule policy, and generally sought to
impose his will on posterity. To my knowledge he did not do
what the neglected Stendhal had done: calculate the exact
date of his resurrection. Nor did he, as Stendhal did, cherish
his future admirers, call them by the pet name of "the Chosen
Few," and project upon them all that was magnificent in himself and in his greatest creations—the dying Julian Sorel, the
Sanseverina, Fabrice del Dongo, the Abbess of Castro.
Definitely not. Compared to Stendhal's relations with posterity, Butler's were what good low comedy is to good *opéra
bouffe*. Butler's relations with posterity were summed up in a
poem he confided to his *Notebooks*. "To Critics and Others"
is in free verse and sounds like a soured Walt Whitman. "*O
Critics, cultured Critics! Who will praise me after I am dead
. . . Oh! How I should have hated you!*" His reason for these
exclamatory execrations? The cultured critics "will see in me
both more and less than I intended." They will *over-* praise
him, thus causing a reaction against him in subsequent generations of critics. These later critics "will go for some future
Butler as your fathers have gone for me." He therefore gives
his affection not to critics but to those "Nice People" who will

be sickened by all the fuss about him. He invites them to "neglect me, burlesque me," and ends by associating himself with the Bard. "There is nothing that even Shakespeare would enjoy more than a good burlesque of Shakespeare." Thus did Butler in his strangely pragmatic visions try to rule the roost of the future.

Because *The Way of All Flesh* is so entangled with its legend—its true legend—I have left the detailed discussion of the work to the final pages of this essay. The novel requires, I think, no very extensive or intensive consideration. It speaks for itself, and bluntly.

There are in it no pockets of ambiguity or symbolism inviting exploration by the curious critic. Its virtues, too, are as obvious as its faults, and the faults are many. *The Way of All Flesh* is not for those "lovers of perfection alone" to whom Ezra Pound directed his poems and James Joyce his novels. Nor is it for the lovers of, or apologists for, *im*perfection—those who are inclined to see in faulty workmanship an assertion of the primacy of "life" over "art." In *The Way of All Flesh* there is a lot of "life" but no more than is to be found in Pound's best poems or the novels of Joyce, Conrad, James, and so on back to the chief founder of the novel-as-art line, Flaubert. True, present day readers have been mainly nurtured on the works in that line and on the criticism arising from it. Faced with *The Way of All Flesh*, those readers may have to make certain concessions to its unmannerly conduct—unless they happen to be wearied by the excesses of the modernist novel in its present state of intermittent decadence and therefore turn to Butler's novel with uncritical relief.

As social history the book is certainly not the bombshell it originally was. Our quarrel with the Victorian age has died down in proportion as our quarrel with ourselves has grown more bitter. Profound changes have occurred in the nature of family relationships. The present situation, with children tyrannizing over their parents rather than the reverse (as parents may see it!), could have been invented by Butler himself, the Butler whose satire thrived on the literal inversion of existing values. What guarantees the book's continuing interest is, partly, the truth and the vivacity of the formula underlying his picture of Victorian manners. In satirizing them he is satirizing the very phenomenon of manners. Manners, he shows, are forms of behavior in which the members of a given class participate more or less unconsciously in whatever period of history. Manners therefore exemplify an element of automatism that remains constant in human behavior. "Stay—I may presently take a glass of cold water—and a small piece of bread and butter." The first part of Dr. Skinner's little speech is Victorian gentility at its most precious; it sounds like Matthew Arnold's prose at *its* most precious. The second part is the giveaway: Dr. Skinner is moved by simple animal hunger. The hunger and the impulse to broach it elegantly, as if tipping his hat to a lady he coveted, are both forms of automatism in a man who, as a headmaster and a distinguished intellectual, has every reason to think himself superior to mere habit or animal appetite. For Butler, manners, when observed from the outside or in retrospect, are seen to be necessary and yet in their extreme forms laughable. For Butler as for Proust, the more superior a person thinks he is, the more striking and funny are the manifestations in him of the automaton.

In the rigor of his formula and the relentless irony it gives rise to, *The Way of All Flesh* was in its time exceptional among novels in English. I say "English" because in certain other ways—and ignorant or contemptuous as Butler was of much

English fiction*—it is very much in the English vein. It tempers the severity of its social psychology with overt idealism. The novel begins and ends with what are really Utopian parables: the picture of Old Pontifex's world and the picture of the world of the mature Ernest Pontifex. The former is made believable by a great deal of affectionate detail. The latter, as already noted, is pure didactic allegory. In both, however, the Butlerian irony is largely in abeyance. A natural harmony reigns in Old Pontifex's life, so far as he is concerned. His drawings ("always of local subjects") are remembered by Overton as "hanging up framed and glazed in the study at the Rectory, and tinted, as all else in the room was tinted, with the green reflected from the fringe of ivy leaves that grew around the windows." Similarly with Old Pontifex as a man of property. For him his possessions extend beyond his house, his workshops, and his grounds to include the distant greenwood and the setting sun. Once this natural harmony is shattered, the troubles begin and the irony sets in with a vengeance. Nature, ignored or perverted, avenges itself on most of the Pontifexes, subjecting them to the tyranny of social and biological necessity. George Pontifex, of the second generation, is an agent rather than a victim of this tyranny. Theobald and Christina, of the third generation, are wholly victims and are therefore enveloped by a certain pathos. Their marriage is the result of a union of pure chance (the card game at which she wins from her sisters the right to woo Theobald) and of virtual necessity (the pressures of family, profession, money, etc.).

---

* Butler thought *Middlemarch* "no good at all" and in his *Notebooks* castigates the Dean of Westminster Abbey for having buried Dickens "cheek by jowl" with the great Handel. He seems to have been equally indifferent or hostile to other major English novelists, as well as to the then new French Naturalists with whom, in his ideas of social and biological necessity, he had much in common.

The marriage remains loveless, static, sterile. Christina and Theobald cooperate in preserving domestic order. Each is otherwise locked up in the private world of his own preoccupations, Theobald in his concern with maintaining his position in the world and his authority in the family; Christina in her daydreams of glories beyond such immediate realities. Thus encased, neither of them can do any lasting harm to themselves or others. In the end their actions meet, not with large successes or disastrous failures, but simply with rebuffs.

As applied to Ernest's parents, Butler's irony is thus of a subtle kind. It is not unique with Butler but it is one of his specialties. It distinguishes him from his English predecessors, Dickens and, to a considerable extent, George Eliot, for both of whom decisive acts must have their decisive consequences. The evaporating of this irony is largely fatal to the concluding chapters of the novel. Ernest is exempted from it when he comes into money and embarks on his planned existence. Without underrating the benefits of money in reasonable amounts and to reasonable people, we can't help noting that Ernest has endured much only to learn what his father and grandfather might have told him: that money, especially inherited money, is absolutely vital to the good life. Butler's psychological determinism here vanishes with his irony. Ernest's treatment of his children is notorious among readers of the book. He gives his children into the care of a bargeman's family living on the lower Thames. Butler presents this transaction as a straight-faced parable of the good life, an "experiment in family living." Psychologically interpreted, it has an unmistakably different meaning. Ernest has simply inverted the family pattern, abandoning his children rather than, like the older Pontifexes, smothering them with self-serving care and righteousness. *The Way of All Flesh* ends by being as loveless as it is—except slyly—sexless. Butler evidently lacked the artistic means or the courage to represent sex and love in the intense degree that he had known them himself. But at least he had the sense not to try to attempt what he couldn't do and what, if he *had* attempted it, would probably have come out mawkish and unreal, wrecking the cold but far from frigid irony that gives *The Way of All Flesh* its peculiar distinction.

As narrative art, *The Way of All Flesh* requires further concessions, although these may again be made by some readers quite willingly. The story bumbles along agreeably while defying many of the novelistic refinements that were in force as far back as 1873, when he commenced work on the book. His inexperience in novel-writing may be blamed for some of its faults: after all, *The Way of All Flesh* was Butler's "first novel" as well as his only one. But there may also be a certain element of deliberation in his defiance of sophisticated novelistic procedures. His known opinions on art encourage this assumption. He preferred Giotto's simple solidity to the work of later painters equipped with the sciences of perspective and chiaroscuro. He preferred Handel's open musical forms to the grandiose syntheses of Wagner. And when we look in *The Way of All Flesh* for the "artist" who looms in most novels of adolescence, we don't find him in the ultimate products of family history, the Little Hannos or Stephen Dedaluses or Marcels, but in Old Pontifex, the family's founder and, as we have seen, "natural" exponent of artistic creation.

Whether Butler had a theory about "the novel" or was simply following his instincts is immaterial. What he did in *The Way of All Flesh* was to disintegrate the novel form into what had originally been its constituent elements: the narrative of romance or allegory, the stage play, and the essay or aphorism. What other novelists had labored to fuse he more or less broke up, or at least let fall more or less apart of their own volition. Thus *The Way of All Flesh* has a far-off resemblance to old chronicles of national or local history—episodic, anecdotal, full of documents, real and invented. The documents, such as Christina's death letter and Theobald's bill of particulars regarding the misconduct of the pupils at Roughborough School, are striking in themselves and an innovation on Butler's part. It was taken up by Joyce, say in the "Hell Fire Sermon" of the *Portrait*, and so passed on into modernist fiction and poetry. In this case instant modernization of Butler *is* possible.

Elsewhere it is not. Butler's use of Overton as narrator looks sophisticated. It promises to put needed distance between the author's personality, which we know was insistent, and the materials of the novel, which were largely autobiographical. But Butler's use of his narrator is capricious. Overton's credentials, including his mysterious affair with Alethea Pontifex, are transparent fabrications. He fades in and out, useful only as a mouthpiece for Butler's wisdom and as a fairy godfather to the plot. The narrative, too, is shaky, tending to lapse into single episodes or sequences of episodes or into impromptu performances of virtuosity on the author's part. And his virtuosity in some things was remarkable. He was a wonderful mimic, a wonderful miniaturist in the representation of character and action. These relatively isolated passages are among the best things in the novel.

There is in *The Way of All Flesh*, despite the general grimness of it, a great deal of simple but exquisite "fun," as when Theobald's tendency to think of himself as a martyr to responsibility culminates in his being actually burned—in effigy

—by Theobald's schoolmates. And Butler's performances in the art of mimicry remain irresistible even when they become ends in themselves, interrupting the narrative. Having, for example, hit upon the idea of reproducing George Pontifex's recorded travel impressions, he develops them into a full-scale burlesque of the mawkish impressions of all sentimental travelers in that Byronic age. True, George's sensibility is peculiarly at odds with his real nature, which is severely practical. So his effusions are correspondingly ludicrous. George visits the Great St. Bernard in the Alps, one of the standard stops on the nineteenth-century Grand Tour. There he writes, among other things: "The thought that I was sleeping in a convent and occupied the bed of no less a person than Napoleon, that I was in the highest inhabited spot in the old world and in a place celebrated in every part of it, kept me awake some time."

George also composes some verses for the visitor's book of the Great St. Bernard. Butler manages shrewdly the shift in tone from George's labored poetic solemnity—

> These are thy works, and while on them I gaze
> I hear a silent tongue that speaks thy praise—

to the rude prose of Butler's own ensuing comment: "Some poets always begin to get groggy about the knees after running for seven or eight lines," etc. This might be Huckleberry Finn remarking on the posthumous works of Emmeline Grangerford; and in fact Butler has more affinities, fortunate and unfortunate, with Mark Twain than with any of his English contemporaries. But *The Way of All Flesh* is no such unintentional masterpiece as *Huckleberry Finn* is. The artistic insouciance that Mark Twain shared with Butler seems to have submitted, in Mark Twain, to the control of some angel of relevance who presided over Huck's mental and physical wanderings and kept them firmly in the picture. It was not in Butler's character to invite, or submit to, dictations from above or, for that matter, from below: the "Unconscious" is recognized and called by name in *The Way of All Flesh* but only as an Idea, one of Butler's many Ideas. It didn't supply the author with any subliminal and unifying passion comparable to the passion excited by the realities of death in the Mark Twain of *Huckleberry Finn*.

Butler adds to George's travel impressions some actual outpourings of Mendelssohn's in the Uffizi. These are prodigiously funny in their self-congratualatory spirit. But they have stalled the narrative, forcing from Butler—or Overton—as he resumes the story one of his jolting and, here, grammarless transitions: "Returning to Mr. Pontifex, whether he liked what he believed to be the masterpieces," etc.

Butler's transitional vehicles often sag ominously, as if the whole narrative were about to break down. At one point he briefly describes Mr. Allaby's relief at finally getting Christina married to Theobald and the bridal couple off on their wedding journey. Then Butler writes: "But what were the feelings of Theobald and Christina when the village was passed and they were rolling quietly by the fir plantation? It is at this point that even the stoutest heart must fail," etc. He couldn't have done it better if he had been deliberately parodying the labored locutions of inept novelists. What follows is, nevertheless, one of the great passages in the novel: the long wearisome ride in the carriage, the muted contest of will between the two occupants, poor Theobald's too easy triumph over poor Christina, and the celebration of this triumph by way of the cheery little supper at the inn. The episode might be something out of the artful Flaubert or Maupassant, except that in Butler there is no denouement in the bedroom.

1967

Max Beerbohm and the Rigors of Fantasy

Zuleika (pronounced Zuleeka) *Dobson* was first published in London in 1911. Other editions followed in Britain and America. The book entered the Modern Library early, when the volumes making up that series were still few, and smelled of frivolity, sin, and oilcloth—or whatever those simulated limp leather covers were made of. Like *South Wind, Zuleika Dobson* was obligatory reading for those literary initiates of the Twenties whose program included, on principle, an appreciation alike of the trifler and the titan: Douglas with Dreiser and Dostoevsky, Beerbohm with Proust and Joyce. In *Aspects of the Novel* (1927), E. M. Forster called *Zuleika Dobson* "the most consistent achievement of fantasy in our time." "Our time" meant, presumably, the Teens and Twenties. When the Twenties ended, Beerbohm rather faded from one's consciousness.

After his death, in 1956, came the modest resurrection. Beerbohm lived again in Ellen Moers's *The Dandy*, in S. N. Behrman's *Portrait of Max*, and, more recently and completely, in David Cecil's *Max, A Biography*.* If he was "easy to forget but delightful to remember," as I wrote some years

---

* For the remarks that follow I am much indebted to these books as well as to J. G. Riewald's *Sir Max Beerbohm, Man and Writer.*

ago, he has since proved to be ever harder to forget and more delightful to remember. Rereading Beerbohm one gets caught up in the intricate singularity of his mind, all of a piece yet full of surprises, as one does in Boswell's Johnson. In *Zuleika Dobson* his mind is in full flower, a tropical bloom, lurid and elaborate, prickly but not poisonous, except to the foolish.

That his drawings and parodies should survive is no cause for wonder. One look at them, or into them, and his old reputation is immediately re-established: that whim of iron, that cleverness amounting to genius. What *is* odd is that his stories and essays should turn out to be equally durable. The mandarin of mandarins, Beerbohm wrote with a kind of conscious elegance that has since become generally suspect. This *nouveau riche* English has for us the fault of shamelessly advertising to the world the lush abundance of its verbal resources. The plain declarative sentence is apt to be set off by a dazzle of rhetorical questions and apostrophes to the reader. Ostentatious connectives, from "indeed" to "however that may be," are *de rigueur*. No word is repeated if a synonym can possibly be found. The attack on the mandarin style, carried out variously by such writers as Mencken, Eliot, and Gertrude Stein, made of repetition a virtue. Into the wastebasket went the book of synonyms. The young Yeats had anticipated the new taste for verbal economy when he criticized a sentence about Hamlet in Oscar Wilde's *The Decay of Lying:* "The world has become sad because a puppet was once melancholy." Yeats asked Wilde why he had changed "sad" to "melancholy." "He replied that he wanted a full sound at the close of his sentence, and I thought it no excuse and an example of the vague impressiveness that spoilt his writing for me."

Beerbohm's mandarinism tended to mock itself, subtly or bluntly. Starting a sentence with "indeed" he went on to apologize in parentheses for the "otiose" word. He avoided not only the vaguely impressive but the crudely *ex*pressive. A friend wrote to him praising the sentence about the lightning in *Zuleika Dobson:* "A sudden white vertical streak slid down the sky." Beerbohm replied: "The word 'slid' was in the first draft 'slithered' which, though more accurate really, looked rather *cherché* and so was jettisoned." Thus he profited from the mandarin abundance while generally avoiding or deriding its excesses.

One now reads Beerbohm with recognitions beyond the powers of those of us who were literary neophytes in the Twenties. The elegant trifler contributed more than one had supposed to literary history. Beerbohm played an essential if deliberately minor role in the famous "revolution of taste" that took place between, roughly, 1910 and 1922. True, he was never a "modernist" in his own tastes, preferring the poetry of Swinburne and the novels of Trollope, Meredith, and James to *Ulysses* and *The Waste Land.* Nevertheless, he discovered before Pound and Eliot did (and independently of Laforgue) the futility and pathos of the dandy and his lady. As a verbal caricature of the London literary life, *Seven Men* parallels at several points Pound's treatment of the same subject in *Hugh Selwyn Mauberley. Mauberley* includes a verse portrait of Beerbohm under the name of Brennbaum. The portrait is, appropriately, a verse caricature of Beerbohm as dandy:

> The sky-like limpid eyes,
>   The circular infant's face,
> The stiffness from spats to collar
>   Never relaxing into grace . . .

Naturally, the famous revolution in taste "went too far." In doing so, it has given work to critics and biographers ever liver would spoil the show. A wink from Candide or Alice or Joseph K. or Zuleika Dobson would bring down in rubble the cunningly constructed worlds of unreal reality they inhabit. A total sobriety of tone is the law of laws for fantastic comedy.

For some twelve years (1898–1910) Max Beerbohm wrote a weekly theater article for the *Saturday Review* of London. He was thus exposed to a good deal of trashy fantasy in dramatic as well as narrative form. Even the ballet came to bore him. Much of what he saw or read in this vein seems to have been delinquent in essentially the same way that much of what is today called "black humor" is delinquent. It broke the law of laws: it failed to take itself seriously enough. What he saw or read was not willfully wacky as the worst black humor is at present. For the Kafkan revolution in fantasy, of which black humor is the sometimes depressing offspring—depressing in its merely mechanical frenzies—belonged to the far future. Thus the action of fantasy was not as yet freely generated in the disturbed psyche, where anything goes, as the action of fantasy was as a rule to be for Kafka and his followers. Nor had history itself as yet reached the extremity of mad inventiveness which today leaves the average fantasist far behind and breathing hard.

It was not willful wackiness but mere waggishness that afflicted fantasy during Beerbohm's London years. An air of holiday high jinks, of forced festivity, hung about it. Preeminent of its kind and in its time was *Peter Pan, or the Boy Who Wouldn't Grow Up.* Barrie's play was beloved by many and derided by a few, doubtless for the same reason: it gave the frankest possible expression to the prevailing vogue for half-hearted escapism. Reviewing *Peter Pan* on its first appearance, in 1905, Beerbohm noted that Barrie had always incarnated

since. Rehabilitating the major Victorians and in some cases the Edwardians has long been a reputable occupation. Tennyson, Kipling, and Queen Victoria herself have recovered from the clawings of Beerbohm's velvet glove.

Yet how exhilarating those clawings were at the time. I mean not only such celebrated caricatures as the one of Queen Victoria attending with majestic patience to a shrunken Tennyson reading *In Memoriam.* More devastating were the drawings that caricatured the political or the literary life in general. There was the bitter series called *The Second Childhood of John Bull,* chiefly inspired by Beerbohm's disgust with the Boer War. There was the series called *The Young and the Old Self,* in which eighteen well-known Edwardians were confronted in the fullness of their age and fame by the specters, gloating or reproachful, of their youthful selves. A real *terribilità* plays about the latter series. It could scarcely fail to impress the literary initiates of any period, from the Twenties to the present.

With the foolish in mind, Max Beerbohm added to the 1946 edition of *Zuleika Dobson* a warning against interpretation. Inevitably his remarks recall Mark Twain's admonitory address to the readers of *Huckleberry Finn.* Critics have generally disregarded Mark Twain's threats, sometimes with deplorable results. Taking our chances, we may dismiss Beerbohm's warning, too. It is only part of the "act," the very stagey act that *Zuleika Dobson* is throughout. If first-rate humorists are never to be taken too seriously, they are to be taken least seriously when they are most at pains to warn us against taking them seriously at all.

Beerbohm maintains that his book is "just a fantasy." No satirical or other serious comment is intended. But this is impossible in the nature of his genre as he names it here.

"Fantasy" must have something which to fantasticate, and what can that something be except "reality" or some aspect of it? "Fantasy" is the rather jejune term for a kind of narrative that was uncommon in Western Europe before the eighteenth century. Nobody, I suppose, would call *The Divine Comedy*, *The Faerie Queene*, and *The Pilgrim's Progress* "fantasies." They are allegories in which the events and characters, however implausible themselves, correspond to principles of morality or religious dogma which had a real existence for their authors. The rise of modern fantasy seems to have had a complicated relation, first to the decline of faith in the reality or efficacy of those principles, and second to the advance of "realism" as a literary mode. Fantasy brings into comic question the nature of belief itself. There was the case of the Irish bishop who is alleged to have remarked of *Gulliver's Travels* on its first appearance, "This book is full of improbable lies, and for my part I hardly believe a word of it."

The great fantasies extend from *Gulliver's Travels* to the *Alice* books to the serio-comic writings of Franz Kafka. The great fantasies embrace not only certain aspects of reality but just about all of it, even in some instances God and the gods. The authors make it their business to fantasticate the realities so thoroughly that, presto!, the realities come to look fantastic themselves.

Their business? Good fantasists are the most businesslike of writers. They go about their creative operations as methodically and with as straight a face as the Lilliputians go about taking inventory of Gulliver's pockets. Nor does Gulliver feel surprise, least of all amusement, at their efforts. This exemplary Englishman is only annoyed by the invasion of his privacy. As with Gulliver so with the other protagonists of comic fantasy. They are themselves quite humorless. A grin from Gul-

the prevailing "child-worship" of the period but that in *Peter Pan* he had outdone himself. Barrie was there seen "in his quiddity undiluted—the child in a state of nature, unabashed—the child, as it were, in its bath, splashing, and crowing as it splashes." Puck's doings in *A Midsummer Night's Dream* were "credible and orderly" compared to "the riot of inconsequence and of exquisite futility" that made up Peter Pan's doings.

Nor was Beerbohm himself an infallible master of fantasy. An early example, *The Happy Hypocrite* (1897), has the interest for us of commemorating a significant moment in his development. As J. G. Riewald has shown, the youthful author of *The Happy Hypocrite* was imitating *The Picture of Dorian Gray* while at the same time trying to free himself from Wilde's influence. *The Happy Hypocrite*, in which a devilish dandy is transformed—not without irony on the author's part—into a loving husband, shows Beerbohm asserting his will to innocence and survival against Wilde's presumed will to the opposite fate. An amalgam of the parable and the fairy tale, *The Happy Hypocrite* is nevertheless a strained performance. So is a much later story, *The Dreadful Dragon of Hay Hill* (1928). This seems to have been written to order by "The Incomparable Max"—the title early bestowed, or perhaps foisted, on Beerbohm by a rival wit, Shaw—rather than by Beerbohm himself. By "Beerbohm himself" I mean the Beerbohm in whom the public and the private man, the insider and the outsider, the precocious child and the preternaturally youthful ancient oddly combined to form what I have called his intricate singularity of mind.

This was the Max Beerbohm who did his best writing (*Zuleika Dobson*, *A Christmas Garland*, *Seven Men*, *And Even Now*) between about 1910 and about 1920—years during which he lived for the most part away from England. *Zuleika Dobson* had been begun and dropped as early as 1898. S. N. Behrman, who has examined the early manuscript, notes that it is "scraggly, written in random columns and riddled with doodles"—that is, sketches for caricatures. Here, Behrman says, "You may watch the struggle between Max's dual careers. Often the graphic seems to gain the upper hand." *Zuleika Dobson* was largely written and was brought to completion in 1910–1911 in a charge of energy released by his resignation from the *Saturday Review,* his marriage to Florence Kahn, an American actress whom he had long kept on the string, and their removal to Italy.

In fantastic comedy, many a familiar jest, proverbial saying, or fashionable phrase comes literally true and many a flower of poesy is born to blush for its presumption. One sometimes says of an unfortunate friend, or despairingly of oneself, that he, or one, is subhuman, a rat, a worm, an insect. In Kafka's well-known story, a certain self-despising salesman wakes up one morning to find that he *is* an insect, complete with many wiggly little legs. Not surprisingly, his remarkable feat of self-realization goes unappreciated by the members of his family, and he presently dies of cruelty and neglect at their hands. The death of Kafka's salesman is paralleled, in a purely comic vein, by the fate of Enoch Soames, one of Beerbohm's creations in *Seven Men.* Soames is the harmless author of a small book of verse called *Fungoids* and a small book of essays called *Negations.* He is nevertheless an avowed poet of the Diabolist school, out of Baudelaire by way of Lionel Johnson, and has written such verses as

> Round and round the shuttered square
> I strolled with the Devil's arm in mine.

Eventually, and much to Soames's surprise, the Devil appears in person and makes off with Soames.

In that story, a single victim is claimed by the process I have been trying to describe—let us call it the process of comic literalization. In *Zuleika Dobson* the same mechanism is flagrantly at work and the victims are many. The casual wish is father to the dreadful deed on an unprecedented scale. The cliché bears watching lest it come true with a vengeance. Oxford dons, one learns, have often remarked that Oxford would be a splendid place if it were not for the undergraduates; Oxford undergraduates have expressed identical thoughts concerning the dons. The dons win in *Zuleika Dobson*. One evening, following the final race of Eights Week, they learn that the undergraduates have drowned themselves en masse in the Isis, as the stretch of the Thames at Oxford is known. "And always the patient river bears its awful burden towards Iffley," Beerbohm writes. This flower of poesy begins like a line from "Lycidas" and ends like something in small print in a guide to Oxfordshire. Iffley is the grubby-sounding place where the locks are that make boating possible at Oxford.

Meanwhile, the crew of Judas College has won the present series of races. Its shell has "bumped" the shell of proud Magdalen. At Judas the dons have celebrated the traditional Bump Supper in splendid calm owing to the scarcely noted absence of the Judas undergraduates. Only Mr. Pedby's illiterate reading of the traditional Latin grace has disturbed the occasion. But this mishap is forgiven when it is realized that memories of the ill-read grace will provide chuckles for generations of dons to come. Mr. Pedby has contributed his hilarious mite to the vast cocoon of Oxford history—bloody, scandalous or hilarious—which Oxford is forever weaving for itself.

In all of Judas College, only Zuleika Dobson is at this moment unhappy and restless. She is the young woman, a conjurer by profession, for love of whom, ostensibly, the students have drowned themselves—all but the cad Noaks, who has chosen a belated and grimmer death. Zuleika has made more Oxford history, one would think, than Mr. Pedby has. Yet as an outsider, and a woman at that, she is ignored by the dons and obliged to spy on the Bump Supper proceedings from a balcony.

In Zuleika's career the literalizing principle is written large. She is a *femme fatale* whose brief stay at Oxford has been actually fatal to hundreds. Surely she has set a new high in the records of *femme* fatality, exceeding the combined tolls of Keats's Belle Dame, Swinburne's Dolores, and Wilde's Salomé. One might expect her to be beaten to death with oars as Salomé is with soldiers' shields. She isn't, nor is she herself visited by any feeling except a resentful loneliness, like that of a popular actress who has made one curtain call too many and is suddenly confronted by an empty house. Whither Zuleika? Zuleika asks herself. After such triumphs, what expectations? True, she has had a gratifying talk with her grandfather. The stiff old Warden of Judas has confessed that he was in his youth an *homme fatal* with many female victims to his credit. What has occurred between the two is unmistakably a "recognition scene." It recalls—probably not accidentally—the scene in *Major Barbara* in which the Salvation Army commander and the ruthless old tycoon slyly discover that each is possessed by the Will to Power and that they are therefore father and daughter after all. Zuleika is somewhat cheered by her encounter with the Warden and presently she finds the answer to her Whither. Consulting her bejeweled copy of Bradshaw she orders a special train for—Cambridge. Nothing can stop a fatal woman so long as she believes that somewhere there are more males eager to be fatalized.

Whether she found Cambridge as compliant as Oxford is not known. Beerbohm never composed sequels, except to other men's works (see his "Sequelula to *The Dynasts*" in *A Christmas Garland*). In 1941, however, a Mr. S. C. Roberts produced a sequel of his own, called *Zuleika in Cambridge*. I have not read the book but gather from Riewald's account of it that her visit to the other university disappointed her. Firmly resistant to her attractions was serious Cambridge, the Cambridge of Milton, Wordsworth, and Dr. Leavis. No lovelorn corpses cluttered the patient Cam. Beerbohm did, nevertheless, reveal snatches of her later history by way of a letter signed Zuleika Kitchener and addressed to George Gershwin, who once thought of making a highbrow musical out of her book. In the letter she berated Beerbohm for misrepresenting her in the book and added a postscript saying: "I was married secretly to Lord Kitchener, early in 1915. Being so worried by his great responsibilities at that time, he no longer had the grit to cope with my importunities, poor fellow."

Nothing came of Gershwin's project. Nor did *Zuleika* ever reach the New York stage in the form contemplated, and long worked at, by Wolcott Gibbs and others. They eventually discovered, what might seem obvious from the start to any but the most obdurate of Broadway adapters, that *Zuleika Dobson* would be nothing without the crystalline surface of unreality wrought by the author for the characters and settings of the book. Release these flies from their amber and they would be just dead flies.*

---

*I learn that an agreeable musical version of *Zuleika* was produced in 1954 at Cambridge and then, briefly, in London. It seems, however, to have been more of a "period piece" than a satire.

"In reading *Zuleika Dobson* as a description of life at Oxford we should be well-advised to allow for ironic intention," Northrop Frye observes in his *Anatomy of Criticism*. Not every reader has been able to make that allowance. The outrageousness of the story has made it a problem to some of its interpreters. To Edmund Wilson the part about the mass suicide of the undergraduates is "completely unreal."

What parts of the book *does* Wilson find "real"? What words of *Gulliver did* the bishop believe? Where fantasy is concerned, there is no accounting for people's credulities.

But Wilson is not alone in his objection to *Zuleika Dobson*, and Beerbohm's dehumanizing of his characters does perhaps ask for a bit of explaining. For me, there is only one moment in the book when it is possible to "feel with" any of them. The Duke of Dorset is watching Zuleika's clumsy performance by moonlight and listening to her arch patter ("Well, this is rather queer"). He is so horribly embarrassed for her that he looks with rage on the other young men to whom his beloved is so recklessly exposing herself ("Damn them, they were sorry for her," he thinks). At this point, one guesses, Beerbohm could not help drawing on his own intimate experience as a friend and lover of actresses, ultimately the husband of an indifferent one whose Pre-Raphaelite ecstasies and graces he found laughable, though lovable, even offstage. For the rest, the author kept his distance from the goings-on in *Zuleika*. So much so that he was surprised when his oldest friend, Reginald Turner, wrote him that—to quote David Cecil's paraphrase of the letter—"he found the characters almost painfully real; he believed in Katie the serving maid too much . . . to take her sufferings in the spirit of comedy." To this Beerbohm replied that he "certainly hadn't realized that Katie and those others were at all real," adding that if "really dramatic scenes

. . . without humanity" were possible in the theater, he "never would have admitted this in the *Saturday.*"

The reference to the *Saturday Review* seems conclusive. Much of the "ironic intention" of *Zuleika Dobson,* including the dehumanized characters, stemmed from Beerbohm's experiences as a theater reviewer for that periodical. *Zuleika* is not only about "life at Oxford"; it is about literature, above all the literature of the contemporary London stage, to which Beerbohm had been for so many years "enslaved" (his word) through his connection with the *Saturday.* His reviews show him to have been often sickened by the theater's hackneyed themes, stock characters, trumped-up motivations, transparent mechanics, and false diction. They violated his common sense, they told on his nerves. So did the conduct, professional and private, of certain leading performers: clumsy "conjurers" and would-be *femmes* (or *hommes*) *fatales. Zuleika Dobson* is life at Oxford seen through the eyes of an inveterate "play-goer," some ideally demoralized veteran of the stalls. Beerbohm, it should be recalled, places the action of his story "in the middle of the Edwardian Age," a time when the theater, bad though much of it was, bulked larger as an institution than it ever has since in Anglo-American culture. Our theater today seems hardly important enough to merit satire, as distinct from kidding, at its expense.

A reading of *Around Theatres,* Beerbohm's collected reviews, is, then, more germane to an understanding of *Zuleika Dobson* than is a short history of Oxford, with maps. The Oxford setting creates itself as one reads, especially the Oxford setting in its legendary or sentimental aspects. Here Matthew Arnold's too memorable paragraph (concluding the preface to his *Essays in Criticism: First Series*) about the "home of lost causes . . . and impossible loyalties" does continual comic service. The parodying of Arnold starts with Beerbohm's first paragraph, where it is Oxford's railroad station and not her Gothic towers that "whisper to the tourist the last enchantments of the Middle Age." We soon learn that these enchantments still prevail elsewhere in the University. The Oxford of *Zuleika Dobson* remains "medieval" in its charm as well as in other, less lovable, ways; and it is still chivalrous, to the point of suicide.

Yes, there have been many Oxfords. There was the Oxford of the various religious revivals, with their Ridleys and Latimers, their Newmans and Puseys. There was the neo-pagan Oxford of Jowett and Pater, when bands of undergraduates are reputed to have marched around chanting the choruses of Swinburne's *Atalanta in Calydon*. There was the eighteenth-century Oxford which to the young Gibbon was wholly barbarous. There was the Victorian Oxford which to Walter Bagehot consisted of colleges that were merely "hotels with bells"— refuges for sporting upper-class youths. There is the Oxford of the present, swamped by the Morris motor plant, made democratic and serious beyond Bagehot's dreams, but still beautiful to look at, still whispering its enchantments and sounding its bells amid the tumult of traffic.

The Oxford Beerbohm knew as an undergraduate in the Nineties was, or seemed to him, lushly end-of-century. It made him, he later said, "insufferable," meaning idle, mocking, snobbish, an adherent of Oscar Wilde's cult and that of past dandies, D'Orsay and Disraeli. He claimed that he had read little at the University except Wilde's *Intentions* and Thackeray's *The Four Georges*. The eating clubs he frequented were exclusive, although not quite so exclusive as the fictional Junta, of which it is said in *Zuleika Dobson* that the Duke of Dorset was for a while the sole member. To the young

Beerbohm, abstaining from the more wholesome undergraduate pursuits was an agreeable duty. Once when he was
out for a stroll he encountered a fellow student with an oar
across his shoulder. "Bound for the river?" the student cheer-
ily asked. "What river?" Beerbohm replied.

His reminiscences of his Oxford life are the caricature of a
caricature, the original having been himself. To his role as an
undergraduate he brought an amused self-consciousness. He
made histrionic capital of his short stature, his large head, his
prominent eyes, and the scrutinizing stare of which they were
capable. His whole earlier history predisposed him to amuse
himself and others, and generally to do what he liked at the
University. The belated child of adoring parents, the youngest
by far of an animated circle of siblings and half-siblings, he had
been early initiated into the Great World by his half-brother,
Herbert Beerbohm Tree, already a celebrated actor when
young Max was still at Oxford.

There, as elsewhere later on, he was the outsider-insider,
capable of mocking things he also cherished, including his own
personality. So if he loved Oxford and mocked it only affectionately in *Zuleika Dobson,* as Oxonians tend to say, he loved it
on his own terms. These involved much skepticism, enough to
set flowing the tricky currents of satire in *Zuleika Dobson.*
Here faddishness is seen to flourish in proportion as Oxford
believes itself to be supremely privileged, proudly possessed
of its own history and legality, grotesquely celibate (if that is
the word), and capable of extending to its dons the privilege
of indifferentism toward the undergraduates, toward everything but the dons' own studies and society.

From Christ Church meadow a mist is described as continually rising and permeating the whole place. A prime characteristic of Oxford, the mist is lovingly evoked by Beerbohm.

The passage has become a famous set-piece, but unlike Arnold's set-piece it is full of double-entendres. The mist is seen to enclose Oxford in a circle of glamor, like a soft-focus photograph. It also shelters the place from "reality," like a smoke screen. Zuleika penetrates and scatters this mist—for the reader. Her presence at the University shows us that its precious faddishness, its cherished weakness for lost causes and impossible loyalties, exist plentifully in the world at large, where they are known, less flatteringly, as the "herd instinct" or "conformity." Zuleika's triumph at Oxford is only a specialized form of the triumphs she has enjoyed everywhere, from Paris to "final Frisco." The great dandy, Dorset, adores her, but so did George Abimelech Post, "the best-groomed man in New York." Self-destruction threatens the herd wherever it exists, although the herd may elect to die in more dignified ways than do the swine in the parable. This Beerbohm saw as early as 1911, with an instinct born of his own highly cultivated idiosyncrasy.

It is not because she is "real" herself that Zuleika disperses the mist for us. On the contrary, it is because she is that most potent of forces, a figment of the mass mind. As a conjurer her skill is nil. Nor is she "strictly beautiful," Beerbohm states in a passage that has been analyzed into its multiple equivocations by William Empson in *Seven Types of Ambiguity* (Beerbohm's type in this passage is Empson's sixth).

It is true that Zuleika has, or acts as if she had, a devouring passion. She wants to love—love, that is, a man self-sufficient enough to scorn her love. Naturally, the man eludes her. Nobody will let her play Patient Grizel. The Duke of Dorset matches her in his own lovelessness and in the impossible demands he makes on women. But all these passions are as phantasmal as the two characters themselves are. The passions are "motivations" of the kind forcibly applied to the personages of inferior drama to make their actions plausible. Complaints against the arbitrariness in this respect of Pinero, who finds his motives in the stock room, or of Shaw, who sometimes supplies them from his intellectual laboratory, recur in Beerbohm's theater reviews. So too with those reversals or, as Beerbohm with his mock pedantry calls them, "peripeties," which keep the moral advantage zooming back and forth throughout the long scenes between Zuleika and Dorset. So tangible does this advantage become in its relentless to and fro that it almost materializes as a ball or a brick.

Dorset is more interesting than Zuleika. He is "motivated" by more than his need to love—by his obligations as a great nobleman and dandy. The Duke is no fraud in these particulars as Zuleika is in her conjurer's role. He is just what he claims to be: the sum of all those titles, residences, servants, decorations, accomplishments, and clothes. Among his accounterments are the pair of owls that have always announced the coming deaths of Dukes of Dorset. The owls really appear on the battlements of Tankerton; they hoot *this* Duke of Dorset to his doom, even in the age of prepaid telegrams. For the other undergraduates he sets the styles of dressing, of loving, and of dying. As a stage duke, Dorset is complete.

The Noakses and Batches are also complete, as stage plebeians. Noaks is a "foil" to the over-privileged Duke. As such he may briefly arouse our democratic sympathies. But his sentiments are soon discovered to be as heavy as his boots and the iron ring he wears to charm away rheumatism. The plebeian creations of Shaw, the great humanitarian, often surprise us by turning out to know their place: the clownish place traditionally reserved for members of the lower orders, from Dogberry to Doolittle. Nor, one suspects, are Zuleika's French maid, Mélisande, and the American Rhodes scholar, Abimelech V. Oover, "strictly" caricatures; they are, again, caricatures of caricatures: the stage French maid and the stage American.

To what in the story itself apart from the mass suicide does Edmund Wilson's cry of "unreal" *fail* to apply? To nothing, I fear. Our demoralized playgoer has "seen everything," the London theater's entire "offering." Not for the world would he have missed the fashionable performances of Greek tragedy in Gilbert Murray's florid English, complete with inverted syntax and doubled negatives, with messengers, *dei ex machina*, and choruses. The busts of the Roman emperors outside the Sheldonian Theater afford *Zuleika* a peculiarly original chorus, helpless, solicitous, whimpering with pity, sweating with fear.

Not that the patent unreality of the story doesn't occasionally pall. Beerbohm's achievement in the art of fantasy is here possibly *too* consistent. The lengthy speechifying, the tireless parodying of motivations and peripeties, make certain scenes tedious. For the wary reader, however, the tedium is continually relieved by all sorts of "tricks" on the author's part—puns, double-entendres, dissonances, parodies within parodies, lyrical set-pieces in the descriptive or historical mode, intrusions of the supernatural, brief realistic "shots," so to speak, as of Zuleika applauding at the concert with her hands high above her head like the thorough professional she is. The ironic vision is, moreover, apt to shift its objects abruptly from one type of stage convention to another. Our playgoer gets his Maeterlinck mixed up with his Wycherley. Romance envelops the moonlight walk of Zuleika and Dorset to her quarters in Judas after the concert and her own im-

promptu performance, the latter a great scene. But crude
farce breaks in when, from her bedroom window, she dumps
on the Duke's waiting figure the contents of a water pitcher
(read chamberpot).

Romance is a recurring attraction in *Zuleika*. The moonlight, the floating mist, the nodding lilacs and laburnums, the
weedy bottom of the Isis—all are summoned on stage from the
greenwood of English pastoral tradition. They remain lovely,
though invariably touched with mockery—the mockery of the
purple patch, of eloquence itself. Eloquence itself, high or
low, is another motif. There are speaking parts for all: the
flowers, the bells, the stony Emperors, together with the
more or less human beings. And oh, the things people *say!*
Nothing in *Zuleika Dobson*, I find, stays in the memory better
than the things people say in it. "She doesn't *look* like an
orphan" (the wife of the Oriel don referring to Zuleika). "By
God, this college [Judas] is well-named" (Sir Harry Esson,
betrayed by a former Warden, as he is stabbed and dies).
"Death cancels all engagements" (The Duke of Dorset). "What
harm has unrequited love ever done?" (Zuleika). "I say he was
not a white man" (Oover of a legendary Oxford libertine). "I
don't know anything about music, but I know what I like"
(Zuleika). "*Je me promets un beau plaisir en faisant la con-
naissance de ce jeune homme*" (George Sand's ghost). "For
people who like that kind of thing, that is the kind of thing they
like" (Pallas Athene, of *The Decline and Fall of the Roman
Empire*). "I, John, Albert, Edward, Claude, Orde, Angus,
Tankerton, Tanville-Tankerton, fourteenth Duke of Dorset,
Marquis of Dorset, Earl of Grove, Earl of Chastermaine,
Viscount Brewsby, Baron Grove, Baron Petstrap, and Baron
Wolock, in the Peerage of England, offer you my hand. Do
not interrupt me" (The Duke of Dorset to Zuleika).

The verbal tricks, the shifts of focus, the imagery of romance, the things people say—all these go to make up the marvelous surface of *Zuleika Dobson*. Indeed, one's pleasure in the book is largely in following the contours of this surface. *It* is real, however cunningly strewn with surprises. It assumes a reader who is capable of responding to it and who is therefore real, too. The author, above all, is real. He is never more so than when he writes, "You cannot make a man by standing a sheep on its hind legs. But by standing a flock of sheep in that position you can make a crowd of men. If man were not a gregarious animal, the world might have achieved, by this time, some real progress towards civilization. Segregate him, and he is no fool. But let him loose among his fellows, and he is lost—he becomes just an unit in unreason."

Unlike its heroine, *Zuleika Dobson* is not an exacting mistress. It is not a book for everyone, the children included. One can enjoy it without claiming too much for it. Whether *Zuleika* is Beerbohm's "masterpiece" is itself open to question. What is almost any writer's masterpiece except a token award for critics to quarrel about? *Seven Men* is as lively and pertinent as *Zuleika* is and has a less taxing consistency of ironic intention. In none of his writings is Beerbohm the fantasist in the same class with Swift or Gogol or Kafka. He was too reasonable to indulge, like the half-mad Swift, in prodigies of invention called forth in the name of Reason. *Zuleika Dobson* is a comic criticism not so much of passion itself as of the fashion for passion, the same phenomenon that Mario Praz was seriously to illustrate and analyze in *The Romantic Agony*. If we can judge by what we know of his love affairs, Beerbohm was not himself susceptible to the grand passions. His early history—to intrude that once more—probably predisposed him to feel affection rather than passion for others, possibly to feel affection more strongly because the exclusive ardors of sexual passion were foreign to him. It need hardly be said that popular Freudianism has perpetuated the romantic agony by putting it on "a scientific basis." To this glorification of sexual passion Beerbohm's entire life and work were opposed. "They were a tense and peculiar family, the Oedipuses, weren't they?" he once remarked.

His opposition arose chiefly from a quality of his mind rather than from a defect of his emotional nature. He had the rococo imagination—so much so that *Zuleika* is closer in spirit to *The Rape of the Lock* than it is to the work of fantasists today, with the exception of Nabokov. Beerbohm saw things as small, discrete, sharply defined, existing in a world that was inexorably finite. From this here-and-now vision came, for one thing, those opinions of his which, often penetrating, sometimes fatuous, are frequently quoted. He objected, for example, that the modern theater lives always in its presumptive future rather than in its present. This opinion is still exemplary. He said of William Morris, "Of course he is a wonderful all-round man but the act of walking round him has always tired me." Amusing but not so exemplary. One is tempted to say that Beerbohm tired rather easily, like a child at an all-day picnic; that his life-long obsession with the tedium of bigness—the bigness of Morris, Shaw, Gibbon, of whomever or whatever, was a kind of childishness or envy. No one else, surely, has ever given so much crafty energy to scaling bigness down, as Beerbohm did, for example, in the thin dummy volume entitled *The Complete Works of Arnold Bennett* which he was at pains to fabricate and which was found in his library at Rapallo. The fifty-odd volumes of Bennett's actual work appalled him. Shaw's reputation struck him as outrageously extensile. But Bennett's literary bulk would no doubt have appalled him regardless of its quality. And he was so oppressed by Shaw's reputation that, as a reviewer, he occasionally missed the point of Shaw's plays.

His opinions are one thing; the imaginary world projected by his rococo imagination and realized in his fiction and drawings is another. In his fiction, if ever in literature, style and substance live in wedded bliss, the perfect midget couple. The English sentence is for him distinctly "an unit," to quote one of his instructively correct phrases. He explores the possibilities of the sentence as thoroughly as Pope did those of the heroic couplet. All known devices of rhetoric and syntax are set to performing for us with unobtrusive gaiety. Thus is bigness mocked by triumphant littleness—bigness and solemnity and the "tragic sense of life." Not that the *materials* of tragedy are lacking in his work. Misery is everywhere potential in it. Throughout *Zuleika Dobson* the strains of the *Liebestod* can be heard swelling, only to dissolve into dissonance. The rococo ethos has been defined by Egon Friedell as a "last craving for illusion," illusion to assuage the painful mysteries of loving and dying. Max Beerbohm had no such craving. For him, loving and dying were mysteries too inscrutable to be encompassed by the slap-happy word "tragedy." Assuagement lay in the contemplation of beauty and folly and in the act of laughter.

1966

Our Man in the Eighteenth Century?

Casanova's *Histoire de ma vie* is one of the most exhilarating of narratives; it is also one of the most mystifying. Like some enormous bird, the last of its fantastic species, the *Histoire* comes to us encrusted with scars yet still proudly levitating in a hostile atmosphere, still holding its own against those who would ensnare and bring it down. The scars are the many doubts cast upon the winged monster by biographers and critics. They have had reason to doubt it: the book *is* a strange bird.

What degree, or what kind, of veracity can be expected of the author of a narrative so full of improbable incidents? Hasn't Casanova exploited the credulousness of posterity just as in the *Histoire* itself he admits, indeed boasts, of having exploited that of the Countess D'Urfé when, claiming to possess occult powers and a helpful oracle named Paralis, he undertook to realize her urgent dream of being reborn as a boy? No court of law would fail to discredit him as a witness on the grounds of his own testimony. Again, was old Casanova in fact the author of the *Histoire*, admittedly a masterpiece of its kind; or was the true author, as someone once

A review of *History of My Life*, volumes 1 and 2, by Giacomo Casanova, Chevalier de Seingalt, translated with an Introduction by Willard R. Trask.

suggested, that lover of hoaxes, impersonations, and pseudo-nyms, Stendhal? And what about the authenticity of the very text of the *Histoire?* Could authority be granted to any of the several versions in which the work used to circulate, since those versions showed striking differences?

True, there exists an international band of literary detectives called "Casanovites." They are, and have long been, intent on establishing what one of them, the British writer J. Rives Childs, has called Casanova's "essential veracity." But surely this is a question-begging term in itself; and the discouraging result of the Casanovite researches is that by documenting certain of Casanova's movements and activities, and affixing actual names to several of his heroines (to whom he gave false names or initials), they have incidentally reminded us of the vast reaches of Casanova's experience that remain unverified and are possibly unverifiable by their very nature. It is one thing to come up with police records or contemporary newspapers proving that Casanova was actually present in a certain city at more or less the same date at which he claims to have been in that city. But it rarely follows that what he claims to have *done* in that city is established. More frustrating still are the attempted identifications of the several women. There is the French woman whom Casanova calls Henriette; she is one of his most believable heroines; on arriving with Casanova at Geneva, where they are about to part, she memorializes the sad, inevitable event by inscribing with a diamond on the windowpane of their hotel room: *"Henriette tu aussi oublieras."* By consulting genealogies and resorting to a good many dubious postulates, the French authority, Charles Samaran, has "identified" Henriette as a certain lady of the Provençal gentry. But since nothing whatever is known about the lady that would connect her with Casanova or afford her a personality, whether or not consonant with Henriette's personality, the attempted identification remains as fruitless in its results as it is tenuous in its logic.* Yet the *Histoire* has kept aloft, in however nameless a void. It is still read by thousands in a variety of dubious texts and unconscionable abridgments, although Casanova himself seems to be less of a culture hero to the advanced public at present than he was a quarter of a century ago.

One quite gratuitous source of Casanovan mystification has, however, been recently removed, that of the text. We now have the initial installment of an excellent English translation by Willard Trask of the first authentic text of the *Histoire* ever to be published. The entire text, in the French in which Casanova wrote it, is contained in six sumptuous volumes with notes, a chronology, and a superb 180-page index. These volumes first saw light in Europe during the years 1960–62. The *Edition intégrale*, as it is called, was the jointly executed project of a French firm, the Librarie Plon, and a German firm, F. A. Brockhaus. The ancient Brockhaus company has been in possession of Casanova's original manuscript ever since it first came into their hands, in 1821, some twenty-three years after Casanova's death. How the manuscript survived, with only slight damage, the menaces of time, war, thievery, and the malversations of editors is a romance in itself. Considering, however, the fabulous nature of the *Histoire*, Mr. Trask is to be congratulated for the sobriety with which, in his

---

* The notes supplied by Mr. Trask draw not only on the Brockhaus-Plon edition but on a German translation of that edition now in progress. He is evidently skeptical of those forced identifications for he omits from his notes to Volume Two, Chapter II the note to the same chapter in Brockhaus-Plon where Bellino-Teresa the pseudo-castrato is said to be a certain singer later well-known throughout Europe. I should add that the researches by the Casanovites have been highly rewarding as applied to Casanova's later life and other particulars.

Introduction, he has told this tale of the manuscript's adventures. It is also to his credit that he has revealed the mutilations suffered by all previous French texts—and naturally carried over into all translations—without crying up in the expected Madison Avenue manner the advantages of the new text. He doesn't have to crow; the many examples he gives of the damage wrought on the *Histoire* by former editors and publishers crow for themselves.

It was one Jean Laforgue, a French professor resident in Germany, to whom the Brockhaus company first entrusted the editing of the manuscript, in the 1820s. Laforgue undertook to correct Casanova's sometimes unidiomatic French. (Italian, or as he liked to say, Venetian, was of course his native lauguage.) The same editor also bowdlerized the text as he was obliged to do if the *Histoire* was to be published at all in those years, or for many years to come. Less pardonably, he supplied clarifications and motivations when he thought the action as recounted by Casanova was obscure. Still worse, he toned down Casanova's anti-Revolutionary sentiments to make them accord with his own more or less Jacobin sentiments. Several decades ago, it became widely known that the existing texts were all largely derived from Laforgue's and were all consequently unreliable, and that the original manuscript lay virtually out of reach in the Brockhaus vaults. This knowledge naturally discouraged interested scholars. From responsible scholarship Casanova got little attention; and since such scholarship when it is applied to worthwhile subjects often unites with good criticism to revive or keep alive the figures of the past, Casanova, lacking such efforts in his behalf, has tended to recede into a semi-Limbo, having been replaced as an eighteenth-century hero by other figures—Boswell, Horace Walpole, Diderot, Rousseau, even the Marquis de Sade—who have been better researched, documented, textualized, or at least existentialized.

Perhaps Bonamy Dobrée's short biography (*Casanova*, New York, 1933) may be taken as a tide-mark in the rise and fall of Casanova's reputation. For Dobrée's too brief but shapely and humane book seems to have been the last book of any general interest on Casanova to appear in English. Certain remarks in the author's Preface suggest that he felt scruples about working from even so up-to-date a text as the *Edition la Sirène* (Paris, 1924–35). His remarks are an apology in the form of a prophecy. "It is probable that we do not lose much in the rephrasing, and it is equally probable that no completely raw text will ever be published; for Casanova called things by their names, and it is odd that though humanity will accept facts, it is often horrified by words."

As prophecy Dobrée's words have proved wrong in all particulars. The "raw text" as now published shows how extensive Laforgue's "rephrasings" often were. On the other hand, the formerly bowdlerized or excised passages now restored turn out to be sparing in the use of "words"—words for the bodily parts and the sexual processes. And just as Casanova's style, freed from Laforgue-isms, gains in terseness, so the scenes of sexual encounter, although they may suffer from the coyness of Casanova's locutions—"charms" for a woman's breasts and lower body, "my steed" for his own penis—have the advantage of including details that help to individualize the scenes and characterize the women.

In the present Englished volumes, there are, for example, the episodes at Corfu involving Casanova and the Signora F. On one occasion the two of them are shown "wiping" themselves off: they have engaged in some act of quasi-coitus. From this and other related scenes the Signora F. emerges as a rather pitiable captive of her situation: the palace on this island outpost of the Venetian empire, her coldly acquiescent husband, her aging official lover, and the insistent young Casanova, ever the born outsider on the watch for his chance to become an insider. Whether from pride or fear or some excess of self-love the Signora F. is a "tease." Once she deliberately though briefly exposes her "charms" to the gaping and gasping youth. Viewing the event in retrospect, Casanova writes, with what strikes me as a certain loveliness of feeling and insight: "I see her staring at herself, lost in herself . . . delighting in her own beauty."

Such episodes as those concerning the Signora F. frequently involve what appear to be familiar motifs from erotic romance and *fabliau*. Our suspicions as to their authenticity are thus aroused, and we recall that he had probably read a lot of that literature from the *Satyricon* to the *Decameron* and beyond. Yet "life imitates art." There is a whole mythology of the modern sleeping-car and it is not all myth. Travel is still a great aphrodisiac. In any case, a wealth of intricate circumstance and realistic detail gives at least an imaginative authority to Casanova's erotic passages. In addition to the Signora F., there is the woman in Rome who, asked by Casonova why she sighs while pulling down her skirts as their carriage halts in front of her palace, replies simply, like Emma Bovary rather than a heroine of erotic romance, "We're home."

For Casanova, love-making is always an occasion for the making of a *scene*. Settings are carefully specified and rendered graphic. The characters are animated by appropriate forms of speech and action, and these may be understated, like the "We're home," or amount to a veritable *beau geste*, like Henriette's words on the windowpane. Occasionally the scene is Hogarthian or Jan Steenian in its rambunctious scam-

perings and debris of squalor. Such is the happening in the
peasant's cottage where Casanova and Father Steffano are set
upon by two lecherous hags. This is an inversion (love among
the lower classes!) of Casanova's frequently idyllic love scenes.
In these idyls the pleasures of intercourse are reflected in the
splendor of the surroundings: the well-upholstered rooms, the
gardens and colonnades, the luminous sunlight, or sudden
thunderstorm. In such scenes, it could be said, the blooming
Fragonard girl is really possessed amid her draperies on that
marble seat under the ornamental urns and elms. Casanova
was the brother of a painter and an acquaintance of Raphael
Mengs, Winckelmann, possibly Francesco Guardi.

Casanova's temper is far more histrionic than painterly. That
part of his mind we call memory, working on what we assume
to have been real events of his past, instantly sets ablaze that
part of his mind we call imagination, with the result that those
events are converted into the kind of scenes referred to above.
This transforming of the stuff of memory into the scenario of
theater commences with what he calls his earliest memory.
Meanwhile he has maintained that his "organ of memory"
developed only with "the beginning of my own existence as a
thinking being," that is, when he was "eight years and four
months old." Casanova's is the classical conception of the limits of recollection; memory is an organ whose beginnings coin-
cide with those of the faculty of reason ("a thinking being").
For the Rousseau of the *Confessions*, on the other hand, as
for the many subsequent autobiographers in Rousseau's tradition, memory begins not at some determinate age or date but
with some happening. The happening is usually domestic, and
often trifling in itself though not generally in its ultimate
significance; and as a rule it is traceable to an age earlier than
Casanova's eight years and four months, if it is traceable at

all. (Henry James was to maintain that his earliest memory was of seeing the column in the Place Vendôme from a carriage at the age of one!) Rousseau tracks his first memory back to what is apparently an age earlier than seven. His "uninterrupted self-consciousness" began with his father's reading to him from the library of romances left behind by Rousseau's dead mother. Often his father would read to him all night long until, "hearing the swallows begin to twitter, he would say, quite ashamed, 'To bed with us; I am more of a child than yourself.' " Rousseau's recall is merely a glimpse, not a scene, but the glimpse brings child, father, and dead mother, books and twittering birds, into a domestic relationship of the utmost poignancy.

By contrast Casanova's earliest recollection is a fully though briefly developed narrative that moves between domesticity and melodrama. He stares at his blood "streaming on the floor" from an unquenchable nosebleed. His grandmother transports him by gondola to a witch's establishment on the island of Murano. There, in a hovel inhabited by a black cat and by several old women speaking a strange dialect, he is submitted to certain magical rites (they include his being locked in a chest) and then sent home with the promise that the bleeding will gradually stop and that he will be visited next night by "a charming lady," unless he reveals to someone the witch's mysteries, in which case he will die. He obeys and is rewarded by seeing ("or I thought I saw," he qualifies) "a dazzlingly beautiful woman come down by the chimney." The lady presents him with gifts in "several small boxes," bestows on him a sort of blessing, and vanishes.

This rather alarming fairy-tale incident seems made to order for the Freudian critic: the terrible nosebleed, the chests and boxes, the threat of death, the visionary lady with her gifts. Casanova's mother was a Venetian actress who gave him as an infant into *her* mother's care, was seldom in evidence thereafter, and eventually abandoned him; while his father, also an actor, died only a few months after the nosebleed scene. Manifestly, Casanova's future as a Great Lover is prefigured in that scene. He will pursue the mysterious maternal charmer all his active life in the various guises of his many loves. Frequently he will seduce or try to seduce women at the expense of husbands and/or brothers, males who often exhibit a dream-like innocence or permissiveness which, as Casanova presents it, savors irresistibly of connivance. Meanwhile he will confess openly to a dread of impotence, thus anticipating a classic Freudian formula for the cause of libertinism. "I have all my life been dominated by the fear that my steed would flinch from beginning another race." But just as the Freudian's eyes begin to glint with clairvoyance, Casanova is, by anticipation, right on top of him. He adds: "and I have never found this restraint painful, for the visible pleasure which I gave [to women] always made up four-fifths of mine." There, complete with the narcissism, you have the whole psychiatric "package"—everything, that is, but the suspicion of "latent homosexuality." And even this, if you want to see it, is "confirmed" by the frequency and the vigor with which Casanova denies any such propensities on his part, while tolerating them in others just as he tolerates masturbation, lesbianism (among young girls), and, in theory, incest.

Again, Rousseau offers himself for contrast. His "case" is more complicated, his inhibitions deeper than Casanova's; and he is therefore by turns more revealing and more furtive than the author of the *Histoire*. And it is interesting to note that their two paths cross, once in connection with the actress-courtesan Giulietta. Casanova's quarrelsome relations with her are recounted in the present English translation (Volume One, Chapter V). They culminate in her demand that the two of them exchange clothes at a ball, which they do while to her annoyance Casanova stares at her body. Observant as he is of women's anatomies, their feet, hands, smells ("I have always found that the one I loved smelled good."), he fails to observe what Rousseau observes, or thinks he observes, when some three years later, himself in Venice, Rousseau is fascinated by the same Giulietta until he discovers that "she had only one nipple" (*Confessions*, Book VII). Was Rousseau "seeing things"? one wonders. Did he transform his own confessed dread of ordinary sex into a deformity on Guilietta's part, thus finding a pretext for bringing his advances to a halt? This he promptly does while Guilietta, bewildered and scornful, remarks "*Lascia le donne, y studia la matematica.*" Rousseau has meanwhile confessed that Guilietta had earlier "put into my wretched head the poison of that ineffable happiness, the desire for which he [Nature] has planted in my heart." This poisoned happiness, as we know from other passages in *Confessions*, consists in his associating women with his dead mother to the extent of wanting to be at once loved and punished by them—literally, perhaps, beaten by them. If Rousseau's inhibitions gave rise to delusions—ultimately to the paranoid conviction that he was the victim of an international conspiracy—they also stimulated his great powers of introspection. And these in turn accounted for the profound novelty of the *Confessions* in their time and for the immense influence that book exerted on later writers. The *Confessions* were original in their exceptional feeling for the *continuity of the psychic life;* the Child is Father of the Man.

Casanova is, or consistently represents himself to be, far more "extroverted" than Rousseau. His histrionic instinct (which Rousseau shared, though intermittently) permits him, perhaps obliges him, to overcome the handicaps of his lowly birth and parentless childhood by the comparatively simple mechanism of playing roles. No sooner is he confirmed as an *abate* than he creates a sensation, sets "the whole town talking" in a favorite phrase, by his performance as a boy preacher.

Eventually he wears out the possibilities of his clerical character. Half consciously he seeks a replacement for it—and through a typical mingling of will and luck finds the replacement. One of Casanova's most brilliant moments occurs. Astride a wild horse he rides, or is carried, across the battle lines in central Italy. Proceeding to Bologna he discards his clerical habit for a soldier's uniform. The uniform is specially tailored to his fanciful design. He is now unmistakeably in costume. And so the masquerade will continue throughout his active life with its peculiar rhythmic alternation of good and bad fortune. There will be a lot of the bad, of sudden descents into the dark night of social obliquity. Once, returning to Venice penniless and friendless he becomes a fiddler in a theater orchestra, joins a gang of delinquents in their wild unprogrammed rebellion against Venetian oppression and hypocrisy, only to bounce abruptly upward once again. He does so by suddenly improvising for himself a new role, that of a physician-necromancer complete with an oracle, the same helpful Paralis. By this maneuver he finds in a credulous old Senator another indulgent "father"—one who, moreover, will hold him in affection and keep him in funds for years to come.

In eighteenth-century lives, real and fictional, impersonation in one form or another is a familiar occurrence. So are such related phenomena as pseudonyms, hoaxes, and literary forgeries. By these means the adventurous outsider could take advantage of the social conditions of the time: the deteriorating despotisms of the Continent, the increasingly ambiguous functions of the patronage system. By similar means but for different ends Thomas Chatterton could acquire a "second existence" as the imaginary Middle English author of quaint and lovely verses. The same tendency persisted into the time of Merimée, Stendhal, and Kierkegaard. Nor did its history end with Balzac's ennobling himself by the addition of a *de* to his name, as Casanova had done with the "de Seingalt." Such practices would be revived later in a more sophisticated form by Nietzsche, Oscar Wilde, Yeats, and others. Their "masks" or "personae" would be assumed with no view to deceiving themselves or others. The end, rather, would be the acquisition of an antithetical self or of multiple selves. By thus recreating, as it were, oneself, one would strengthen one's creative power as applied to thought and art. And so on into our time, when in black humor fiction acts of impersonation are, however, exclusively "subjective," accomplished momentarily and by the magic of alcohol, narcotics, and orgiastic sex.

Casanova is, or represents himself as being, the most "objective" of the classic impersonators in history or fiction. Indirectly but unmistakably he gives a social as well as a psychological explanation of his behavior. He is the forsaken child of actors. But he is also a native of histrionic Venice. There almost every parish has its much frequented theater; the annual Carnival goes on for weeks with a continuous round of spectacles and with crowds of costumed and masked merrymakers. In ordinary times, however, the wearing of masks is permitted only to members of the patriciate and their hangers-on. And Casanova, confided by his dying father to the guardianship of the noble Grimani family, well educated at Padua with their assistance, becomes one of the hangers-on. He thus acquires a position that was not his by birth and that he therefore clings to with conspicuous firmness throughout his career. Meanwhile the ambiguity of his own social status is reflected in the duplicity, as he sees it, of the Venetian oligarchy, which maintains the outward appearance of piety and decorum while in many cases pursuing in private not only the usual pleasures of sex and gambling but the heretical satisfactions of necromancy. Its hypocrisy makes the patriciate fair game for the gifted adventurer, though it by no means guarantees his continued success. For Casanova Venice becomes the model of all aristocratic Europe. The city's very configuration—the narrow streets, the *casini* (or hide-outs) of the pleasure-bent patricians, the canals, bridges, islands—and, of course, the convenient gondolas—form a sort of scrambled chessboard where victories can be won by the clever and venturesome player, if only briefly.

Casanova's Venice is a Venice never painted by the festive Canaletto or the moodier Guardi. Indeed he never really visualizes the city except at one climactic moment: in the course of his now famous escape from the Leads, the prison beneath the lead-plated roof of the Ducal Palace. He and his companion in flight have made their way to the steep palace roof. While the bells of San Marco boom midnight they sit precariously astride the roof-tree wondering what to do next, for Casanova has as usual made careful plans while leaving much to luck. Desperately waiting for luck they gaze about them. On one side is the guarded Palace courtyard, on another the shallow little canal, on another the mountain mass of San Marco's domes, on still another the Riva pavement, all of them invitations to death or recapture. Beyond the Riva, however, are the Lagoon, the boats, the islands, the mainland, the frontier, freedom. Luck now abruptly, and almost comically, manifests itself in the shape of a ladder left behind on the roof by workmen. After further exertions and perils, the two fugitives simply walk down the grand staircase, proceed out on the Riva, leap into a boat, and are off.

End of the greatest episode in the *Histoire*. But not of course the end of Casanova or even of his Venetian career. He will return to the labyrinthine city, eventually to serve as a spy for the very Holy Inquisition that formerly imprisoned him. The trouble with being a free spirit is experienced by Casanova long before it is known to André Gide and the heroes of his novels. The free spirit, remaining human, is tempted to *demonstrate* his freedom. In doing so he commits a gratuitous murder, as Gide's Lafcadio does, or, like Casanova, he indulges in other forbidden games, thus unwittingly joining the least free of social groupings, the criminal class. Luck, together with his lasting charm and bravado, saves Casanova at last, though not in the way he has expected. Instead of making his fortune once more, he finds refuge with Count Waldstein at Dux in Bohemia, becoming the castle librarian.

Even then, in 1785, he had thirteen years to live. It was no foregone conclusion that he would produce the *Histoire* and in the Preface be able to make his boast of "*Vixi:* I have lived" and by way of that book live on in the eternity (figuratively speaking) of literature. Long before he announced that he had "lived," he was already old, toothless, cantankerous, the almost penniless pensioner of the patient Count, the butt of the servants when the master was absent. He had then tried, and would try again, to reach his ideal audience by other kinds of writing: a mathematical treatise, a five-volume philosophical romance à la Voltaire. All these efforts failed to win him a public except one: his account in published form of a story he had often told *viva voce*, that of his escape from the Leads.

Related with immense zest, the story had gained for him a multitude of hearers; news of it had preceded him in his travels; so had news of his other exploits and entertainments.

He could improvise verse on the instant, quote Horace and Ariosto at length, crown feeble witticism with devastating witticism. It was, in part at least, as a kind of minstrel of the salons that he had made his way among Europe's dispersed courts and seats of the gentry. From Naples to Petersburg many a duke had been kept awake by his performances—the duke, his wife, his mistress, his wife's lover, the local archbishop, and the attractive young girl, or preferably pair of girls, listening in the shadows. What Casanova did finally was to resume, by way of the *Histoire*, the most innocent of his former roles, that of entertainer. Meanwhile the French Revolution had intervened to assist him in his choice, not of a role now but of a vocation. He hated the Revolution and its consequences for the aristocratic society which, generally corrupt, credulous, and bungling though he depicted it in his book, was still "reality" for him. It seems to have been in 1789 or thereabouts that he embarked seriously on the writing of the *Histoire*, evidently making use of notes composed earlier. With the discovery of his vocation and subject he also discovered, or re-discovered, his ideal body of readers. He wrote, the Preface says, "to provide a most worthy subject for laughter to my well-bred audience, for such is the society which has always shown its friendship for me and which I have always frequented." Always? The delusion no longer mattered. He goes on to clinch his point. "To write well I have but to imagine that my readers will belong to it [the well-bred society]."

I have implied that the best test of Casanova's "veracity" is the quality and the consistency of his imagination as shown in given episodes. A precarious sort of test, I admit, but, with all respect to Casanovite documentation, the only one that so far suggests itself as possible. Judged by this standard, the Constantinople episodes in the present volume are inferior fictions —and no documents have so far been produced to validate those episodes. In certain of them he seems to be inventing at second hand. His models, all based on conventionalized ideas of the Orient, show through. For his conversations with Yussef on comparative manners and morals, the models could be anything from the *Lettres Persanes* to *Rasselas* to the *Princesse de Babylone*. The voyeuristic orgy with the sodomite Ismail (those Turks!) is fancy pornography, perhaps out of the *Arabian Nights*. The scenes in which Yussef offers Casanova his daughter in marriage and then exposes him to the lust of Yussef's wife are another matter. Casanova is here indulging without restraint his own erotic-familial fantasies.

What, by this pragmatic test, are the more *convincing* passages? There will be more of them, I think, in the later volumes than in the present ones. Casanova seems to grow up with the progress of his narrative. There will be the passages recounting his first arrival in the Paris of Louis XV, his youthful joy at escaping from the hypocrisy of Venice into the relative candor of French court society. At Paris, characteristically, he heads straight for the place where the "action" is, the Palais Royale, and then on into the drawing rooms of delightful people and, by way of the State lottery, to the attainment of what is to remain his highest point of prosperity. There will be his sentimental journey with the believable Henriette and his increasingly detailed portraits of other individuals. These include an outrageous Irish mercenary soldier and rake, named Morphy, a sort of alter ego whom in his hard way Casanova loves for once (he usually hates his own kind, from Cagliostro to the poor French soldier in Corfu who ventures to impersonate LaRochefoucauld). In the present volumes there are marvelous things too: the portrait of Senator Bragadin and his circle of well-bred cranks (all belong to families listed in the *Libro d'Oro* of Venice for the year 1297); his account, already mentioned, of the fantasy uniform he puts on in Bologna (one thinks of the young cleric in *Le Rouge et le noir* admiring his mirrored self in what he thinks is the privacy of the vestry); the arm torn from the corpse by Casanova and thrust at his enemy who, waking suddenly in the dark, finds himself clasping a dead hand and—goes mad. The Bellino-Teresa episodes are striking, though padded out with tiresome conversations reminiscent of classical French drama. These episodes owe their grotesque fascination to the remorseless energy, the cruel avidity, with which Casanova pursues the boy-girl and forces her at last to reveal her sex.

In these volumes as elsewhere in the *Histoire*, it is true, the exhiliration of the narrative is qualified by Casanova's theatrical excesses, his overplaying of scenes, his will to remain on top of every situation and several paces ahead of his reader. As narrator his personality is at once too insistent and too impoverished in complexity of feeling and thought. He lives by a code, that of the man of pleasure; he is the too literal disciple of the materialist Gassendi. The code, like most codes, is inflexible: a dagger in the belt. Only in certain love scenes where in his rapture he attains to a state of parity with the woman, achieves a status which allows him to give as well as take pleasure, and to provide for his women as a gentleman does for his family—or a good son for his mother—only then does he really escape from his histrionic compulsions.

For all his egocentrism and his "insincerity" the Rousseau of the *Confessions* establishes with the reader an intimacy quite beyond Casanova's scope. No single character in the *Histoire* exists as Rousseau's Mme. De Warens exists, in the intricacy of her relations to herself, to others of her ménage, to her activities, to her house and the surrounding landscape. Nor does any object acquire the luminosity, the precious singularity, of things in the *Confessions:* the periwinkle in the grass at Chambéri; the walnut tree at Bossey; the bare backsides that a woman accidentally shows to the King of Sardinia when, watching his equipage pass, she tumbles in her excitement; the father who says, "To bed with us, I am more of a child than yourself." Such things acquire their luminosity, their singularity, because they occur in a rich medium of Time and at once mark its passing and signify its recapture in the memory. For Rousseau Time—Time in the modern sense of a fifth element that conditions our lives at every instant—is again a discovery that later writers will develop. Casanova, on the contrary, is unaware of Time except when, intermittently, someone he has known in the past reappears on the stage of his life to remind him of Time's passing. Space is Casanova's medium—the distances between cities, the relation of room to room within houses, the dimensions of the imaginary theater in which he and his creations perform. For intimacy this winged monster of an *Histoire* substitutes comprehensiveness, variety, the perspective of grandeur. Casanova's light, as distinct from Rousseau's, is a magnificent, artificially intensified beam that never was on land, sea, or the candle-lit stages of Venetian theaters.

1967

Truman Capote's Score

Poor dead Bonnie Clutter appeared to a friend in a dream. "To be murdered," she wept. "No. No. There's nothing worse. Nothing worse than that. Nothing." *In Cold Blood* is strewn with snatches of pregnant speech, with glimpses of things that grow and grow in the eye of memory. None of these particulars surpasses the grimly clinching effect of Mrs. Clutter's dream speech.

For the still living Mrs. Clutter, moreover, the horror of being murdered herself had been triply compounded. Roped to her bed, her lips sealed with adhesive tape, she was the last of four members of her family to be despatched by two youthful intruders, entire strangers to the family, in the Clutters' roomy farmhouse on the plains of western Kansas one moonlit night in November of 1959. At intervals she heard the gun-shots—in a single instance possibly the gaspings of a slit throat as well—that announced the deaths, one by one, of her husband, her fifteen-year-old son Kenyon, and her sixteen-year-old daughter Nancy. For some reason Nancy Clutter's lips had been left untaped. Her head turned to the wall and away from the flashlight beamed on it, the shotgun levelled at it, she was able to plead briefly with her killers, again possibly within hearing of her mother across the hall: "Oh, no! Oh please. No! No! No! No! Don't! Oh, please don't! Please!" Mrs. Clutter's turn to be flashlighted and blasted at close range came next. Was her death a deliverance that she welcomed? Among her pitying, grieving, haunted friends in the small town of Holcomb, some hoped that it was. A dim comfort glimmered in the thought.

No other comfort was at first to be found in any aspect of the seemingly inexplicable massacre of this respected, in part beloved, family. Even those natives of the place who resorted to fanciful theorizing and secret finger pointing seem to have done so out of pure fear—a fear too burdensome to find support in religious patience or rational wait-and-see. Here and there, speculation survived the very capture and conviction of the criminals. It was suggested that still darker forces and larger figures hovered in the infinitely contorted and receding backgrounds of an occurrence so monstrous itself, so unprecedented in local history, as the Clutter murder was. Up to then, Holcomb and its environs had made up a somewhat "backward" community. A degree of frontier austerity, religious and moral, persisted in those hinterland fastnesses despite all the well-filled grain elevators, the ranch-type houses, the television sets, the outdoor movies, the teen-age dating. Overnight, as it were, Holcomb had joined the mid-twentieth century. The ages, alike of faith and of rational doubt, had been quickly passed. Our time of suspicion, this sinister synthesis of faith and doubt, of fierce conviction and mad ratiocination, had been reached.

Thus is Holcomb's brutal coming of age pictured in Truman Capote's *In Cold Blood*. The picture, if I have it right, provides one of the numerous "angles" that exercise the mind as well as chilling the blood while one follows Mr. Capote's intricately circumstantial account of the Clutter murder, its causes and aftermath. There is of course a considerable public, generally indulgent, often profitable, for books that reconstruct, whether in a wholly journalistic or a partly "fictionalized" form, one or another of the more significant criminal episodes of the recent or distant past. To the perennial, the probably aboriginal, appeal of crimes and criminals there is sometimes added a sentimental, even an ironically patriotic, motive when the given episode has occurred in the United States. From Jesse James to Loeb and Leopold, from the perpetrators of the Saint Valentine's Day Massacre to the Lindbergh kidnapper and beyond, our celebrated delinquents have become a part of the national heritage. They figure in a sort of *musée imaginaire*, half Madame Tussaud's, half Smithsonian, of American crime.

In Cold Blood is the best documentary account of an American crime ever written, partly because the crime here in question is not yet a part of the heritage. Only in the region where it took place was the Clutter murder large-scale news. Generally ignored elsewhere (there have since been so many other virtually gratuitous rampages of blood and sex), the Clutter affair has been spared the attentions of the memorialists. Its horrors, its meanings, its supposed relation to the *Zeitgeist* have gone unexplored. For Mr. Capote the incident is pristine material; and the book he has written about it is appropriately and impressively fresh.

But if *In Cold Blood* deserves highest marks among American crime histories, it also raises certain questions. What, more or less, is the narrative intended to be; and in what spirit are we supposed to take it? While the book "reads" like excellent fiction, it purports to be strictly factual and thoroughly documented. But the documentation is, for the most part, suppressed in the text—presumably in order to supply the narrative with a surface of persuasive immediacy and impenetrable omniscience. Nor are the author's claims to veracity set forth in any detail elsewhere in the volume. They are merely asserted in a brief introductory paragraph wherein his indebtedness to several authorities ranging from the Kansas police to William Shawn, editor of *The New Yorker*, is acknowledged. With all respect to the author, how can anyone be sure that the book's numerous angles, including Mrs. Clutter's dream speech and the social portrait of Holcomb, are in any reasonable degree authentic? To ask such questions of a book that is otherwise so praiseworthy may be captious; but to praise without asking is foolish. For these are years not only of neurotic suspiciousness but of much that is really, and grossly, suspect, in art as in politics. As the present writer has at times felt obliged to remark in print, a lot of what passes for sociological observation is only private fantasy, the pulse not of the patient but of the hypochondriac healer at the bedside. "Parajournalism" is Dwight Macdonald's perhaps too glamorous-sounding term for this "creative" reportage or social criticism. And parajournalism is detestable because, to the many real crises that now lurk and loom, it adds another and quite unnecessary one, a crisis of literary truthfulness.

I am myself convinced that *In Cold Blood* is not parajournalism. Its general authenticity is established, for me, by what I hope to show is a species of internal evidence. I do nevertheless wish that Mr. Capote had gone to the trouble of taking us into his confidence—perhaps by way of an appendix explaining his procedures—instead of covering his tracks as an interviewer and researcher, and of generally seeming to declaim, with Walt Whitman in one of his seizures of mystical clairvoyance, "I am there . . . I witness the corpse with its dabbled hair, I note where the pistol has fallen." A journalist turned poet, Whitman went on to write what was unmistakeably poetry, so far, at least, as its frankly visionary immersion in man's total experience was concerned. At present, all reportorial writing aspires to the condition of poetry, or of myth or—in the still more abused word—of "story." *In Cold Blood's* similar aspirations are, as I say, largely justified by its unique excellence. Meanwhile, the questions have proliferated, mostly in conversation, since last autumn, when the work appeared serially in *The New Yorker.*

Some of these questions had to do with documentation. Others were more intangible, "personal," and, as I now think, impertinent. Given, for example, the preoccupations of Capote's early fiction, its nostalgia for states of innocence together with its fascination with deformed or precocious or odd-ball types of human creepiness (that Miss Bobbitt in "Children on Their Birthdays"! That New York City dream collector in "Master Misery"!)—given, in short, Capote's repertory of fictional themes, to what extent did he impose it upon the actualities of the Clutter case, "identifying" with one or another of the figures in the case and distorting this or that situation? In their original form such speculations have, as I say, proved to be mostly irrelevant. But they were not without justification if one considers Capote's seeming possessiveness toward his subject, his determination to make the subject his *very* own, to the point of refusing to share with the public the means by which he has done so.

Perhaps his reportorial activities, which I understand were arduous and prolonged, are another story, to be made public later, like Gide's *Journal of "The Counterfeiters."* Meanwhile Mr. Capote, interviewed by a *New York Times* reporter, has suggested further reasons for his suppressing documentation. The book, he says, is an attempt at what is in effect a new genre, the "non-fiction novel." To this claim the only possible retort is a disbelieving grin. The book chills the blood and exercises the intelligence just because it reports, without much novelistic comment or simplification, what one is persuaded really and horribly *happened*. Nor do "genres" as such really matter; certain of anyone's favorite books—*A Sentimental Journey, Walden*—are *sui generis*. If anything, Capote has perfected an old form of journalism and done so by virtue of qualities peculiar to his subject and to himself. Not the book's admirable essence but its glittering aureole of fame achieved and money made in heaps is what is likely to attract imitators.

Whatever its "genre," *In Cold Blood is* admirable: as harrowing as it is, ultimately though implicitly, reflective in temper. Capote's possessiveness toward his subject is understandable in view of the industry, intelligence, and passion he has brought to the book's making. One's belief in its merits deepens on rereading *In Cold Blood* in its present form as a volume. Indeed the book has the special merit of *requiring*, and repaying, thoughtful attention even while it tempts one to devour its contents with uninterrupted excitement. Many of the original questions are effectively answered, and the speculations silenced, by rereading the work in all its astonishing abundance of provocative detail.

This abundance flows chiefly from two circumstances: the character of the two criminals and the nature of Capote's participation in the proceedings. To speak first of the criminals: one of them, Richard Hickock, combined a high IQ and a gift of almost total recall with a marked deficiency of imagination and feeling. The other, Perry Smith, had imagination and feeling in fearful and wonderful plenitude. Smith was a disappointed *poète maudit*. Repeatedly he dreamed or daydreamed of vague paradises, of great winged creatures that did injury to others in return for the injuries done to him. He cherished writing of any kind, his own or that of others, so long as it applied directly or indirectly to himself. To his partner's annoyance he packed almost everywhere with them his boxes of old letters and other documents. In effect this bulky, messy, assorted archive was at once an apologia and a guarantee of identity for this fugitive who in his thirty years had led several rather different lives and been as many varying selves. So the archive, or some part of it, went with them to Miami, to Mexico, across the deserts of the American West, into the bars or motels where the two men took shelter, into a car which, as hitchhikers, they planned (and failed) to make off with after doing in the driver. In the end, of course, this background material, together with the foreground material supplied by their confessions, formed part of the court record and hence came to Mr. Capote's knowledge.

Factually speaking, what Smith remembered about the crime itself and about their subsequent wanderings was less extensive than Hickock's memories. But the recollections of both were in substantial agreement. Naturally Smith's memories included things that escaped Hickock's less impressionable mind or that didn't concern him. Among them were the brutality and neglect to which Smith had been subjected as a child, the suicides of a sister, a brother, and the brother's wife. Among his memories, too, was the far-off presence of a second sister, Bobo, and her success, thus far, in eluding the family curse. Bobo had acquired a respectable husband, three children, a house and home. This good fortune on her part seems to have made Perry despise Bobo in proportion as he envied her. It made him express a strange wish concerning her, express it repeatedly and almost to the end—he and Hickock remained quite unrepentant during their trial and the long years they spent in the death house of the Kansas State Penitentiary until, in April of last year, their original sentence of death by hanging was finally carried out—Smith wished that his sister Bobo had been present that night in the Clutters' house. In his mind, obviously, her precarious respectability got connected with the manifest respectability of the Clutters. On first seeing their large farmhouse and extensive grounds by moonlight, he thought them "sort of *too* impressive"; and he almost succeeded in convincing Hickock and himself to abandon the "score," as Hickock called the felonious job they had undertaken.

No doubt Smith's voluble confessions to the police and, one gathers, his conversations with Capote, contributed much to the abundance of circumstantiality that characterizes *In Cold Blood*. Inevitably they also awoke in Capote, as surely they must in almost any reader, a kind of sick compassion and wonder. That so much suffering could be taken and given by a single youthful human creature is a fact that unsettles the intelligence and works with desperate confusion upon the emotions, especially when one comes to know the creature as intimately as one does Perry Smith in the pages of *In Cold Blood*. A half-breed and, virtually, an orphan like the fictional Joe Christmas of Faulkner's *Light in August*, Perry Smith has exactly what Faulkner's killer lacks, a personality.

Does, then, the author seem to identify himself with *this* particular specimen of human oddness, who is even short-legged like several of Capote's early characters? Beyond a point, definitely not. Any such sentimental conjunction of egos or alter-egos is precluded by what is gradually revealed about Perry Smith in and between the lines of the book. Smith's excess of imagination and feeling was his undoing and that of the Clutters. It was his blandishments, as contrasted with Dick's bullying, that reassured the Clutters as to the probable intentions of the two intruders, and caused the Clutters to go to their deaths without resistance, perilous as resistance must have been in any case. Perry's will to deceive—perhaps to deceive himself—was matched by the Clutters' will to believe, which in turn sprang from simple shock and fear. Moreover, it was Perry who, after thwarting Hickock's intention of raping Nancy, sat down at her bedside for a pleasant chat about horses, which she loved, and other innocent things. It was Perry who thought Mr. Clutter a nice gentleman at the very moment that he put the knife to Mr. Clutter's throat. Finally, it was Perry who pillowed his victims, tucked them in their beds, or otherwise made them as comfortable as possible, considering that he had also used his ex-seaman's skill to tie them up and that he was soon to slaughter them, one by one. That Pal Perry is no Pal Joey, and thus a projection of the author's fears or desires concerning himself, becomes certain, if only because the *facts*, again, make it impossible. Perry Smith is a heel to end all the heels in modern American fiction.

Not that the slaughter itself was a foregone conclusion. True, "no witnesses" had been Hickock's slogan from the start. But during their four-hundred mile drive to Holcomb, Smith had thought of avoiding detection by masking their faces with women's stockings—black ones. Their attempts to secure these unfashionable articles failed, and the whole stocking-hunt forms one of the more grotesque elements in the wonderful configuration of choices and chances, identities within differences, appearances and realities, which shows everywhere in Capote's narrative.

Between Hickock and Smith, tensions developed during their lengthy occupation of the Clutters' house. Besides keeping Hickock away from Nancy, Smith annoyed him by crediting Mr. Clutter's insistence that there really was no safe in the house. Dick, on the other hand, kept searching for the safe, his whole "score," and the self-esteem that went with it, being at stake for him. Except for these tensions, they might have left the Clutters tied up and unharmed, making their escape with the small portable radio, the pair of binoculars, and the fifty-odd dollars in cash they did find and take. But something, or everything together, awoke in Perry Smith a hallucinated state of mind. He took leave, not merely of his senses, but of his very self, amorphous as it was at best. He was suddenly someone else, the observer of a scene in which his other self was fated to act out its essential impulses. The cutting of Mr. Clutter's throat confirmed Perry's sense of his doubleness. By this act of gratuitous violence, this former petty thief, and, like Dick, parolee from the state prison, became what he had earlier dreamed about and bragged about being, a killer, the avenging bird.

Here, then, is some of the internal evidence (or my version of it) that persuades me *In Cold Blood* is to be read as *fact*, its author's claims to the contrary. Even the propriety of his including Bonnie Clutter's dream speech is thus established, apart from its great dramatic value. He got it, directly or indirectly, from the dreamer herself, an acquaintance of Mrs. Clutter's and the wife of the local police investigator whose involvement in the case was urgent throughout. Similarly with the portrait of Holcomb and its environs. This is as convincing as any such sociological panorama is ever likely to be, especially because of the presence in it of other, somewhat more worldly, "enclaves" beyond the Clutter circle, which is strictly Methodist, Republican, temperance, and 4-H Club. Within and roundabout the Clutter group itself there are also significant differences, despite the seeming harmony. Unlike the others, Bonnie Clutter is a "mental," a partial recluse, subject to bad "spells," convinced that she is unneeded in her generally extroverted family, and given to guilt-stricken gestures and monologues. Then there is Bobby Rupp, the neighbor boy whose teen-age romance with Nancy Clutter has been firmly discouraged by her father because the Rupps are Catholic. Indeed, suspicion fixes, unofficially and briefly, on Bonnie Clutter herself; while Rupp is promptly submitted by the police to the formalities of an interrogation. Thus do those grotesquely opposite numbers, the stranger and the friend, the normal and abnormal, the killer and the killed, shade into one another.

As for Capote's part in the proceedings, it consisted in his making himself so thoroughly familiar with the circumstances and the surviving people involved that he was able to feel himself almost a participant and to make the reader feel a participant also. Thus the various possible clues and suspects are introduced, not with the mechanical trickery of a detective story, but as they might have been dreamed up by the natives or pursued by the police from day to day on the spot. Meanwhile, in alternating chapters, we are made aware of Hickock and Smith, parolees on the loose, meeting at distant Olathe, Kansas, consuming their root beers and aspirins, or vodka orange blossoms, planning the job in their shrewd but halfbaked way, and starting on the long drive to the isolated farmhouse which neither of them has ever seen, which only Hickock has heard about, from a former cellmate who, several years earlier, had been one of Mr. Clutter's field workers, and whose account of the Clutter setup included a money-filled safe which isn't, and never was, there.

In short, Capote has it both ways, the mystification and the clarification. And the narrative evolves through a succession of firmly written scenes—scenes that are occasionally, I think, *too* slickly executed and that end with too obtrusive "curtains." These, unfortunately, embrace a concluding graveyard scene where the weather and the sentiment—Life Goes On—are unmitigated Hollywood.

But no known film maker could easily convey in his medium that elusive interplay of the gratuitous and the determinate which makes *In Cold Blood* at its best both artful and lifelike. True, Perry Smith, although thoroughly individualized, is also a clinically perfect type of the misfit turned psychopath and the psychopath turned killer. But his partner? Nothing in Hickock's antecedents accounts for his becoming a criminal on this scale of brutal inconsequence. In so far as the crime has a definable and possibly remedial cause, it lies in the nature of prisons, the kind of mentalities and associations apt to be fostered by prisons. For the rest the cause is something in the relationship of Smith and Hickock, a relationship so involuted and internal that it can be made believable, as Capote does make it, not through any of the usual formulas of partnership or palship, but solely in the shifting minutiae of their behavior from incident to incident. How, moreover, to represent in any medium less flexible than Capote's other significant relationships? For example, that of Mrs. Clutter and her daughter, the mother who feels herself displaced and the daughter who, in all apparent humility and sweetness, has filled her place? Or that of the two principal fathers, Nancy Clutter's and Perry Smith's, who never of course meet but who are, each in his own place, Kansas and Alaska, and in his own way, embodiments of free enterprise and the pioneering spirit?

Until now, Truman Capote's literary record has been somewhat uneven. A series of well-written, never quite negligible, passes at literature has made it up. At last, in a small Kansas town disrupted by a peculiarly horrible and bewildering crime, he seems to have found, for a time, a sort of spiritual home, complete with a lovable police force. At least he discovered there a subject equal to his abilities. These appear to have required that he profess, and no doubt sincerely believe, that he was composing a non-fiction *novel*. In a way, Capote's claim is the more believable because it perpetuates, by inversion, an ancient literary impulse: the impulse of romancers to create a fiction within a fiction. The tale twice told of Cervantes or of Hawthorne, the story shaped within the consciousness of some imaginary observer (Henry James and others), are of this tradition. Capote's inversion of the tradition is itself a striking response to the present-day world and to the tendency noted earlier in this review: the tendency among writers to resort to subjective sociology, on the one hand, or to super-creative reportage, on the other. As Lionel Trilling once observed, it is no longer poetry but history, preposterous current history, which beggars the literary imagination and requires us to attempt a "willing suspension of disbelief." But it is surely to Capote's credit that one cannot quite suspend one's disbelief that *In Cold Blood* is a novel.

1966

Wilson
without
Reputation

This volume* is a reissue—with alterations and omissions duly acknowledged in the Preface—of a book made out of the author's experiences in Europe (chiefly England, Italy, and Greece) during the final terrible months of the Second World War. The writing of it was undertaken on assignment for *The New Yorker* and the results were first published as a volume in 1947. To this series of vivid "sketches among the ruins," as Wilson calls them, are now added some *Notes From a Diary of 1963–64: Paris, Rome, Budapest*. The *Notes* were also published, quite recently, in *The New Yorker*. But they show less of the alertness of someone writing on assignment, more of the fatigue of an aging—though far from moribund—tourist writing on his own. Piecemeal, often imprecise and cranky, the *Notes* are, conspicuously, from a diary. Occasion is nevertheless found for including in them a lengthy account—more like a good encyclopedia article than a diary entry—of puppeteering.

First mention is here given to Wilson's book rather than to Wilson himself for a special reason. Increasingly, it seems to have become impossible for anyone to write about any of his books without remarking at length on his "reputation," a loom-

---

* *Europe Without Baedeker*, by Edmund Wilson.

ing phenomenon. The causes of the Reputation, and the value of it relative to the value of that widely despised commodity, literary criticism in general, is one of the stock subjects of the higher journalism at present. Sometimes the much eulogized Reputation is dis-eulogized, declared to be overblown. By and large, however, it forms a spectacle that excites only praise— praise, moreover, of the peculiarly gratifying kind that appears to give pleasure to the giver, as well, presumably, as to the receiver and to that part of the public which, to its credit, rejoices in a well-earned success story.

With a single reservation, the present writer is at one with the praisers. To me Edmund Wilson has been an indispensable figure almost as far backward in time as my literary memory extends. Yet—here is the reservation—Wilson is frequently eulogized, not only on his own merits but at the expense of other, lesser critics. Exclusiveness reigns here as it does not reign, to any such extent, in the departments of fiction, poetry, or drama. The implication seems obvious: Criticism is tolerable, in fact admirable, only insofar as it is represented by the work of a single major figure; otherwise it is suspect.

One rural editor put the matter graphically when he wrote that, compared to Edmund Wilson, all other living critics are as mice scampering around the Master's feet. Wilson was evidently sent a copy of the editor's remarks, for he replied (the reply was promptly published), "Thanks for the plug." No doubt he thought the occasion too trivial for further comment, thus failing to disassociate himself from the vulgar invidiousness of the "plug." Yet the rural editor was only doing what, as I say, other writers have done repeatedly with more finesse: elevated Wilson, that is, while humbling most others of his profession. Generally the humbled are said to belong to some narrow, conspiratorial circle, say the "New York Critics" or the "new Critics"—the latter group, incidentally, a collective dead horse which continues to be flogged, so persistently and with so little discrimination that it has acquired the status of an immortal scapegoat, flayed all over, the life long since gone out of it, but still good for a passing kick. How seriously is Wilson himself involved in this process of making him into a Moloch or Minotaur? One can't confidently say, except to note that he has given tacit consent to the process and even at times gone victim-hunting on his own. A habit of swagger, often recklessly cruel, is common among longtime survivors who have made it. The aged Yeats, Shaw, Churchill, and Gertrude Stein afford precedents, not to mention the abominations in this line of the aging, but as we now know half-demented, Hemingway.

What is most disturbing about Wilson's attitude, as I understand it, is the extent to which it seems to represent a concession to present-day literary attitudes and manners and thus to be at odds with the attitudes and manners of Wilson's own literary generation in its prime. On the whole, literary manners today are awful—virile and exciting, yes, but absurdly vindictive, self-advertising, and in the long run self-destroying. Dog eats dog, or at least cat cat, only to find that he has made an unappetizing spectacle of himself. (Truman Capote's overblown campaign of self-publicity for *In Cold Blood* accounts for many of the equally silly and quite irrelevant attacks on his fine book.) Contemporary literary manners rest on assumptions peculiar to this inflationary age, an age habituated to the imminence of "explosions" in all things, from culture in general to literary reputations in particular. To expect immediate recognition is common; to develop acute paranoia when recognition fails to materialize in full and without qualification is not uncommon. The times are, or seem to be,

magnificently astir; anything can happen, and does, with consequences, for writers, that are about equally inspiriting and
demoralizing.

Quite different literary manners still prevailed when, in the
Thirties, I first knew Edmund Wilson. They prevailed, I
mean, with him and, I would guess, with other of his contemporaries such as Cummings, Stevens, Tate, Dos Passos, and—
despite their resounding public roles—Pound and Eliot. Not
that these writers were merely "modest." Inwardly, at least,
they seem to have felt immense pride, the natural concomi-
tant of their shared ambition to make new the fiction, poetry,
or criticism of the English-speaking world. The very size of
their ambition nevertheless qualified their expectations of immediate fame. Nor did their intense rivalries and loyalties take
the form of public feuding and acts of mutual demolition to the
extent that similar rivalries and loyalties (if any) do today. Yet
each of those older writers—the good ones—gave the impression of being a fully self-made self. Marvels of individuality,
intricate, prickly, often hermetic, they confirmed Hopkins's
claim that every first-rate literary talent "is like a species in
nature, and never recurs." Even so, most of them conceived
of the literary life as an affair, so to speak, of adjoining ateliers,
in each of which the single talent thrived in proportion as it
gave assent and aid to a common cause, that of remaking, as
I say, art and literature. D. H. Lawrence was the great exception, a genius trapped in an age of genius; and it is Lawrence's
pugnacity, or a travesty of it, along with Hemingway's more
visceral approach, that has helped to fix the literary tone of the
present age.

Like others of his generation, the Wilson I knew in the
Thirties and early Forties showed a marked diffidence toward
public opinion, friendly or hostile. The "atelier," his and that

of the rest, was open to qualified outsiders. There you could spend an entire evening in distinguished company without once mentioning—as today it would be fatal to fail of doing—the "work" of one's host or hosts. The diffidence was charming, merely assumed though it may often have been in conformity with the prevailing manners. It was also, possibly, a useful form of self-restraint. As a member of a younger generation, I recall the times when, on making the acquaintance of one or another of those older writers, I violated the code. Warned though I had been, for example, against referring to Dos Passos's work in his presence, I found Dos Passos so friendly and in his bashful way so communicative on our first meeting—again in the Thirties—that the warning was forgotten. While talking alone with him about a woman we both knew I let fall the suggestion that she reminded me of a certain character in *U.S.A.* With that the author of *U.S.A.* turned crimson and stammered something unintelligible. To the distress I already felt was added the pang of realizing that Dos Passos was exerting himself just in order to *spare* me distress.

With Wilson, whom in those years I saw more often, the diffidence was less pronounced though in its own way it was inescapable. When, occasionally, he spoke kindly of something I had written, he spoke with conviction but very quickly, as if any talents I might possess were to be taken for granted. When, however, I undertook to review *To the Finland Station* and found little in it to object to, he sent me a postcard saying that he would have appreciated more criticism. Had I been guilty in his eyes of the unpardonable sin, as it then was in the best literary circles, of logrolling? Another time, talking with him about Yeats, I said that the chapter on Yeats in *Axel's Castle*, which I had just been rereading, had survived very well all the more recent hullabaloo about that poet. "No, no,"

Wilson replied, again with conviction but quickly, "It's very dated. It won't do at all." And just as I had not meant to logroll before, so now the intention of flattery was far from my mind. In fact, our conversations had by this time become difficult, even slightly irascible, owing to my inability to cope with Wilson's conversational tactics—those habits of flat contradiction and of one-upmanship to which he has since confessed, not at all ruefully, in print.

He several times conveyed dissatisfaction with other of his writings, doing so, however, always with authority, even with pride, never as if asking for reassurance or offering extenuation. In short, the dissatisfaction was genuine beyond a doubt. And whatever it may have owed to literary manners, it owed more to his now celebrated pioneering spirit. As his eulogists have often noted, Wilson's pioneering spirit manifests itself in numerous ways. He continually explores and settles new literary territory. He also revisits, scrutinizes afresh, and alters for republication, the quite sizeable world of his own past writings.

That this expansiveness takes its toll in the form of occasional superficiality and poor judgment is equally a feature of the legend. While bestowing honors on some second-rate Sicilian or Canadian writer, Wilson is capable of ignoring or condescending to the first-rate talents that exist—literally—under his nose. This limitation has had its advantages; it has made work for less ambitious critics. To poor Richard Blackmur, for example—"poor" because so often associated with the New Critics and sacrificed with them to Moloch Wilson—was left one of the essential critical jobs of the century. I mean the making more or less accessible to the common reader the American modernist poets—poets who, in certain cases, were once Wilson's neighbors and acquaintances in the Village and who wrote for the same periodicals. To them he never really gave the time of day. Yet theirs turns out to have been probably the most substantial achievement of his generation, their very modes of life testifying to the kind of moral character, the capacity for long and sustained efforts against odds which, in other instances, have so often fired Wilson's critical imagination. Still his expansiveness is a prime reason for his indispensableness. To it he owes, above all, the forceful narrative momentum of his essays, that effect of a venturesome critical expedition whose outcome is the more eagerly awaited because not readily foreseen.

Europe Without Baedeker made little stir in America on its first publication; it is nevertheless indispensable Wilson. Here as in his other travel books he is, most literally though in his own fashion, the pioneer. His fashion is the opposite of those travel writers, from Gautier and Stendhal to Doughty and the two Lawrences, who deliberately visit and write up places which tend to be highly exotic and which therefore require of the traveler and writer that he submit his usual sense of himself to the exquisite ordeal of transplantation or at least of adaptation. The exotic in this sense interests Wilson little, and the perilous luxury of self-surrender even less. Rather, it is in places that lay claim to a considerable culture, old or new, fine or foolish, and that therefore stimulate the social critic's faculties, rather than the impulses of the seekers of self-knowledge, which form the subjects of his travel books: those about the Soviet Union in the Thirties, the American hinterlands during the Depression, or the new state of Israel. And it is not surprising to find him describing, in *Europe Without Baedeker*, his encounters in war-demoralized London with a French prostitute who, unlike her bedraggled and bedevilled English co-professionals, preserved the self-esteem and decorum of a native Parisienne. "Odette was in good shape and handsome, and conducted her commerce with men with the same sort of efficiency and dignity with which she would have run her shop. She was scrupulously hygienic, and availed herself of every resource to eliminate both squalor and risk."

Thus Wilson in his best eighteenth-century manner. In fact, and for reasons to be considered later in this review, his well-known affinities with the writers of the English Enlightenment are very much to the fore in *Europe Without Baedeker.* Thus women of all ages and degrees of respectability make frequent and candid appearances in the book, chiefly for the simple reason that women strongly attract Wilson. Essentially, though, he remains the social critic where women are concerned. Their condition as affected by the War is an enticing clue to the condition of Europe's culture in general; and it is the conjunction of the two, wretched Europe and wretched if often courageous women, that brings the cool pathos of the book to a not infrequent simmer. For the rest, Wilson here takes sexual passion for granted. It is a *Ding an sich* just as sex probably was for Hume when he wrote that "the two greatest pleasures of life are study and society," doubtless including in the word "society" his relations of all kinds with women.

One reviewer of *Europe Without Baedeker* has politely noted that the book is "dated in several particulars." The truth is that the book is dated in a great many particulars—so radically dated that it is no mere period piece but a historical document of lasting merit and interest.

As viewed by Wilson in 1945, Europe comes as close to looking like an apocalyptic mess as is compatible with his obvious determination to avoid high-keyed impressionism and blanket judgment. His effort, on the contrary, is to see things one by one, and in themselves as they really are. Hence the mosaic-like form of the book, the clusters of relatively brief and discrete passages that make it up. Read in succession, these carefully wrought and placed little pieces of observation work both ways upon the reader's mind. Europe's misery is seen in all the variety of its kinds and degrees and in all the horror of its appalling generality. The misery manifests itself in the condition not only of single women but of families, and in that of persons and groups undergoing the slow torment of displacement. Here too there are different kinds and intensities of suffering. A White Russian family that Wilson visits several times in Rome has been displaced for decades; homelessness is for them almost a way of life, although one of the sadder ways; and while their eminently refined faces are further emaciated by hunger, the ladies can nevertheless conjure up, when they have to—and as it were out of their recollections of old Russian gentility—a meal that Wilson makes sound attractive. At the other extreme are, for example, the brutalized London prostitutes and the homeless *ragazzi* of Italy. The latter are not only emaciated; they are white with the papery whiteness of corpses; they beg, thieve, and pimp in a world that is all timeless jungle, without past gentilities or future promises.

Meanwhile, in its political aspect, *Europe Without Baedecker* is equally devastating although far from perspicuous regarding what have since proved to be Europe's powers of recovery. Wilson sees the war as having exacerbated the nationalism and racism of Europeans. The worst of their native traits are thus written large as in a caricature. For him, the English in their late-war extravagances of manner are the hardest to take. Englishmen of the upper classes are still determined to run the show in Italy, Greece, and Yugoslavia. Those whom Wilson encounters seem, on the average, to be trying to submerge any consciousness they may have of the absurdity involved in their continuing to exercise a power that in fact they no longer possess. The condescension and the hypocrisy with which the English have, in their heyday, treated the peoples of "inferior" nations are thus at present grotesquely exaggerated. On this subject, Wilson is funny in a deadly sort of way. English conversational tactics, which to him resemble a kind of mental judo, are described with special precision and gusto, perhaps because they recall Wilson's own conversational habits. One of these tactics, however, is certainly not his. It consists in a last-ditch resort to gross irrelevancies or alleged forms of inside dope on the part of those Englishmen whose opinions are seriously challenged. Wilson quotes one such official who, in his efforts to run down Marshal Tito, is finally reduced to saying, "Why Tito's not even his name! His real name is Josef Broz!"

Here Wilson might have said something not by way of excusing such conduct but of generalizing it. Surely there is a Pall Mall clubman ready with a snub or a bit of supposed scandal in almost everyone when he is hard-pressed enough. For example, a kindly Yugoslav professor, a woman, whom I first met in her country and saw last year in New York, said of the rebellious Mihajlo Mihajlov, who was on the staff of her own university and whose prosecution by his government I hesitatingly mentioned to her: "Well, you know," she said, "whatever the rights and wrongs of it all, Mihajlo is a very *disagreeable* person." Seeing that she was really upset by "it all" I decided not to ask her if disagreeableness was a criminal offense in Yugoslavia.

Between the seemingly hopeless London, Rome, and Athens of Wilson's book and the giddily revived London, Rome, and Athens of the present, the contrast is great. But if the book thus appears to seethe with irony, the irony is of course projected on it by the reader as he puts together the two pictures of Europe, Wilson's in 1945 and the one left in the reader's mind by his own more recent travels. Looked at together, the two pictures raise strange doubts, not as to Wilson's veracity but as to the soundness, the very "reality" even, of this resurrected, and swinging, Europe—or of anything.

To be sure, there is something in Edmund Wilson's temperament that may have made him especially responsive to the catastrophic-seeming aspect of Europe in 1945. That something is an elegiac, even on occasion apocalyptic, strain in him, a strain that has generally mingled oddly with its opposite, the tendency in him to an assertive rationalism and self-reliance. The elegiac note was sounded in his work as early as *Axel's Castle*. There the author was saying not only Hail but also Farewell to Proust, Joyce, and company and calling Proust's world, resoundingly, "the Heartbreak House of capitalist culture." But criticism, not prophecy, is Wilson's business, in *Europe Without Baedeker* as elsewhere. His goodbye-to-all-that side has misled him at times. It is nevertheless connected, as a similar among-the-ruins pathos was in Gibbon, with all that is best in his work—the wonder, the richness, and, at times, the very glory of it. What I have in mind is his imagination of greatness, a greatness that is not Nietzschean, not the property of a disciplined elite, but that, nourished as it often is on adversity and on the courage and the intelligence ideally called up by adversity, can manifest itself in inconspicuous individuals as in celebrated ones and in any state of culture short of barbarism. Hence, in *Europe Without Baedeker*, Wilson's feeling for the aged Lampedusa and his work, a feeling I don't share. Hence also—to give another dubious example—his comparison of *South Wind* to

The Marble Faun, a comparison which is intended to stress Hawthorne's sturdy Yankee moralism as against Norman Douglas's frivolity but which actually arises from a misreading of *The Marble Faun* in several important particulars, and from an unawareness that Hawthorne raises the most profound questions, moral and theological, but evades them miserably at the end. There the young American hero finally formulates these questions only to back away from them when his beloved Hilda, the "Daughter of the Puritans," objects. "O Hilda, guide me home!" he then promptly cries, a cry that is about the sorriest surrender to the moral tyranny of the Little Woman in all American fiction.

Hence, on the other hand, the many instances in *Europe Without Baedeker* in which Wilson does convincingly depict the triumph, often muted and minimal, of character over circumstance. So doing, he gives the impression, doubtless unintentional, of trying to perpetuate English traditions which the English themselves, he may have felt, are no longer in a position to sustain. So he here combines the common sense of Hume with the moral feelings of Sterne, so delicate, equable, and profound, applying both to a subject, the decline and fall of Europe, that requires for proper understanding something of Gibbon's complex but forthright fusion of historical and moral judgments.

By saying all this I may seem to be loading with significance a book that is perhaps only a very good specimen of the higher journalism. For me, however, the book in its present form—with the hasty and sentimental pro-Americanism of the original version partly cut away—is a small but perfect revelation of Wilson's powers—powers that have, as noted above, been so much eulogized that his "reputation" tends to loom larger than his actual work. Yet *Europe Without Baedeker* gives much new evidence of Wilson's powers. Even the glimpses of cities, landscapes, and states of weather, though always brief and restrained, are peculiarly fresh and expert, as when he remarks that one "looks out, in a commanding view . . . over the infinite lines and planes of Rome, all gray-blues and dry pale buffs, which are matched, during the winter sunsets, by the pale blues and pinks of the skies, in which the eternal swifts restlessly flock and twitter." (If this recalls the swelling cadences, the dying falls, and the omnipresent relative pronouns of the Heartbreak House of capitalist culture, the Proustian influence is nevertheless much less apparent in *Europe Without Baedeker* than it is elsewhere in Wilson's writing.)

Rome's infinite lines and planes are there, immutably one hopes, and so are the swifts, whose twitterings, however, are now apt to be drowned out by the roar of evening traffic. Just as immutably there, in Wilson's pages, are the figures of human endurance, of greatness *in petto,* portrayed as they are cannily and without guff or gush: that French prostitute in London, the White Russian ladies in their shabby Gianicolo villa, a pair of Italian youths who, for the equivalent of ten cents a day, make a profession of hunting for mines and booby traps—it is a perilous profession requiring much physical deftness and technical skill, qualities that the youths take considerable pride in displaying. Among the celebrated there is Santayana, whom Wilson, like many other pilgrims of the time, goes to see in his refuge at the Blue Nuns' convent. Santayana professes to be ignorant of Wilson's very name, let alone his work: he thus risks arousing in Wilson the impulse to mischief which others have registered apropos of Santayana—those, I mean, who are not moved by him to extremes of piety. Still, Santayana talks, and Wilson talks, and between them they provide the future author of *Europe With-*

out Baedeker with material for a portrait that allows for both Santayana's undoubted splendor of mind as well as his rather self-conscious and exclusive *grandezza*.

One concludes that Wilson is after all a modified Nietzschean type. The greatness in himself is nourished by his happiness at discovering elements of greatness in others. For Wilson—and never more strikingly than in the gloomy *Europe Without Baedeker*—people, like books, cities, landscapes, and historical events, exist not merely to be judged, severely critical though he is capable of being. Rather, they are something to get excited about, in however restrained a way, when they give any sign of meriting excitement.

1966

Flaubert
and *The Sentimental Education*

The Sentimental Education was first published in the Paris of 1869, thirteen years after the triumphant appearance there of *Madame Bovary;* and the later novel has remained ever since in the long, long shadow of the earlier one, waiting for full recognition. The reasons for this preference may seem cogent, at least to the "average" reader of novels. Thoroughly original in its conception and its language, *Madame Bovary* still rests on the ancient formula of sin and retribution and so moves steadily toward a decisive end: the suicide of Emma and the ruin of her family. Emma's adventures dominate the action; one's attention is the more acute for being fixed on a single line of development.

True, Emma is a wretched woman, and her character and culture are relentlessly dissected by the author. Yet she has the advantage for any reader of being violently real in her physical presence. Her lush, irritated sensuality works on one's own sensuality, even to the moment when, agonizing on her deathbed, she "stretches out her neck" and "glues her lips" to the crucifix offered her by the priest. Emma dying is the same person as Emma living, the literal embodiment of unlimited *desire*. One might say that she has turned into the very stuff of her daydreams: the stuff of sex and body, of the money, jewels, carriages, draperies, and yards of dress goods she has coveted. And Emma's ghastly "materialization," so to speak, has a pathos about it. The impoverished *mœurs de province*, the phrase Flaubert uses for the book's subtitle, defeat her efforts to escape them. Confined to her dismal province, she feels permanently excluded from Paris, where all the good things—sex, money, jewels, and the rest— presumably abound.

In *The Sentimental Education* bountiful Paris is itself the scene of most of the drama. The characters are numerous and rather better endowed than Emma is with culture and experience. Nevertheless they come to ends which for the most part are not decisive ends at all; they just fade away into nothingness. The Paris of *The Sentimental Education* is "sick" in much the same secondary sense as that word has today. And during Flaubert's lifetime it was one thing to represent the provinces as "sick," quite another to represent as "sick" a great city, the capital of a great nation's culture as well as its government. On its first publication *The Sentimental Education* was condemned by all but a few of Flaubert's contemporaries as ailing itself: politically perverse, morally squalid, and an aesthetic failure. Until recently the book has been stuck with that reputation, so far as the large public is concerned, while *Madame Bovary* has continued to flourish.

Nothing in recent literary history is better known than the contagious fame won by *Madame Bovary* in its time and after. Emma's appeal to readers was equalled by the appeal of the novel itself—its subject as well as the sophistications of its form and language—to young novelists in all the novel-producing countries. Flaubert's new, exacting realism was adapted to the life stories latent in other provinces, remote from France, where young men and women yearned for other capitals: Moscow, Madrid, New York, even Chicago.

Implicit deep within *Madame Bovary,* however, is a theme which only the greatest of Flaubert's progeny have laid hold of—insofar as it was not given by their own experience—and the theme becomes quite explicit in *The Sentimental Education;* though publicly neglected, the *Education* soon acquired an underground reputation, especially with writers. This theme was the existential one: the perception of a growing estrangement from "real experience" and the "lived life" —vague terms for elusive but powerful feelings—on the part of individuals living in whatever locale, provincial or metropolitan. This perception was at the heart of Flaubert's idea of modernity; he and Baudelaire were the first "modernists," not solely because of the innovations they brought to the art of writing but because each developed powerful conceptions of the nature of modernity itself.

The history of Flaubert's influence, as the author of both novels and tales like *Un Cœur simple,* is formidable. It has been a history not of imitations, which don't matter, but of transformations—unpredictable, brilliant, self-perpetuating. Among the novelists strongly affected there was Henry James, especially in *The Bostonians;* and later there were Proust and Joyce (not to mention the several French writers who were Flaubert's immediate disciples). The least predictable episode in this history was the infusion of Flaubertian spirit, together with the Baudelairean-*Symboliste* spirit, into modernist *poetry,* chiefly the earlier poetry of Eliot and Pound. As Flaubert had fought for a prose that was as well written as poetry, so Pound fought for a poetry that was as well written as prose— meaning, in part, Flaubert's prose: its precise rhythms, its acutely particularized images.

Of the two poets, Eliot was the more susceptible to the existential theme, as localized in his "Unreal City." Bored, restless, and afraid, the people of the Unreal City are sub-liminally anxious to hear the saving Word but can only hear the comforting commonplace: "Cousin Harriet, here is the *Boston Evening Transcript.*" Our knowledge of Eliot has helped us to identify and understand the function of common-places and banalities in *The Sentimental Education.* Mme Arnoux remarks to Frédéric: "Sometimes your words come back to me like a distant echo, like the sound of a bell carried by the wind." Mme Arnoux talks like Eliot's too baffled, too articulate "lady of situations" in her several guises. The Flau-bertian tradition has been a two-way thoroughfare.

Where Flaubert's influence is concerned, however, qualifications are called for. To his literary progeny Flaubert was assimilable only in part. He was a difficult father figure whose testament was full of discriminatory clauses that seemed to require contesting. His pessimism was too unyield-ing, his work a triumph of artifice over art, his style a medium too solid to transmit the possible varieties of feeling implicit in his subjects.

Henry James objected that Flaubert "had no faith in the power of the moral to offer a surface." This delicately phrased judgment is convincing if one agrees with James about how "the power of the moral" asserts itself upon the "surface," that is, in the necessarily aesthetic style and form of any good novel. For James "the moral" makes itself felt through a series of identifications between the best in the author and the best in his readers, with the characters acting as agents in the transaction: those of his characters, I mean, who at *their* best are capable of reaching states of consciousness about them-selves and their situations, and then of acting decisively on the data of consciousness. For James, experience is the great teacher and the lesson is the primacy of mind, mind as awareness. In his own subtle fashion James was captivated by the *Bildungsroman* conception of literature. Flaubert was not. James's New World idealism was alien to Flaubert's conception of the average human potential in the age of modernity, itself a manifestation of the sovereignty of the average. *The Sentimental Education* is a negative *Bildungsroman*. With the characters, the education by experience doesn't "take." They learn nothing. For readers, the novel is an *un*learning of indefensible sentiments and ideas.

Among Flaubert's other putative descendants, Eliot and Proust found different exits from the Flaubertian Limbo. For Eliot, the saving Word is really *there*, even if it comes to us garbled and attenuated, offering partial epiphanies and precarious conversions. For Proust transcendence is the peculiar privilege of the artist, a conclusion that gives his wonderful big-bodied novel, clamorous with suffering, a very small head.

Only Joyce among "moderns" surpassed Flaubert in greatness while possessing a similar vision of human limitation; both writers were of course renegade Catholics. Joyce's Dublin, like Flaubert's Paris, is incurably stricken (Victor Brombert* astutely diagnoses the particular Parisian *mal* as a universal susceptibility to *prostitution*). Dublin epiphanies range from the frankly false to the merely promising. The immanence of myth deflates reality. Molly Bloom is more Molly than earth mother. In Dublin nothing really happens, nothing transcendent. Dubliners simply reveal, for the reader's pitying or amused contemplation, the general lifeness of life: people are what they are, not in any past or future imagined by them, but in what they feel and do and imagine at any given moment or hour or day in their lives.

---

* *The Novels of Flaubert: A Study of Themes and Techniques* (Princeton, 1967).

But there was at least one great difference between them. Flaubert's doctrine of "impersonality" in art was equally an item in Joyce's literary creed. But impersonality can be "cold" or "warm." Joyce's is warm in the profoundly, elusively tempered way that the impersonality of Shakespeare and Cervantes is "warm." Flaubert's is cold, with variations here and there. His relationship with his characters tends toward incompleteness; a void is formed which the author's brilliant irony is seldom capable of filling. This, to me, is the most problematical element in his work; yet it is not the whole story of his work. What Mark Van Doren has written about Thomas Hardy, another implacable ironist, is true of Flaubert too: "He is that most moving of men, the kind that tries not to feel yet does." Flaubert does feel, almost in spite of himself, especially when his subject is the betrayal or exploitation of the helpless: Emma Bovary's husband; the servant woman in *Un Cœur simple;* and, in the *Education*—among several others— Dussardier, the worker who is the captive and victim of his bourgeois friends. The pity that comes easily to certain other writers is the more moving in Flaubert because to him it comes hard, when it comes at all.

A recent English, very English, critic condemned *The Sentimental Education* as "an attack on human nature." One admits the charge is true, while wondering what is so great about human nature that it should be declared immune from attack. Flaubert's aloof, melancholic temperament caused some of the bleakness of his vision, as any writer's negations or affirmations owe something to his temperament. Yet the bleakness is also inherent in an Old World skepticism, a pre-bourgeois *désabusement* concerning human nature as manifested in society, the only form in which human nature can be known. In Flaubert the moralism of, say, Montaigne, Pascal, and La

Rochefoucauld survives, with the newly bourgeoisified Paris rather than feudal Paris as the object of his censure or derision. Invoking a writer's traditions is an easy way of making him respectable. Flaubert was the rare kind of writer, later celebrated by Eliot in a famous essay, in whom a strong sense of tradition interacts with great originality to produce the "new, really new work."

His more immediate precedents for *The Sentimental Education* were, it would seem, the comprehensive eighteenth-century satires, among which *Candide* and *Gulliver's Travels* were intimately known to Flaubert. Like those earlier satires, *The Sentimental Education* is an attack on the whole modern spectacle of human *bêtise*, imbecility. Indeed, the *Education* has always been taken with the wrong kind of seriousness by critics who are insufficiently tough-minded or are too humorless to see that the book is essentially if often deceptively comic, anticipating the pure comedy of *Bouvard et Pécuchet,* his next—and last—important work. "Deceptively" because the comic effect of the *Education* is generally subdued to conform to the generally dreary realities of bourgeois existence. The method of the satires was comic fantasy touched here and there with realism and pathos; Flaubert's method is realism touched with the fantastic; many episodes of *The Sentimental Education* are as outrageously comic as anything in *Candide.*

Candide was one of Flaubert's "sacred books"; and the *Education* forms certain relationships with it that are worth noting. Both narratives move at a frantic pace, "cresting," like a flood, in a pair of major phenomena, the Lisbon earthquake and the 1848 Revolution; in both narratives, too, the episodes are strung along a continuous thread of romance: Candide's enduring devotion to his much put-upon dream girl, Cuné-

gonde, and Frédéric Moreau's devotion to *his* much put-upon
Mme Arnoux, a rather mature dream girl. While a playful
irony attaches to Candide's affair, an irony that is alternately
light and corrosive informs Flaubert's account of Frédéric's
affair.

The two heroes are, however, essentially unlike. Candide is
a thoroughgoing "innocent" whose continuing innocence is
guaranteed by his incorruptible good will. Frédéric is innocent only by virtue of the Romantic literary convention which
tended to attribute this quality to the young, so long, at least,
as they stayed young. (Flaubert's ironic subtitle to *The Sentimental Education* is *L'Histoire d'un jeune homme*.) In his fine
study of the novel,* Harry Levin calls the mature Frédéric
"a dilettante who has survived his innocence." I would only
object that Frédéric's innocence and the good will it rests on
have been subject to corruption from the start. So while Candide gets his reward, is at last reunited with Cunégonde, and
they are left cultivating their garden, Frédéric loses Mme
Arnoux, the possession of whom he has always blown hot and
cold about, and is left cultivating his memories.

I mention these parallels with *Candide* not to pronounce
The Sentimental Education a classic by association but, again,
to affirm Flaubert's originality. In part, the originality of the
Education consists in his bringing to bear a comic perspective,
infinitely variable in its intensity, on a mass of "real life" characters and stories which normally were subject to serious, or
occasionally serio-comic, concern, especially in popular novels
of the time, like Octave Feuillet's *Roman d'un jeune homme
pauvre*.

In a larger sense, Flaubert's manner here is an adaptation of
the traditionally French manner of working within deliber-

The Gates of Horn: A Study of Five French Realists (Oxford, 1963).

ately confined borders, the success of the performance depending, like the success of laboratory experiments, on just this principled selectivity. The Anglo-Saxon way is different, sometimes causing philistines of that community, even important philistines like D. H. Lawrence, to belittle the energy of French creation. On this subject V. S. Pritchett* remarks, "We [English] tacitly refuse to abstract or isolate a subject or to work within severe limits. . . . A native instinct warns him [the English writer] that he could learn more than is good for him. He could learn, for example, final fatalism and acceptance."

In *The Sentimental Education* it was Flaubert's feat, and one that followed from his comic aims, to have made an epic novel out of an accumulation of anecdotes. The novel is epic because the fates of numerous characters and of a major revolution are embraced in the action; it is anecdotal because each episode recounts—as I think anecdotes do by nature—the momentary defeat or the equivocal victory of someone in a particular situation. In *The Sentimental Education* each episode extracts from the given situation a maximum of irony and then, having made its point with a precision consonant with its brevity, is caught up in the furious current of the enveloping narrative. By itself, anecdotal irony is self-contained, a blind alley. It is irony for irony's sake, such as is apt to inform the anecdotes that circulate in any group of acquaintances, real or fictional, getting from the reader or hearer only a laugh or amused sigh or a murmured "How typical of him!" Superior anecdotes make for superior gossip as distinct from mere talebearing. And the doings of the members of the circle—mostly career-bent intellectuals and their women—that centers on Frédéric Moreau in the *Education* make for superior gossip.

---

* "A Love Affair," in *Books in General* (Harcourt, Brace & World, 1953), p. 104.

However, the irony itself isn't *finally* of the blind alley kind, as the following episode should make clear.

For years Frédéric has been trying at intervals to seduce Mme Arnoux, the faithful wife of his friend, the art dealer Jacques Arnoux. Finally she consents to a rendezvous in a room Frédéric has rented and beautified for the occasion. But she doesn't show up. And after hours of frantic waiting and searching, Frédéric takes his whore to bed in the same beautified room, a case of defiance combined with thrift. Later she wakes up to find him weeping and asks why. "Because I am so happy," he says, meaning the opposite. In itself the outcome of this little episode may deserve no more than a snort of recognition. "How typical of Frédéric!" But this primitive response doesn't stick. There's more to it.

The episode crawls with implications, not only amatory but domestic and political; and promptly caught up in the narrative stream, it goes to feed the rising flood of irony which will at last engulf the novel's entire scene, figuratively speaking. The whore, as I unjustly called her, is really a *lorette* or kept woman, Rosanette Bron, called *la Maréchale*, and is at present the mistress of Jacques Arnoux. Rosanette is beautiful and weirdly charming, by turns affectionate and mean, wonderfully vulgar in her taste for lush boudoirs and Turkish parlors complete with hookahs, and no happier in her profession than Frédéric and his circle of fellow intellectuals are in theirs, but a cut above them in her prodigious if futile vitality.

Mme Arnoux, for her part, has failed to keep the rendezvous because, her young son having come down suddenly with a violent croup, she takes this as a judgment on her for her proposed betrayal of what she instinctively values most: husband, children, home; and for years to come she will rarely see the importunate Frédéric. Meanwhile, searching the streets for her, he hears a noise of rioting on the distant boulevards. "The pear is ripe," he soon reads in an excited note from his friend Deslauriers. Deslauriers is trying to involve Frédéric in the political struggle against the degenerate monarchy of Louis Philippe, an involvement that Frédéric, busy with his love affairs, prefers to avoid. In short his amatory mix-up coincides with the outbreak of those disturbances which, extending from February through June, will be known to history as the Revolution of 1848.

As reported by Flaubert, the uprising generates its own irony and contributes to the epic, or mock-epic, character of the whole novel. It is not only the political "commitments" but even more the personal "motivations" of the participants that naturally fascinate the novelist—the participants including people of all political persuasions, not least the rich banker, Dambreuse, a former conservative who promptly declares himself a republican.

And just as their motivations, better and worse, color the actions of people during the Revolution, so the actions are sometimes heroic, oftentimes fatuous and self-serving. Flaubert's account of the uprising is, again, episodic, his tone dispassionate. He doesn't want to make a monumental set piece out of an event which will turn out to be, from his viewpoint in the novel, a tragic farce. So he touches in more or less detail on such episodes as the abdication and flight of Louis Philippe; the eruption all across Paris of political meetings and street battles; the sacking of the Tuileries palace by a mob; certain incidents connected with the gradual concentration of power in the middle classes and their military force, the National Guard; certain incidents connected with the corresponding loss of power by the working classes; their final defeat; the imprisonment of hundreds of them in vaults beneath the Tuileries facing the Seine where they are left to starve. In one instance an imprisoned youth who screams too insistently for bread is shot to death by Old Roque, Frédéric's miserly home-town neighbor who has hastened down to Paris to take his stand in the National Guard and who commits this decisive act in defense of private property (the memory of it sickens him a little, but not for long).

So the Revolution itself is caught in the embrace of Flaubert's irony. Just as the proletariat is put down by the republican middle classes, so those classes are presently put down—or bribed to surrender—by Louis Napoleon when, in his coup of 1851, he converts the Second Republic into a Second Empire with himself as Emperor. Flaubert soft-pedals this development, possibly because Napoleon III was still in power and his censorship still in effect when Flaubert wrote the novel. But the implications of the coup are made clear. Louis Napoleon has dreamed of playing the same role that his uncle, Napoleon the Great, played when, in 1799, he proclaimed the First Empire, with himself as Emperor, thus terminating the Great French Revolution of those years, and leaving France, with its burden of half-resolved problems, to a century of intermittent turmoil. Two years after the *Education* appeared, Napoleon III would be defeated by the Prussians and driven from France. Paris would again be the scene of a working-class uprising (the Commune) which would again conclude with the slaughter of rebellious proles.

Flaubert's own politics, if any, were protean in the extreme. One might call them, paradoxically, a politics of noncommitment, except that he did now and then react impulsively, and stupidly, to events. He had been no more than a spectator of certain actions in 1848, having been in Paris at the time more or less by chance. But his instinct for detecting the convulsions at work deep within the society was steady, profound, and, alas, prophetic. What Henry James called, in a misguided attempt at reductive wit, Flaubert's "puerile dread of the grocer" was a dread of the entire acquisitive culture which corrupted, or threatened to corrupt, grocer, banker, and worker alike. Flaubert was far less knowledgeable about society than Balzac and Dickens were. Nevertheless, as concerns his visionary pessimism and its effects on his art, there was a point in his refusal to identify his fortunes with those of any existing or pre-existing social class, aristocratic, big bourgeois, little bourgeois, or proletarian. Having no faith in the power of the social—that is of reformism or revolutionism—to offer a surface, he made what he could of his unimpeded, unqualified bleakness of vision. He made, chiefly, *The Sentimental Education*, and the world has now caught up with the bleakness.

"The first time as tragedy, the second time as farce," Karl Marx wrote of the *coups d'état* of the two Napoleons, in words that have been too often quoted since. Flaubert views the events of the years 1848–1851 in a similarly theatrical spirit, though with less hopeful implications for the future of France and its working class than those entertained by Marx.* In

---

* For a modern account of the 1848 Revolution in its pan-European as well as its French aspects see Lewis Namier, *1848: The Revolution of the Intellectuals* (1946). Namier's judgment, supported by the failures of revolutionary or irredentist uprisings in Central and Eastern Europe and in Italy, is close to the judgment of Marx and of Flaubert: "In February 1848, in Paris, political passions devoid of real content had evoked revolutionary phantoms [phantoms of the Great Revolution]. . . . Once more the traditional revolutionary cries were heard, but there was no élan, no sacrificial zeal. . . . All over Europe the middle classes paid lip-service to the 'people' and its cause, but never felt altogether secure or happy in its company. . . . They wanted the revolution to enter like the ghost in Dickens's *Christmas Carol*, with a flaming halo round its head and a big fire extinguisher under its arm." Tocqueville's *Souvenirs* (1893), cited by Namier, include his reminiscences of the 1848–1851 period, in which Tocqueville was himself a participant; his appreciation of the courage and desperation of the working-class actions in Paris is moving. In the same connection I should call attention to Edmund Wilson's pioneering essay, "Flaubert's Politics," in *The Triple Thinkers* (1938).

1835, as a boy of fourteen, Flaubert had observed in a letter to a school friend that "our century is rich in bloody peripeties." Such peripeties, as they affect the characters of the *Education*, bring the harsh comedy of the novel to a climax. The tragic farce of the revolutionary years is a large-scale political manifestation of the farces, bitter or merely ludicrous, enacted by the characters in their individual lives.

The fiasco of 1848–1851 hastens and intensifies all the processes at work in the novel. The temporal process is one of these; it pervades everything, and accordingly accelerates in the years following the Revolution. Yet there seem to be two kinds of time at work in the *Education*, and since the two interact in devious ways, neither is easy to define in itself. The first and more obvious may be identified with what we call "clock time." It consists of the hours, days, months, and years—often specified by Flaubert—during which Frédéric and his circle pursue the objects of their various ambitions. The wretched painter Pellerin boasts that "art, learning, and love—those three faces of God," are solely on view in Paris. And Paris, insofar as it is assumed to enjoy this exclusive privilege, represents the pure present, an eternity of *now*.

Generally invisible to the characters, therefore, are the great monuments of the city's past. In Flaubert's descriptive patches, they appear rarely: furtive reminders of what Frédéric and company tend to ignore. Frédéric is first seen aboard the steamer bound for his home town of Nogent-sur-Seine. As the steamer pulls away from the quay and up the Seine, he gazes regretfully back at the city. "He peered through mists at bell towers and buildings whose names he did not know," while glimpses of Notre-Dame and the Cité merge in his eyes with glimpses of riverside "warehouses, yards, and factories." Caught in the unlimited present, physical Paris is to the characters a faceless configuration of streets, shops, cafés, restaurants, and residences, among which they hustle, trying to meet or avoid meeting one another, and generally contesting for place and preferment like the checkers on an immense checkerboard.

By contrast, the countryside is reserved for holidays and duty visits, and there time's action is naturally decelerated, at least for the Parisians; sooner or later they must be off to the metropolis. It is the presence in the country of the Parisians and the Parisian idea that injects into these rural scenes the peculiar Flaubertian compound of yearning dreariness and elegiac charm. Here as in *Madame Bovary* some of his greatest passages are devoted to bringing out, through people's behavior, through the look and feel and smell of trees, rivers, gardens, palaces, and houses, this intermingling of past and present France, of artificial and natural time, of pastoral "poetry" and realistic "prose." No country scene in the novel is without its intrinsic serenity, no country scene fails to excite an intrinsic anxiety in the minds of characters and, perhaps, readers alike.

In the two chief country-based episodes, one in Frédéric's home town of Nogent, the other at Fontainebleau, love itself partakes of these contradictions, flowering on the serenity, withering with the anxiety. At Nogent as at Fontainebleau the presence of the past is complicated: in both places there are pasts within pasts. At Nogent Frédéric wanders with Louise Roque among waterside gardens strewn with the broken statues and ruined pavilions of a Directoire "folly." Louise is the neighbor girl, once an illegitimate waif, now a potential heiress, who has always adored Frédéric. Since he is at present low on funds and she will have money, it is now vaguely understood between them that he will propose marriage.

Together they sit on the river bank and play in the sand like children, Louise hinting that the clouds are floating toward Paris.

Her passion for Frédéric is awkwardly but violently physical; she envies the way fishes live: "It must be nice to glide in the water and feel oneself stroked all over." The two have reverted to their own pasts, but not for long. On the premises there is a big wood shed, and when Louise suggests they go inside it Frédéric is embarrassed and ignores the suggestion. She breaks into frank reproaches—the frankest and truest he ever gets from anyone—and the pastoral idyl limps to an end. The Parisianized Frédéric has refused to play his appointed role in the idyl. And Louise is left to ripen within the retarded medium of rural time—to ripen, alas, into bitterness.

The idyl motif recurs with variations in the later passage that describes the visit of several days that Frédéric and Rosanette pay to Fontainebleau hoping to get away from the turmoil of revolutionary Paris. Here too there is a monument to an earlier past within the perennial splendor of the great wooded park with its radiating carriage roads, its sunny clearings, deep glens, and outcropping of ancient rock. The monument is the Palace itself, heavy with grandiose mementos of Henry II and his mistress Diane de Poitiers. The Palace excites in Frédéric one of his sudden "frenzies of desire," this one "directed toward the past." But Rosanette is bored and weary and can only say, "It brings back memories." In a way it does. But *her* memories concern herself—her past as an impoverished working-class girl in industrial Lyons, turned *lorette* at the age of fifteen. Her thoughts concern herself *and* Frédéric, whom she too adores, momentarily at least, dreaming of a lasting affair with him. ("One day she forgot herself and told her age; she was twenty-nine and growing old.")

They daily explore the forest in a carriage, happy with each other, feeling a "thrill of pride in the freer life." Yet misgivings shadow their pastoral excursions. They recall other lovers, she Arnoux in particular, he Mme Arnoux. Each yearns discreetly for the lover who is absent. By turns the forest soothes and disturbs them. The vistas into its dark interiors gloom at them; the rocks take on the shapes of wild beasts coming at them. One day Frédéric finds in a newspaper Dussardier's name on a list of men wounded at the Paris barricades. Dussardier is a young man of heroic size and strength, the one authentic worker in Frédéric's circle. It is late June and the workers are making their last stand. Frédéric and the reluctant Rosanette leave for the city, Frédéric finally getting into Paris alone, past barriers and guardposts manned by suspicious National Guardsmen, past ruined barricades and shot-up houses, to the attic room in the house where the wounded Dussardier lies.

Meanwhile Flaubert's Paris, citadel of the pure present, is also subject to the workings, barely perceptible though they are, of natural time as distinct from artificial or clock time. Natural time flows through the city with the river, drifts across its skies with the mists and clouds, manifests itself in the succession of day and night, in the changing seasons, in the winter wind that reddens Rosanette's cheeks, in the setting sun whose rays—in Frédéric's rather mercenary imagination—cover buildings with "plates of gold." If he is more susceptible than others are to these presences, it is, again, never for long. Pausing on bridges, he has exalted visions which, however (as Harry Levin points out), quickly resolve themselves into dreams of instant acquisition.

Parisian epiphanies, Parisian dreams. Yet it should be said that, whatever Flaubert himself thought of the city—and his pleasure in it was intermittent—he shapes the Paris of the

Education to his own selective purposes in the novel. Those purposes have their bit of common truth vis-à-vis the real Paris. Surely Paris was, and is, a great city if there ever was one. It lends itself to satirization (in how many works besides the *Education!*) because its sillier inhabitants are tempted to believe that the city's greatness rubs off on them, causing them to feel unduly self-important.

Pellerin's "three faces of God" slogan is the reduction to nonsense of this Parisophiliac madness. Pellerin himself, like so many of Frédéric's *copains*, suffers from this gratuitous sense of privilege. Haunted by the idea of art, he never makes it as an artist in fact. The actual endowments of *les copains* are unequal to the expectations they have of themselves as Parisians or Parisianized provincials. They remain artists and intellectuals *manqués*. Flaubert knew that they were special types of the Parisian. Scattered through the pages of the *Education* are the names of actual, and variously distinguished, men of the period. Corresponding to Pellerin there are Géricault and Delacroix; to the sometime littérateur Frédéric, Hugo, Chateaubriand, Lamartine; to the radical Sénécal, Proudhon, Barbès, Blanqui, Louis Blanc. The Paris that harbored such men has, we may think, eluded time in all senses, and lives on in an eternity of deserved fame.

The varieties of time are merged into a single powerful force by the happenings of 1841–1851. As the crisis deepens, Flaubert's characters undergo the same rapid changes of heart—from fear to exaltation to final disgust and fatigue—experienced by the populace at large. Individual weaknesses come glaringly to light; everyone grows confused, demoralized, desperate. Even Dussardier is confused. The good if simpleminded prole has been beguiled, as many proles actually

were, into fighting with the bourgeois National Guard during
the June days. Now, his huge body stretched wounded on his
bed, he begins to suspect that he has fought on the wrong side.
He has assaulted a fellow worker at the barricades. Presently
Dussardier himself is shot to death by a policeman newly
recruited to keep order in Louis Napoleon's Second Empire.
The policeman is Dussardier's old friend and mentor, Sénécal,
once known as "the future Saint-Just," long a strenuous advocate of Socialist discipline, scientific logic, proletarian literature, and progress. Sénécal's motivation has been in excess of
his Socialist commitment. His real commitment is to power,
even if exemplified in the lowly figure of the policeman with
uniform and gun.

No other incident connected with the general decline is as
lurid—and prophetic—as this one. Frédéric and the remaining *copains* merely prey on others, and on each other, in their
abasement before the *new* God of three faces: sex, money, and
power. Much that happens in the new situation is merely
ludicrous. There is "the magazine" and *its* change of heart.
Les copains have long struggled to start and keep going the
precious periodical without which no intellectual circle is
complete. Their periodical now ends up as a gossip sheet.
Frédéric's development is scarcely more interesting. He ter-
minates his quest for greatness by trying, and failing, to marry
money.

Only one member of the group survives intact, preserved
by the remarkable system he has imposed on his life. He is the
stern republican, Regimbart, known as "the Citizen," and his
system consists of his rushing around Paris each day in order
to be present in the same cafés or restaurants at the precise
hours he has scheduled for his presence at these establish-

ments. Regimbart's regimen has constituted *his* career. Come revolutions or *coups d'état*, he remains the useful Parisian citizen, a sort of human clock, a walking landmark.

One tends to dwell with special delight on Regimbart and others of his type in the circle of *copains* that surrounds Frédéric Moreau. Frédéric, for reasons that I will go into later on, is not himself a compelling character, although he is the occasion for much anecdotal amusement. Nor are the habitués of that *other* Parisian scene, the Dambreuse salon, compelling either. The rich banker Dambreuse, a bourgeoisified nobleman, and his sleek fashionable wife, later widow, whom Frédéric woos for her money, are puppets; their world is a pastiche of Balzac's world. Flaubert had no such imagination for the aristocracy as Balzac and Proust had.

Regimbart and his type are not puppets. Regimbart, Sénécal, and Pellerin, for instance, are lively grotesques, literal embodiments of their obsessive ideas. Frozen in their characteristic attitudes, they are like figures in Daumier, just as the milder people and their characteristic settings, the studio scenes, the rural scenes, recall those of Courbet. There is, I believe, nothing quite like *les copains* elsewhere in literature, whether in the intellectual milieu of Dostoevsky's Petersburg or of Joyce's Dublin. Only in Paris, where the cultivation of arts and ideologies counts for so much in the *high* French culture, could such debased types of the artist and ideologue as Frédéric and company be found in such profusion.

No doubt the type of the intellectual *manqué* fascinated Flaubert, and for reasons that form part of the well-known Flaubert legend. Acknowledged master though he became at the age of thirty-six with his first publication, *Madame Bovary,* he had in him at all times a good deal of the perpetual amateur, the compulsive dreamer, the man of obsessive ideas.

Born in 1821, he was admittedly, proudly, a belated Romantic. Precociously literary from childhood, he was given to revering, as if they were holy relics, certain images of past beauty: old stones recalled from a visit he made to the Acropolis; old paintings in oil or glass studied in cathedrals or museums; old books—*Candide*, *Don Quixote*, Rabelais—continually reread and pondered through the years; old professions, like sainthood, monkhood, and prostitution; old friendships and exalted moments in his life. Familiar too as part of the legend is the detestation he nourished for the present, the age of "the grocer," as a corollary of his passion for the past. The present was given over to the worship of commodities, so much so that people, their possessions, their careers, their speech, their very dreams belonged to the commodity realm.

Divided souls like Flaubert's were of course common in the emergent industrial democracies of the mid-century and on into our own time. The type has produced connoisseurs, collectors, critics, professional travelers, and, when the luck was good, fine writers, major and minor. Flaubert became a major figure in this tradition, partly by practicing in his literary work a unique form of the division of labor. He split his writings into historical fictions and fictions of contemporary life, while composing all of them with the same attention to style and form. To the world of his historical fictions (*Salammbô*, *La Tentation de saint Antoine*, *La Légende de saint Julien l'hospitalier*, *Hérodias*) he assigned the qualities he worshiped in the past: the heroism, idealism, romance, beauty, and so on; while to the novels of contemporary life (*Madame Bovary*, *L'Éducation sentimentale*) he relegated, so to speak, his sense of the modern materialization of life. As he practiced it, the division of labor had its limitations. It was mechanical. Whether for this reason or another, the bulk of his work was small in an age when novelists were prolific, almost by definition.

The bulk of his *un*published work was considerable. He lived amid a clutter of dormant manuscripts, the continually expanding archives of his restless creative spirit (many of these items have recently been exhumed and put into print). There were the notebooks; the first drafts; the more or less completed works that never saw print (among them an earlier version of *The Sentimental Education*); the assorted early projects that remained fragmentary; the plays that were unproducible or, if produced, as *Le Candidat* was, were flops; the fairy tale briefly worked at in collaboration with friends; the *Dictionnaire des idées reçues*, a compilation of clichés to which he added items through the years and which was to have formed an appendix to *Bouvard et Pécuchet*, the great extravaganza of which he had completed ten chapters when, in 1880, he died.

In addition, letters to friends poured from him in daily profusion: they now fill thirteen indispensable volumes in the posthumously published *Corréspondance*. The letters testify in dizzying detail to the quality of Flaubert's mind. His mind was more than chaotic: protean. It was by turns adult, juvenile, kind, cruel, masculine, feminine, myopic, prophetic, supremely fantastic, supremely intelligent.

Given his genius, there were advantages in being, as Flaubert was, subject to epileptic seizures. He could produce extraordinary masterpieces and still live with his devastating knowledge of the precariousness of everything, one's genius included. To George Sand he confessed when he was quite old: "One doesn't shape one's destiny, one undergoes it. I was pusillanimous in my youth—I was afraid of life. One pays for everything." The condition of his existence was that he remain vulnerable, and for this too he ungrudgingly paid—to the extent, finally, of surrendering to his grasping niece, whom he loved, and to her feckless husband, who faced bankruptcy, much of the income on which his precious independence had rested, and then of looking about for jobs, as librarian or whatever, to support him in his old age.

As the letters make clear, Flaubert himself was not the Flaubert of the invidious literary legend contrived by critics, whose praise for Flaubert's "technique" has been relative in intensity to their distaste for his unseemly habit of self-exposure, his *extremism*, in his novels as well as in his letters. The letters show that Flaubert was not the "confident master of his trade," the "technologist of fiction" that some critics have called him. His kind of realism, compounded of observation, research, and certain specialties of style and construction, was no foolproof method. It was a looming *idea*, which he sought always to realize in different ways in his writings. Great innovator in fiction as he was, he re-created his innovations from work to work. Each work was a fresh start, preceded by anxious deliberation, accompanied in the actual writing by attacks of self-doubt, depression, panic, boredom, disgust. True, his pride in his Idea and his finished work was great, and so was the almost Johnsonian authority he exercised over other writers of his time. Yet the pride and the authority rested on a consciousness, acute and pervasive, of possible failure. The great artist in Flaubert represented a continually renewed triumph over the artist *manqué* in him.

His bond of sympathy with *les copains* and their women, when they have women, is therefore firm—firm in the degree that the sympathy is negative. Among them we find, perhaps, a couple of more or less "lovable rogues," if the traditional phrase really applies to Arnoux and Rosanette; one betrayed "saint" (Dussardier); and one woman (Mme Arnoux) who remains a veiled figure of presumptive goodness until, at the last, unveiling herself, she shows *slight* traces of being what was called in old novels about fallen women "damaged goods." But the fates of all, in particular that of Frédéric, involved the broader problem of human freedom, a problem that is broached more explicitly, with more philosophic flair, in French literature than in most other literatures.

French writers in the tradition of Montaigne and the rest generally raise the question in a negative manner. They harp on the data of human *un*freedom: the perverse impulse of people to enslave themselves to false ideas, ruinous passions, unwarranted pride. In this matter, again, Flaubert perpetuates a tradition by transforming it. His characters abase themselves before the very phenomena of their time that are presumed to liberate them. There is the prevailing idea of progress itself. There are the comforts and luxuries, the printed books and periodicals, the lithographed art works ("the sublime for sixpence") provided by the new industrialism. Most ironically, there are the promises explicit in social revolutions ("No more kings! Do you understand? The whole world is free!"). Enslavement to material affluence and vocational opportunity produces its own kind of moral failure. Frédéric, in whom this kind of failure is enlarged, as under a microscope, names it when in the final scene he casually remarks to Deslauriers, "Perhaps we let ourselves drift from our course."

Drift! Flaubert did indeed have a faith in the power of the moral to offer a surface, and drifting is perhaps the precise word for the moral sickness of his Paris. A man like Frédéric is incapable of fully recognizing the operation on himself of this universal force, which motivates our achievements while surviving them, prompts us to make commitments while working to eventually undermine them. A Frédéric is congenitally unable to reach those ideal states of consciousness which signify the power of the moral for Henry James. Drift is one of those elemental human phenomena, like hunger, of which James is perfectly aware but which he keeps in the background of life, for his own admirable purposes as a novelist of moral dilemmas and decisions. Drift occupies both the foreground and the background of *The Sentimental Education*.

Given this general concern with human freedom, French novelists are fairly consistent about the degree and kind of volition allowed to the characters in their fictional worlds. In general, Stendhal's is a world of the probable, Zola's of the necessary, Flaubert's of the plausible. The "average sensual man" of common realism is largely of his making. But Flaubert brings to this humdrum domain the dashing energy of primary creation. His mastery of the *invention juste* equals his better known mastery of the *mot juste*, or precisely chosen word. Perhaps, as I said, his inventions owe something of their apposite brevity to the anecdote—the *ideal* anecdote which after making its ironic point goes on to waken in the reader amusing recognitions, poignant identifications. Ourselves may be Frédéric. Among our friends may be a Deslauriers, a Pellerin, a Sénécal, a Louise Roque, a Rosanette.

Even so, Flaubert's invented actions have a remarkable way of being unpredictably predictable. He seems to affirm the plausibility principle of realism, its capacity to liberate rather than to confine the imagination, by often stretching things to the verge of *im*plausibility. His intellectuals *manqués* and their women lend themselves readily to this kind of testing. In the men, the ambition to create is strong but the relevant concentration, patience, and intelligence are nil. And it would seem to be the very extravagance of their exertions in this moral void that makes for much that is grotesque, fantastic, and ironic in the spectacle of their existence as mirrored in the *Education*.

By way of illustration, two highly developed scenes, first the masked ball and second Frédéric's last important enounter with Rosanette:

At Rosanette's ball, Frédéric and many of his acquaintances are present. Most of them come dressed as gypsies, Turks, angels, sphinxes—an assortment of standard disguises. Quite naturally, the party's mood changes from hour to hour, going from gay to raucous to boring. But as the dawn light comes through the windows, surprising everyone, the mood turns desperate. The entire scene—people, costumes, furniture—resolves itself into a tangle of debris, a riot of hysteria. "The sphinx drank brandy, screamed at the top of her voice, and threw herself about like a madwoman. Suddenly her cheeks swelled; she could no longer hold back the blood that choked her. She put a napkin to her lips, then threw it under the table." For Frédéric "it was as if he had caught sight of whole worlds of misery and despair—the charcoal stove beside the truckle bed, the corpses at the morgue in their leather aprons, with the cold tap-water trickling over their hair." The ball has become a *danse macabre*, as so many death-in-life party scenes were to become in Proust, Mann, Joyce. Yet the symbolism of Flaubert's scene is qualified by the everyday realism of it. The remaining guests leave to go about their business. Pellerin has a model waiting. A woman has a rehearsal scheduled at the theater. "Hussonet, the correspondent of a provincial journal, had to read fifty-three newspapers before lunch."

Symbolic invention also contends with mere plausibility in the second of these exemplary scenes. Rosanette had originally become Frédéric's mistress because, terrified by the first uproar of the Revolution, she had thrown herself into his arms and because he had at last summoned the brute nerve to take advantage of such a situation. As a professional, Rosanette has since had other lovers besides Frédéric. But she still longs for money, sex, *and* affection. Her vitality is more and more concentrated in her hunger for some kind of lasting attachment. But with whom among the several men in her life? Arnoux? Frédéric? The actor Delmar? She doesn't know, nor would most of these men be available for a lasting affair, even if she did know. Well, there *is* Frédéric, of whom she is fond and whose vagueness of temperament makes him seem available, especially since Mme Arnoux, his dream girl, seems to him unavailable.

Rosanette has a child by Frédéric but the child, a boy, dies in early infancy. Rosanette is frantic. "We'll keep him, won't we?" she asks Frédéric and wants to have the skinny little body embalmed and preserved indefinitely in her rooms. Instead Frédéric suggests that Pellerin be asked to paint the dead baby's portrait. Pellerin arrives promptly. No commission is unacceptable to him so long as he can paint the subject in his own manner—that is, as he says, in the manner of Correggio's children. Or those of Velasquez or Lawrence. Or of Raphael. "So long as it's a good likeness," Rosanette says. "But what," Pellerin cries, "do I care about a good likeness? Down with realism! I paint the spirit." He decides to do the portrait in pastels.

The result when shown to Frédéric is a mess. Painted in wildly clashing colors, his head resting "on a blue taffeta pillow among petals of camellia, autumn roses, and violets, the dead baby is now unrecognizable." But the little corpse remains unburied for an unspecified time, while Rosanette keeps gazing at it, seeing it as a young child, a schoolboy, a youth of twenty. "She had lost many sons. The very excess of her grief had made her a mother many times over." The idea behind all this seems Balzacian or Dickensian in the extravagance of its pathos, but the passage remains pure Flaubert in its understated brevity. Another tragic farce has been played out, in miniature.

Frédéric Moreau is not one of Flaubert's triumphs of invention as applied to character. He is scarcely a character at all, and the fact that he is by intention the novel's unheroic hero, a prototype of the modern anti-hero, doesn't alone explain his dimness. Like Bloom and many lesser modern examples of the type, the anti-hero can be a character among the other characters in a novel, visibly occupying space as they do, making himself felt as they do by his physical presence, the sum of his distinctive modes of speech, gestures, movements, whatever. Apparently Frédéric was his author's alter ego, the sum of Flaubert's own refusals and malingerings; and one's alter ego is apt to be a shadowy creature by nature. Frédéric is all symptoms and no "surface." Flaubert knows him too well, sees through him with a clairvoyance that dissolves its object. The author's self-punishing hand is monotonously present in his hero's thoughts and actions.

The actions can be marvelous in themselves. For example, Frédéric decides to become a politician during the Revolution and so goes to make a speech at a noisy meeting where speakers are shouted down with slogans ("No more matriculation!" "Down with university degrees!" "No, let us preserve them;

but let them be conferred by the people"). When Frédéric's turn to speak finally comes, the platform is seized by "a patriot from Barcelona," who harangues the audience in his native Spanish, a language nobody understands. Frédéric leaves the hall, disgusted with politics as a vocation. Frédéric is Flaubert to the extent of having the same birth date and background that Flaubert had: the provincial home town, the superior social standing, the forceful widowed mother.

Dim though he is, Frédéric has an essential part to play as the center of the innermost circle of characters. His symptoms, as distinct from his character, become interesting when he is seen in relation to the other members of the circle. Those who make it up are, besides Frédéric, Deslauriers, Arnoux, Mme Arnoux, and Rosanette. In the economy of the novel, these five are reserved for intimate inspection at the point in their personalities where social and emotional charges explosively meet. The five of them form a series of interlocking triangles, which are subject of course to frequent interference from the "outsiders": Mme Dambreuse, Delmar, the lurid, enigmatic career woman, Mlle Vatnaz. What brings the five together, apart from their social ambitions, is an intricate configuration of emotional states: love and lust, love and marriage, love and friendship, love *in* friendship.

Primary, by reason of its unparalleled duration, is the friendship of Frédéric and Deslauriers, the poor, mistreated, lonely, unloved, and unlovely youth who becomes a lawyer by profession but will do anything that promises to relieve his desperate poverty and self-hatred. On Frédéric's part, the friendship is based on habit plus his need, from time to time, of Deslauriers's special kind of devotion. Deslauriers, however, really loves Frédéric, with a love that is definitely though

discreetly shown to have a physical side to it.* In his eyes
Frédéric's good looks have something "feminine" about them.
This impression explains, or perhaps justifies for him, the
warmth of their frequent embraces, which otherwise are just
manly Latin hugs. It explains much else: Deslauriers's jealousy of Frédéric's friends; in one case his resentment of his
own mistress, whom he cruelly denounces when she intrudes
on the scene of one of their embraces; the fits of animosity that
punctuate his relations with Frédéric; his conviction that
Frédéric with his intermittent income owes him not only a
living, so to speak, but a share in the hearts and beds of
Frédéric's women, whom Deslauriers covets one after the
other. In his milder way, Frédéric is subject to a similar tangle
of feelings for the Arnoux, husband and wife. Fond of the
rascally, philandering, amusing, good-natured Arnoux, a gour-
met of life, an attenuated Falstaff, Frédéric covets Arnoux's
women, his wife and Rosanette, his mistress. The whole affair
thrives on feelings which are, variously, filial, maternal, paternal, and sexual. Rosanette, on the other hand, is, as we have
seen, given to bestowing her pent up affections on whoever is
available, including her dead infant, although Arnoux is her
favorite. "I'm still fond of the old goat," she tells Frédéric at
Fontainebleau.

Any mere initiate into the deeper psychology can see that
Frédéric's instability, emotional and vocational, arises from his
unconscious desire to remain a child, with a child's privilege
of changing his mind and his allegiances at will; to the inevitable question, "What will you do when you grow up?" the
child, like Frédéric, has at his bidding any number of answers.
Frédéric is by turns "the future Sir Walter Scott of France,"

---

* On this subject I am indebted to an unpublished study by Philip Lopate.

a painter, a politician, a man of the world. The friends and lovers who surround him make up a substitute family, complete with possible fathers, mothers, brothers, and one "kid sister" (Louise). His sexual desires for them are at once stimulated and constrained by the quasi-incestuous implications of the desires.

His protracted, never consummated, affair with Mme Arnoux must be understood in the light of these subconscious impulses. Critics have always tried to view the affair as a genuine sublimation. It is the Great Exception, the Saving Grace, in a novel that is otherwise totally disillusioning. One commentator, Anthony Goldsmith, the translator and editor of the Everyman's Library edition of the *Education*, sees the affair as a "pure romance," exempt from the evils of the World, the Flesh, and Time. To another, Victor Brombert, whose study of the novel is the most accomplished I know of, "Frédéric acquires nobility" from the affair. "For the sake of this 'image' [that of the unattainable Mme Arnoux] he has in the long run given up everything."

Such ideal interpretations rest partly on the established fact that Flaubert transferred to the Frédéric–Mme Arnoux affair certain of his own memories of a boyhood infatuation, also never consummated, for a certain Mme Elisa Schlésinger, whose husband was, like Arnoux, feckless and faithless. Doubts have nevertheless been recently cast on the nature and the duration of Flaubert's love for Mme Schlésinger.* It is supposed that he loved her, as he did others—for example his sister, who died young, and a male friend who also died young—*in memory* only, and his memory, as we have noted,

---

* See Benjamin F. Bart, *Flaubert* (Syracuse University Press, 1967), p. 639 passim.

was a wonderful storehouse of sacred things and moments. He actually saw Elisa rarely in later life, and probably saw her not at all after she and her husband moved to Germany, where she died at a great age, following a series of confinements in a mental hospital. There she was visited by a friend of Flaubert's who reported that Elisa, thin and whitehaired, was a lovely woman still.

To examine at all closely the passages in the *Education* that concern the Great Affair is to suspect that, in adapting the original relationship to his purposes in this novel, Flaubert gave it a searching look. In the *Education* there are, to be sure, charming scenes between Frédéric and Mme Arnoux. Troubled by the conflict between her fondness for Frédéric and her attachment to husband, children, and home, she is touching. Mme Arnoux speaks little, and what she does speak are quite conventional sentiments. Yet she means them, and her speech is the more affecting because it is so unlike the loud, self-serving, sloganeering speeches of *les copains*. Frédéric's part in the affair is another matter. He alternately admires her from afar and tries to seduce her. His doing this may be only "human," but does it make him "noble"? On the contrary, one agrees with Mme Arnoux that her son's sudden illness is a kind of judgment on her and on Frédéric, and that she is right to avoid him.

Yet in the long run she *is* corrupted or half corrupted, though not entirely by him. Arnoux's ventures into "the popularization of the arts" have gone from pretty bad to atrocious, financially and artistically. Only a loan from Frédéric has saved him from disgrace, and following this episode the Arnoux family has disappeared into Normandy for some sixteen years. The Mme Arnoux who after this long separation suddenly turns up alone one evening in Frédéric's Paris apartment is much changed by her sufferings, her isolation, and the sheer impact on her of natural Time.

The scene that follows between them has been described as "heartbreaking." It is heartbreaking chiefly in its falseness, in the sad failure of the two to rise to this putatively great occasion. There are exchanges of reminiscence, professions of eternal love, all in the kind of language that must have been taken for passionate in popular novels like *Le Roman d'un jeune homme pauvre.* Frédéric is "drunk with his own eloquence"; while Mme Arnoux, her former restraint gone, is all breathless banalities. Telling him how she often broods by the sea, she says: "I go and sit there on a bench; I call it 'Frédéric's bench.' " (It sounds no better in French.) Her sufferings and her age have made of Mme Arnoux a sentimentalist.

Frédéric, for all his rapture in this interview, lies to her twice. She has brought him, in a velvet purse embroidered by her own hand, the money owed to him by Arnoux. He makes no move to refuse it. When she finally removes her hat and Frédéric discovers that her hair is white (like Elisa's), he suspects that "she has come to offer herself to him." He recoils from the suggestion for reasons which, as Flaubert lists them, build up to a stunning anticlimax: "he was seized with a stronger desire than ever—a frantic, ravening lust. Yet he also felt something he could not express—a repugnance, a sense of horror, as of an act of incest. Another fear restrained him—the fear of the disgust that might follow. Besides, what a nuisance it would be! And, partly from prudence, partly to avoid tainting his ideal, he turned on his heel and began to roll a cigarette." What can the poor woman do but exclaim, "How chivalrous you are!" and depart forever, after first cutting off a lock of her white hair to leave with him as a souvenir? Do his wildly mixed motives add up to chivalrousness or "nobility"? And how can Frédéric be said to have "given up everything" for her image when his entire existence has been a series of uncompleted moves on the checkerboard of life? The big scene is a deliberate fiasco.

One's skepticism about Frédéric and the Great Affair is confirmed by the final chapter, often called the "epilogue" of the *Education*. Frédéric, now in his forties, and Deslauriers have been reconciled after a long separation on *their* part and are alone together. Reliving their pasts, they hover between mild regrets, mild complacencies, and tentative self-reproaches. ("Perhaps we let ourselves drift from our course.") They end by recalling an incident from their boyhood. In his first chapter, Flaubert has sketched in the little incident very lightly, leaving it to the mature Frédéric and Deslauriers to clarify the importance which the incident has—for them. As boys in their teens at Nogent they had decided one Sunday to visit the town brothel. On arriving inside, Frédéric bearing a bouquet of flowers, they had been laughed at by the girls and Frédéric, embarrassed, had fled the place, and because as usual Frédéric had the money, Deslauriers had fled too. Recounting the story in detail, the two men agree on its significance: "That was the best time we ever had."

That a long crowded narrative should conclude in this flippant manner has shocked many readers. Other long crowded novels end with real denouements, in which the complications of the plot are unraveled, the hero is reformed, and the ironic tensions are relaxed. For *this* long crowded novel, however, Flaubert's epilogue is the perfect ending. The original brothel incident makes a miniature anecdote. That

incident, as recalled and moralized by the middle-aged participants, is the apotheosis of the anecdotal form. It resolves
nothing, leaves the hero unreformed, and perpetuates into
the indefinite future the ironic tensions, the equivocations of
drift, and the operations of the World, the Flesh, and Time.

1971